LANGUAGE ARTS FOR THE CHILD

Ivan J. Quandt
Temple University

PRENTICE-HALL, INC. *Englewood Cliffs, N.J. 07632*

Library of Congress Cataloging in Publication Data

QUANDT, IVAN J.
  Language arts for the child.

  Includes bibliographical references and index
  1. Language arts (Elementary)   I. Title.
LB1576.Q36 1983   372.6   82-11313
ISBN 0-13-522623-6

Editorial production/supervision by Marion Osterberg
Cover photo courtesy of Ken Karp
Cover design by Miriam Recio
Manufacturing buyer: Ron Chapman

Printed in the United States of America

10   9   8   7   6   5   4   3   2   1

ISBN 0-13-522623-6

Prentice-Hall International, Inc., *London*
Prentice-Hall of Australia Pty. Limited, *Sydney*
Editora Prentice-Hall do Brasil, Ltda., *Rio de Janeiro*
Prentice-Hall Canada Inc., *Toronto*
Prentice-Hall of India Private Limited, *New Delhi*
Prentice-Hall of Japan, Inc., *Tokyo*
Prentice-Hall of Southeast Asia Pte. Ltd., *Singapore*
Whitehall Books Limited, *Wellington, New Zealand*

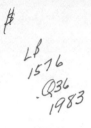

CONTENTS

PREFACE

The child is the most important part of a school and of a language arts program. Teachers deal with more than speaking, listening, and writing. When they teach language arts, they deal with and teach children. It is the child's ability and confidence to communicate that provides the purpose, motivation, and energy of the program. Both ability and confidence are important for the child because each is needed to become an effective communicator.

This is a text about helping children become better communicators. It is designed to give teachers the understanding that is necessary in developing sound language arts programs and to provide practical ideas for implementing the instruction. It gives detailed attention to speaking, listening, and writing instruction. In addition to dealing with the skills for each of these areas, it provides techniques for building confidence among learners who are growing as communicators. Approaches to evaluation of each aspect of language arts are also included. The final chapter shows how to apply these techniques to various special learners and how to organize the entire program.

Many people have directly and indirectly helped to construct this text. Countless researchers and authorities in language arts have contributed theories, knowledge, and ideas that provided the basis for much of the material. Hundreds of pre-service and in-service teachers have given practical support to the teaching ideas presented. I acknowledge their help and I thank them all. I am especially grateful for the patience of my family, the expert typing skills of Mary Ann German, and the valuable help with the special education section provided by Anita Rauch.

Ivan J. Quandt

CHAPTER ONE
WHAT IS
LANGUAGE ARTS ?

Scene A

"OK, boys and girls, get out your language arts books," said Mr. Lopez.

"Oooh," groaned the class in unison.

"Why are you groaning?" asked the teacher. "Don't you know how important language is? If you don't learn the language that I teach you here, how will you ever get by when you're older?"

"Ooooh," groaned the class a little more quietly.

Scene B

"OK, class, we've been talking and reading about ants. How would you like to 'publish' our own book about ants?" asked Ms. Schmidt.

"Hey," said Bob.

"Great," said Jerome.

"And if we do it well, maybe we can start our own publishing company," added the teacher.

"We like it," implied the face and body language of the class.

Everyone who lives with or near other people learns how to communicate. With no formal schooling, people easily develop the abilities to express needs, barter, show anger, ask questions, and maintain a livelihood somewhat equal to that of other people in the society who also have no formal schooling. If we lived in a society with low levels of technology, with little need to communicate outside of our immediate environment, and with somewhat uniform occupations and status, we probably would have little need to advance our communication abilities by attending a school.

We live in a society that is quite the opposite, however, and it is assumed by almost everyone that children should be taught how to communicate well by attending school. Most schools, in fact, have set up elaborate systems for teaching children to listen, speak, read, and write. Reading and writing especially have received much attention, and society in general has usually demanded that schools do a good job of teaching these abilities. Furthermore, our society has generally offered career and status rewards to its members who are highly effective in their use of communication. Ironically, while society's demands for reading and writing are louder, through its systems of job interviews, political campaigns, television and movie stardom, labor negotiations, and so on, it seems to offer larger rewards to individuals with better *speaking* abilities.

In such a complex society, the role of the school in developing communication abilities is anything but simple. The inconsistency of society's demands and rewards is only one of the contributors to this complexity. Another factor is a frequent discrepancy between what a community expects from its schools and what it is willing to pay. Another is a lack of agreement among educators themselves about what and how to teach for the sake of communication.

One of the most complex aspects of the school's role, however, is related to the children that fill the schools. They come to school with the task of learning to communicate well under way, and even after they arrive, much of their language growth occurs away from the school. This puts the school in somewhat the same position as that of a barber whose customer started to cut his own hair at home and then came to the barber to "fix it up." The school must take whatever language and communication ability the learners bring and attempt to develop it to a level of effectiveness. This presents two types of challenges.

First, it is obvious that every child is unique in the amount and type of communication ability brought to school. Individual differences are the unavoidable result of a system that places the responsibility for teaching children to speak and to listen in the home. They are of various types, for communication has a variety of facets. And these differences are quite extensive, for the factors that surround language growth vary so greatly from one child to the next. While conformity is certainly not a desirable goal, such great individual differences make the task of the school quite complex.

The second challenge to the school results from the way humans develop language. Language is not learned in isolation from other parts of development, but as an outgrowth of total life experiences. Of the many factors in language growth, special importance is attached to the emotions and attitudes of the child. Emotional interference affects many aspects of child development, but is particularly evident in the development of language.[1] A child's attitudes, emotional makeup, and language seem to be closely intertwined. When the school attempts to deal with language, then, it must deal with the total child. The school cannot eradicate any language that it regards as inappropriate and replace it with "good" language, because this would also destroy part of the child's emotional strength. Emotions and attitudes, therefore, cannot be ignored. The task of the school is indeed complex and challenging.

LANGUAGE ARTS AND THE TEACHER

In order to meet the challenge of developing communication abilities, almost all schools include in their content plans (curriculum) a daily subject called "English" or, more commonly in elementary schools, "language arts." Although reading is also a language art, it is normally treated as a separate subject. Regardless of its name, this part of the curriculum is designed to teach children to listen, speak, and write.

Teaching language arts has at least one thing in common with teaching any other subject. Decisions must be made about what to teach and how to teach it. With the complex challenges that face today's schools, it is not surprising to find that many schools and teachers allow textbooks, in effect, to make those decisions for them.

There are many fine language arts textbooks available from various publishers and they can be valuable teaching tools, but it is wrong to allow such materials to be the sole guide for making decisions. When teachers regularly decide what to teach on the basis of what comes next in the textbook, they are ignoring individual differences. When the methods or techniques of teaching are limited to textbook teaching, the emotions and attitudes of the learners are usually ignored.

When the school attempts to deal with language, it must deal with the total child. (*Upper left—Leslie Deeb; others—Ken Karp*)

The best source of decision making about content and teaching methods is the teacher. Decision making by the teacher, however, must also be based on reasonable objectives. Without appropriate goals and objectives to guide them, some teachers use their language arts planning time to search through lists of teaching activities. Entire resource books are available with hundreds of language arts lessons and activities. In addition, teachers often trade good ideas or pick them up during graduate or in-service courses. The use of such resources is excellent and should be encouraged, but only when activities are selected on the basis of teaching objectives.

Often, a school or school district offers the teacher some assistance in the selection of language arts content in the form of a *curriculum guide.* In a few states, there is also a state language arts guide that gives general help. The degree to which these guides are actually of assistance and the degree to which teachers are expected to follow them varies from one situation to another. Frequently, such guides list objectives and some specific teaching activities. The ideal language arts curriculum guide is specific enough to offer teaching ideas and yet general enough to allow the teacher flexibility in setting up the program.

An opposite situation arises when there are no apparent objectives. When there are no objectives, the teacher's primary and recurring question becomes, "What should I teach tomorrow?" Then, teacher and learners may wander aimlessly through a maze of unrelated lessons and practice activities.

A method for selecting language arts content and teaching techniques that is based on objectives might use the following steps:

1. On the basis of the teacher's interaction with learners during the first weeks of the school year and of planned diagnosis, the teacher determines the needs of the learners.

2. On the basis of the learners' needs, the teacher's previous experience, and possibly a school curriculum guide, the teacher determines the general language arts goals for the year (for examples, see Box 1–1).

BOX 1–1   *EXAMPLES OF LANGUAGE ARTS GOALS*

GOALS   Do the following this school year:

Raise the verbal confidence of those who need it (two-thirds of my class)

Improve the verbal expression ability of each individual

Overcome the extreme lack of writing confidence in six individuals

Build the writing confidence of the remaining class members

Expand each individual's creativity and expression in writing

Provide each individual with adequate spelling and writing skills

---

3. On the basis of general goals, specific objectives are developed that deal with the skills, abilities, and attitudes that need to be taught or provided. The manner in which the objectives are worded is unimportant, but their existence is essential (for examples, see Box 1–2).

OBJECTIVES The seventeen learners who need confidence will:

Actively participate in mime and choral speaking activities

Participate in puppet dramatics using adequate voice volume

Contribute actively to small group discussions

Converse with me privately during conferences

Occasionally contribute to whole-class discussions

Volunteer for role playing

4. On the basis of the objectives, content for the language arts lessons or activities is selected and teaching techniques are developed. Language arts textbooks, activity books, and other resources may be used, but selections are made on the basis of objectives.

The advantages of a program built around teacher-made objectives are high potential for teacher enthusiasm and for meeting the needs of learners. When teachers are involved in planning the program, they not only understand its purpose but develop a commitment to it. The enthusiasm that is thus generated is usually spread to the children. In addition, the program is more often geared toward the needs of the learners and is therefore more likely to build positive attitudes. The results are a higher level of motivation and more effective learning.

Effective learning is dependent upon useful content and enthusiastic teaching. When learners sit through lessons and complete their assignments or homework simply because they "have to," they develop negative attitudes that interfere with learning. They come to see language arts as just so many tasks to complete. When children (or adults) don't understand *why* they are expected to learn, there is probably very little learning.

Although teacher-made objectives don't automatically overcome these potential problems, teachers' decisions based on such objectives are more *likely* to engender motivation and learning because of the teachers' enthusiasm and the useful content. The purpose of all the pages that follow is to give the teacher and the potential teacher the background that is necessary to make good decisions about language arts.

CHOOSING GOALS AND OBJECTIVES

When teachers set goals and objectives, the right ones need to be set. The overall goal of language arts instruction must be to make better communicators of the learners. When consideration is given to the specific language needs of children, it must be done in relation to their ability to communicate. The school must help the child become more effective and efficient in giving and receiving messages.

A secondary goal is to help learners appreciate the beauty of literature and language in general. As important as the aesthetics of language are, however, they must remain secondary to, and in some cases vehicles for, the primary goal of developing communication.

In order to limit objectives, language content, and teaching techniques so that they deal with communication development and language appreciation, it is necessary for the teacher to be selective. This is not a simple process, for communication involves more than a set of skills. Attitudes are of equal importance with all the skills of language.

One of the most important attitudes that the learner holds is the one toward himself or herself. Individuals who view themselves as verbal people have the confidence to speak more; those who see themselves as good writers have the confidence to write more. Confidence affects all areas of communication. Building confidence, then, is not just a desirable by-product of the language arts program. It requires as much attention as the skills of language.

In order to intelligently determine objectives, language content, and teaching procedures, the teacher needs to understand two major aspects of communication. First, he or she must understand the *nature of communication*. This includes knowing what it is, how it functions, and its various levels and forms. In addition, the teacher must understand language acquisition. This includes knowing how the ability to communicate is acquired and what the school can do to promote that acquisition.

THE NATURE OF COMMUNICATION

Communication is the sending and receiving of some type of message. Sometimes the sender simply records the message for his or her own later use (example: grocery list), sometimes it is designed for a specific receiver (example: personal letter), and sometimes it is for a general audience (example: campaign speech). The sender may decide to speak the message, write it, transmit it by codes, express it through art, or hire planes to skywrite it. The forms and modes of communication are almost limitless. However, the most common by far is oral communication, the spoken word.

There is more to communication than simply sending and receiving words, however. In nearly every case, the sender has a thought or a concept that he or she wishes to communicate to someone else. The sender must rely on past experiences to decide what words and other forms of communication to use to express the thought. The receiver, on the other hand, must translate the message once it is received. Because the receiver has a different experience background than the sender, the words and any accompanying voice tone or gestures may have different meanings to the two people. Sometimes the intended message and the receiver's interpretation are quite similar. Sometimes they are quite different. Seldom, however, is the message interpreted by the receiver in exactly the same manner as it was intended by the sender, because they are basing their communication on different experience backgrounds.

Two Levels of Communication

One reason that communication is somewhat difficult and less than precise is that messages are received at two levels. The most obvious is the overt level. The intended message is interpreted in terms of its content and apparent meaning. But the message is also received and interpreted at the covert level. This means that, while interpreting the overt message, the listener or reader is also looking for hidden and subtle meanings. Even beyond this, the receiver is making judgments about the sender while listening to the message. The sender's character, values, level of education, and possibly even intelligence are frequently judged by listeners or readers. The "correctness" of the language, the vocabulary, the voice tone and expression, and the body language may all contribute to the impression that is made. Sometimes this covert communication may be quite weak compared with the more obvious overt level, and frequently the receiver is not consciously aware of it at all. However, it is usually there.

The importance of covert communication varies from situation to situation. When two classmates complain to each other about their schoolwork or when an audience becomes enthralled with a good storyteller, for example, almost all of the attention goes to the content of the message, to the overt level. There are situations, on the other hand, where the more subtle covert message is stronger than the words. When an applicant stares at the floor and stammers through his comments during a job interview, the interviewer gains a strong impression of the applicant's confidence and initiative. When a racially biased customer is waited on by a salesperson with a definite minority dialect, the sale is affected. When a student writes an application for graduate school with spelling or punctuation errors, the application reviewers make judgments about the student. The judgments made in these and hundreds of other situations may not be fair or right, but they *are* made.

The elementary language arts program seldom deals directly with covert communication. Textbooks say very little about it. Lessons and activities are almost never developed to improve it. Yet, teachers tend to be aware of its importance and to teach its value to their students. Much of the rationale for correct spelling, good handwriting, and other writing skills is stated in terms of the impression it will make on readers rather than in terms of more effective overt communication. Likewise, good usage and standard spoken English are stressed because these factors have an influence on listeners. Sometimes teachers overemphasize these factors at the expense of other types of language development. Good language arts teachers attempt to develop both overt and covert levels of communication.

Four Forms of Communication

The language arts program is usually organized around overt communication. That is why language arts is usually divided into four categories: speaking, listening, writing, and reading. Speaking and writing are *sending* forms of communication, while listening and reading are *receiving* forms. Obviously, speaking and listening are paired, as are writing and reading. In fact, it would be just as proper to speak of only two forms of communication, speaking-listening and writing-reading. As will be shown later, all of these forms greatly overlap.

Of course, there are forms of communication which technically do not fit into any of these categories. For centuries, the navy used semaphore (flag signals) by day and light codes by night. Smoke sig-

	Covert	Overt
Listening		
Speaking		
Reading		
Writing		

FIGURE 1–1 Levels and forms of communication.

nals, drum rhythms, and other symbols and codes have been used by various cultures. Body language is used by everyone nearly all of the time. Because in a school setting they are by far the most useful, however, speaking, listening, writing, and reading are the forms of communication contained in most language arts programs. As a result, they are the four areas around which this text is organized.

LANGUAGE ACQUISITION

The second major aspect of communication which a good language arts teacher must understand is how it develops. It is not only necessary to know how language is acquired, but also important to know what can be done in a classroom to help that process along. All of the chapters in this text except the first two deal with methods for fostering and encouraging language growth. At this point, it is necessary to examine the process of language acquisition itself, especially as it unfolds in the years prior to formal schooling.

There is a normal order in which a child acquires the four common forms of overt communication. Although there are obvious exceptions with blind and deaf children, most individuals learn first to listen, then to speak, and finally to read and write somewhat simultaneously. A more detailed account of this sequence will be presented shortly.

Why Children Are Able to Learn Language

Before dealing with the sequence for language acquisition, it makes sense to look at how it is possible. Why are humans able to communicate through abstract language? There are three human attributes that make language learning possible:

1. The human mind has the ability to understand, order, and combine varied and complex symbols.
2. Humans, including young children, have a felt *need* to communicate.
3. By experiencing language in his or her environment, the young child is able to discover how the language system works.

The first of these, the ability to think symbolically, separates humans from all other forms of life. Although some animals have very simple signals that they can communicate, and certain birds have almost humanlike voice ranges, no creature can begin to approach the language ability of even a young child. This human ability allows us to make specific descriptions or to convey abstract attitudes and emotions.

Language, however, would never develop in the individual if that person did not have a *need* to communicate. If crying brought us everything we needed, we would remain in that infant stage of communication. Even the infant, however, quickly discovers a need for more precise communication. It has been recognized for some time that a child will begin talking later in life if the need for communication is reduced. For example, a child frequently delays his or her first words if an older sibling regularly interprets and speaks for him. Eventually, however, everyone develops a need to communicate, and a delayed beginning seldom has lasting effects on later language.

The need to communicate leads the young child to learn the language of the people in her or his environment. This particular language is learned not only because it is the one that is heard, but also because it is the one that makes communication with others possible. Listening and speaking are normally the forms learned, because they are the ones needed. If the need changes, so does the form. In a study of deaf children born to deaf parents, Bellugi found that these children learned sign as a first language as early and as well as hearing children learn to speak.[2] The fact that children learn the language of their environment, then, is further evidence that language develops out of need.

A third and important reason that children are able to learn a language is that at a very early age they are able to discover how the language "works." First proposed by Noam Chomsky, this theory holds that as young children experience the language in their environment they begin to understand how words relate to each other, to understand the structure of language.[3] In other words, they do not simply learn the meanings of words and string them together; they develop an understanding of the grammar or syntax of their language. They are, of course, unable to *describe* this grammar or syntax, but they are able to use it.

Evidence for this theory can be found by observing children who are in the process of learning language. Young children frequently use grammar that isn't found in adult speech. Statements such as, "she bringed a lunch," "the sheeps," or "he gots it" are common. These incorrect statements usually follow grammatical rules, however, and give evidence that the child has learned some generalizations about grammar. The child is not randomly putting words together, but is overgeneralizing. Experience with language has taught the individual some generalizations, but when, and when not, to apply them has not yet been mastered. In the example, "she bringed a lunch," it is clear that the learner has a well-established concept of past-tense verbs. As young boys or girls have more and more experience with language, their speech becomes more like that of the adults in their environment.

A Sequence for Learning Language

Further evidence that these are the three reasons children learn language can be found by looking at the sequence that children typically follow in acquiring language. Linguists have studied the language development of children in a number of countries and languages over the past two decades and have found the following general sequence to be true in all situations. The steps in the sequence, however, are not completely discrete. One step merges into the next, and there is much overlap.

1. From birth, babies are normally able to make sounds. For some time, however, they babble and experiment randomly. The babies are apparently not able to distinguish one sound from another either in hearing or making noises. They are able, though, to use noise productively. They cry in reaction to discomfort or fear.

2. Babies begin to distinguish among sounds. Anastasiow reports that at approximately five months, they begin to determine that speech sounds have meaning. This is one of the most significant steps in language acquisition.[4]

3. At the same time that babies begin to exercise some control over their other behaviors, they begin to control some of the sounds they produce. They begin to experiment with their own sounds intentionally. The experiments may include voice intensity and pitch as well as various sounds. It is during this time that parents frequently believe their baby has said his first words because the experiments may include "ma-ma-ma-ma" and "da-da-da-da."

4. Although this is a step that only some children experience, eager parents are sometimes able to get their babies to parrot certain sounds upon request. When, "say 'bye-bye' " is repeated often enough, children will sometimes repeat the sound in order to receive the reinforcement from their parents which follows.

5. Eventually, children do begin to speak, using words that have meaning to them. A common time for this to occur is between one year and one and one-half years of age. They use utterances which are based on the language they have experienced. The

utterances are frequently limited to a single syllable, but they communicate meaning in the context of the situation. For example, a child might say "door" and that could mean "this is a door," "will you close the door," or "I will close the door," depending on when and where it is used. Children at this stage will usually learn a key word or syllable from a phrase they have heard often and use that word to mean the entire phrase.

6. By approximately age 18 months, children have usually expanded the length of their utterances to two, three, or even four words. These longer utterances are used like the single-word messages, however. That is, each utterance is a unit or a complete message. The phrase does not sound like adult language, but it does keep adult word order. This is not because these children understand grammar, but because they have been reinforced for imitating adult language that they have heard. Thus, a child might say, "Mike go school," because Mother has often said, "Mike is going to school." The child does not yet understand how language works and cannot yet arrange words logically. But children of this age can learn many such utterances and use them meaningfully, especially when parents give them confidence through positive recognition. Such utterances are sometimes called *telegraphic messages.*

7. Next, children begin to expand their utterances in two ways. The messages become longer as the children fill in more words. As more language is experienced, these eager learners bring their telegraphic messages more into line with adult speech. "I go store" may become "I wanna go to store." The other type of expansion is in delimitation. That is, the children learn more exactly when it is appropriate to use a certain utterance and when it is not. At this time, then, it would seem that language learning is a matter or remembering a statement for every occasion.

8. About the same time that they find their communication needs becoming too complex for whole-language units, children develop the ability to generalize. Having developed confidence in themselves as communicators, they begin to see how language works. Although they could never state them, children develop generalizations about grammar and begin applying them independently. The result is frequently an overgeneralization, as described earlier, so that their speech at this time seems less adult than it did during previous steps. "She runned away" and "he

gots it" become typical remarks. This may be alarming to some parents. Smith, Goodman, and Meredith warn, however, that if children are overcorrected during this time they may be discouraged from trying out generalizations and remain in a less effective whole-unit stage.[5]

9. While the young learners are still developing new generalizations, they begin to refine the ones they have. In fact, this process continues to some extent for many years. Preschoolers become aware of when a generalization (for example: add s to a noun to make it plural) is true and when it isn't. They also gain control over the interrelationships of parts of speech and language patterns. They are able to make grammatically correct statements that they have never heard before. Strickland and Loban conducted extensive research which shows that by the time children are in kindergarten they understand and use all of the basic sentence patterns of the adult speech in their environment[6] (although some, more complex, patterns take several additional years to learn).

10. Under the right conditions, children will next begin to read and write. Determining what the "right" conditions are, however, is a source of much controversy. On one hand, schools have set up elaborate systems of readiness training and initial reading instruction. On the other hand, a small percentage of children from various intelligence levels and socioeconomic backgrounds learn to read on their own with no formal instruction. Many factors have been linked with initial reading success, but three key ones should be mentioned here. Children need to see that written language "works" much like spoken language. They must feel a need to communicate through written language before reading and writing instruction will have a very large impact on them. Finally, they must have the confidence that they will succeed in reading and writing.

11. After children have a reasonable command of their language, they are able to become creative with it, to invent their own words and patterns. Few children ever develop this ability very extensively, however, because parents, the school, and society are much more concerned with conformity of language than with creativity of language. Adolescents typically rebel against this conformity for a time by using a few slang expressions of their own, but the individual still does not invent language during this

period, since adult pressure for conformity is temporarily replaced by peer pressure. In reality, only a very few of our society
are given, or take the opportunity to develop, language creativity.

12. At some point, children begin to be aware of the covert level of
communication. At the present time, it is not known when this
occurs. Six-year-olds sometimes ridicule a peer because he or she
"talks funny," but it is doubtful that such judgments are very
discriminating. By the time students are in junior high school,
however, they seem quite prone to make numerous judgments
about their peers on the basis of their use of language. Perhaps
this is a type of communication that develops very slowly and is
linked to the development of social values and personal attitudes.

It should be pointed out again that these twelve steps are not
necessarily discrete. One step may still be partially in effect long after
another begins, and there is much overlap. At the present time, however, this sequence seems to be the most accurate that research and
theory combined has to offer.

The Nature of Language Learning

There are some common elements in all of the above steps. In fact,
regardless of whether language acquisition is divided into twelve steps;
into six stages as proposed by Smith, Goodman, and Meredith; or into
some other scheme, these common elements exist.[7] The first element
is discovery. The second is an experience base. The third element
found at any point in language learning is purpose, and the final one
is confidence.

Basically, children discover how language works on their own. Of
course, they have to be surrounded by language models for discovery
to be possible, but they sort through the endless array of noises and
voices by themselves. Parents, and later teachers, correct children
when their language doesn't conform, but little planned instruction
typically occurs prior to entrance into school.

One of the reasons children are able to discover the sounds and
generalizations of language is that communication is almost always
related to experience. Words and messages are not learned in isolation. When the infant recognizes such key words as "milk," "mommy,"
and "daddy," he or she does so out of need. But it would be impossible
to learn the words if the child had not experienced the real people and
things these words represent. Evidently, we learn concepts and relationships through experience, and then we connect them to language.

Thus, a rich and varied set of experiences is an important element in learning language.

The reason that children bother to discover language and the reason they put forth the energy to associate experience with language, is that they have a purpose. The purpose is in the *use* of the language. Halliday emphasizes the connection between language and its use.[8] He points out that the two are learned simultaneously and cannot be separated. When a child sees Mother offer a ball and say "Do you want to play with the ball?" he or she realizes the language must be connected to the action. When the child hears "Turn on the TV" and sees someone stand, walk, and turn a button to make a picture appear, the words are associated with the action. When the language fits the child's purpose, it is learned. Frank Smith asserts that this is the only way language in any form is learned; if a child perceives no purpose for a segment, or form, of language, it will not and cannot be learned.[9] Children have a general need to communicate, as described earlier, and this need is translated into specific learnings as specific purposes are developed. The amount that is learned and the verbal expression of the learning will be limited by the step in language acquisition within which the child is growing, but at any stage of development the child must see a purpose in learning.

The final element that is common to all language acquisition is confidence. It is not known how much confidence is needed at any given step or even how to measure it with the same precision that we measure skills. It is evident, however, that children who believe they are good speakers, listeners, readers, or writers tend to excell in that area. The rate at which communication ability develops and the extent to which it is learned are affected strongly by the child's level of confidence.

THE ROLE OF THE SCHOOL
IN LANGUAGE DEVELOPMENT

The discussions above would almost seem to imply that the school is not needed in the growth of the individual's language. But this is far from true. Since children come to school already listening and speaking, some educators feel that the role of the school is limited to teaching reading and writing. But this is not accurate either.

When the overall goals of language arts instruction were described early in this chapter, it was pointed out that the language arts program must help learners become effective and efficient communicators. This is the role of the school in language development. Help for children in becoming effective and efficient is provided by applying what is known about language acquisition to the classroom. This involves a number of factors.

Applying the Elements
of Language Acquisition

All that we have learned about language acquisition should not be lost when children enter school. There, they should continue to develop language and communication abilities in the same manner as before. While it is true that as children mature they are more able to deal with abstract learnings, school-age children learn language through discovery when there is a perceived purpose, just as preschoolers do. Therefore, one of the roles of the school is to set the conditions so that children can make discoveries about language and so that they have purposes for learning it.

Of course, discovery and purposeful activities are not as easy to arrange in school as they are in the home. In many homes, they simply happen naturally. In school, teachers have a large group of learners to guide, expectations about curriculum to fulfill, and decisions about teaching strategies and content to make. The one-to-one relationship, so perfect for language learning at home, cannot even be approached in school. Yet, the school must not let this obstacle keep it from doing as much as possible to set the conditions for discovery and purposeful learning.

Recognizing the Importance
of Attitudes

In order to help learners become effective and efficient communicators, the school must recognize the importance of attitudes in language development. Attitudes are difficult to measure on tests, so the exact relationship between attitudes and language growth has not been clearly established by research. Most language authorities agree, however, that attitudes heavily influence language growth.

One essential type of attitude has already been discussed. Learners must see a purpose for their language arts activities. If students view language arts as a boring time slot, a series of meaningless workbook pages, or a necessary evil, language growth will be slow at best. If, however, language arts is seen as a way to discover better ways to communicate in order to fulfill life-related needs, language growth will be at its best. The learners' views of language arts have a large influence on how much learning occurs in school.

A second type of attitude has to do with the learners' views of themselves. Commonly known as *self-concept,* this attitude also affects the students' learnings. Learners who have positive self-concepts about learning will learn more quickly and thoroughly.

Self-concept can be a factor in any form of communication. Nearly everyone has experienced the difference between fear and confidence when talking in front of a group. The effect that confidence, or the lack of it, has in such a situation is obvious. Confidence, or a positive self-concept, has a similar effect on writing, reading, and even listening. So, then, a major role of the school in language development is that of building positive attitudes toward language and toward self.

Teaching Skills

Of course, there are skills of communication that must be taught. Spelling, handwriting, punctuation, usage, word recognition, and other skills would not develop very well for most children without some direct instruction. But even when we teach skills, our knowledge about language acquisition and the effect of attitudes must not be overlooked.

SUMMARY

Language arts can be more than a time slot to fill, more than a series of pages to cover, and more than a collection of activities to complete. It can be a meaningful program built around objectives and based on the teacher's understanding of language, its acquisition, and the needs of the learners. The goal of the program is to develop individuals who can and will communicate effectively and efficiently.

The teacher in Scene A at the beginning of the chapter realized the importance of learning to communicate, but the program for developing the ability to communicate was evidently anything but meaningful. Whether the groans from a class are audible or just mental, a negative reaction like the one this class gave is not uncommon when the language arts program is little more than the completion of activities in the textbook. Perhaps this class reacted so negatively because they saw little in the textbook or in their language arts lessons with meaning for their lives.

The class in Scene B had an attitude about language arts that was clearly more positive than that in Scene A. Making a book about ants had real meaning to them, perhaps because the study of ants in science class was interesting to them. If the teacher in this situation could take advantage of the interest and motivation to improve whatever language abilities were included in the objectives, this classroom would probably produce much more language learning than the first.

It isn't necessary to abandon the language arts textbook in order to develop a meaningful communications program. Such texts often contain many useful ideas and general plans. But the textbook and all other resources must be used selectively to build programs that work toward the objectives. An essential ingredient in any program, regardless of the goals or objectives, is a purpose with which the learners can identify. Students who have a purpose, that is, they know *why* they are doing what they are doing in language arts, are much more likely to develop communication abilities from the program.

NOTES

1. Nicholas Anastasiow, *Oral Language: Expression of Thought* (Newark, Del.: International Reading Assoc., 1971), p. 12.

2. Ursula Bellugi, "The Language of Signs and the Signs of Language" (paper delivered at the Michigan Conference on Applied Linguistics, University of Michigan, January, 1971).

3. Noam Chomsky, "Language and the Mind," *Psychology Today,* 2 (February 1968), pp. 48–51.

4. Anastasiow, *Oral Language,* pp. 13–15.

5. E. Brooks Smith, Kenneth S. Goodman, and Robert Meredith, *Language and Thinking in School,* 2nd ed. (New York: Holt, Rinehart and Winston, 1976), p. 23.

6. Ruth Strickland, "The Language of Elementary School Children," *Bulletin of the School of Education* (Bloomington, Ind.: Indiana University), 38, no. 4 (1962); Walter Loban, *The Language of Elementary School Children* (Urbana, Ill.: National Council of Teachers of English, 1973).

7. Smith, Goodman, and Meredith, *Language and Thinking in School,* pp. 21–24.

8. Michael A. K. Halliday, *Exploration in the Functions of Language* (London: Edward Arnold, 1973).

9. Frank Smith, "The Language Arts and the Learner's Mind," *Language Arts,* 56 (February 1979), pp. 118–25.

CHAPTER TWO
LINGUISTICALLY SPEAKING

Scene A

"What do I think of linguistics?" Miss Kress repeated the question from a colleague in the teachers' lounge. "Not much! As far as I can tell the only difference between the new 'linguistic' language arts books and the old ones is a lot of different words. They use so many new names for old ideas I can't keep it straight. All the parts of speech have new names! I don't like it."

Scene B

"What do I think of linguistics?" repeated Mr. Abdurian. "I'm glad I've learned something about it, because it's helped my language arts teaching a lot. I've learned how important speaking and listening are for children. The time that I spend on speaking and listening will probably really pay off in my teaching of reading and writing. I've also learned that language learning is more effective when children actually *use* language. I think linguistics is very helpful."

In recent years, a wealth of information about communication and language has been added to our storehouse of knowledge. One of the main contributors to the increase in language information over the past several decades has been the science of linguistics. In their study of language, including English, linguists have learned a great deal about its structure and the way it functions. Much of what they have learned has influenced education and probably will continue to do so.

Linguistics is the study of human speech and all of its components and modifications. It includes the study of the nature, structure, change, process, and functions of language. As a result, there are a number of fields of linguistics, each with its own speciality. Some of the more common fields of linguistics are listed below:

Morphology—the study of word formation

Phonology—the study of the various sounds of speech

Historical—the study of how language has developed, including etymology, the study of word origins

Comparative—the study of language families and their various dialects

Descriptive or structural—the analysis and description of language as it exists today

Generative or transformational—the study of how a language functions

Psycholinguistics—a combination of psychology and linguistics (Chapter Twelve explains how psycholinguistics can be applied to reading.)

The last three fields have special significance for the classroom; therefore, a more detailed examination of them is appropriate.

THREE KEY FIELDS OF LINGUISTICS

Two of the fields of linguistics which have the greatest significance for language arts teaching are based on types of grammar that bear the same names. Therefore, it is important here to briefly look at grammar. A common way to describe English grammar is to divide it into three types. Traditional grammar from sixteenth- and seventeenth-century England is basically a set of rules defining how English ought to be. Descriptive linguistic grammar is a description of the way English is actually practiced. Generative or transformational grammar is a description of how simple sentences are generated and transformed into every possible phrase and sentence structure of English. These three types of grammar are described again in Chapter Eight.

Two of the fields of linguistics that have been defined above can be associated with two of these three types of grammar. While some linguists specialize in the study of language history, there is no field of linguistics devoted to the advancement of traditional grammar. The two fields of linguistics which are based on the other two types of grammar are *descriptive,* or *structural,* and *generative,* or *transformational.*

Descriptive Linguistics

The branch of linguistics commonly known as descriptive or as structural is concerned with describing, analyzing, and formalizing language patterns as they exist in our language.[1] Reacting against the prescriptive rules of traditional grammar, structural linguists began in the 1930s to describe and catalog all observable features of English. In order to describe language, they first had to analyze it.

The analysis proceeded from form to meaning. First, they identified the smallest units of speech, called *phonemes.* The phonemes of a language are all of its meaningful, minimal speech sounds (examples: pronunciations of b, t, m, ch, aw). Then they studied the smallest units of meaning, called *morphemes* (examples: ill, fix, staple, –ness, pre–, s). Finally, they analyzed how morphemes are combined to form phrases, clauses, and sentences. Structural linguists have theorized that every communicated message has two levels: a deep structure (the underlying meaning of the message) and a surface structure (the words or other features of the stated message).

Structural or descriptive linguists have contributed much to our understanding of English. They revised the definitions for parts of speech so that they now match the structure of English rather than the structure of Latin (see Box 2–1). They discovered the role that spoken language plays in the process of learning to read and write. They have given us new insights into regional and cultural dialects and into "standard" versus "nonstandard" English.

Generative-Transformational Linguistics

The branch of linguistics known as generative or transformational is concerned with how English functions. It assumes that all sentences of a language are based on simple subject-predicate constructions called *kernel sentences.* When these basic sentences are written or spoken, however, they are usually transformed into more complex messages.[2]

BOX 2–1 *STRUCTURAL LINGUISTIC PARTS OF SPEECH*

Some parts of speech can be defined in terms of what can be done to the word; others, in terms of what words they go with or *pattern with;* and still others, in terms of what they signal. There are two general categories: main word classes and function words.

Main Word Classes

Main word classes are words to which an unlimited number of words can be added.

Noun   A word that can be made plural or possessive:
(Boys, Girls, Elephants, Kittens) like to play.
Bill ate the (cake, carrot, breakfast, moth).

Verb   A word that can change from present to past and, except with forms of *to be,* requires an added s when patterned after *it, she, he:*
Amy (talks, runs, grew, shouted).
Mr. Smith (saw, wanted, likes, eats) them.

Adjective   A word that *could* follow the word *very* and precede a noun (although it does not always do so), and that can follow a linking verb:
Terri is very (smart, tall, pretty, sad).
The (huge, young, friendly, awful) boy stood next to me.

Adverb   A word like *sometimes, brightly, happily, down, sweetly, never:*
Tom played first base (poorly, often, carefully).
She threw the disk (angrily, down, hard).

Function Words

Function words aid in providing structure for the sentence or other unit of language. Only rarely is another word added to any of them.

Noun marker or determiner   A word which signals that a noun follows. Included are *the, a, an, this, that, those, these, each, every, my, our, your, their, his, her, its,* all numerals, and other words that indicate number:
I saw (the, a, this, your) dog.

Pronoun   A word that substitutes for a noun:
(He, She, It) is very large.
Miss Jones saw (you, us, them, it).

Intensifier   A word such as *very, somewhat, extremely,* or *quite* that patterns with adjectives or adverbs:

The tiger was (extremely, rather, very) dangerous.

I do my work (very, quite, somewhat) slowly.

Auxiliary   A word which signals that a verb follows. Such auxiliaries as *have, has, had, do, does,* and *can* may also serve as independent verbs:

He (did, can, will) see the rock stars.

Sally (was, is) helping me.

Subordinator   A word such as *who, which, when, although, because, unless, before,* or *after* which joins a subordinate (conditional) clause with an independent clause:

You can't have dessert (unless, until, before) you eat your dinner.

(Before, After, While, When) you go home, write to me.

Conjunction   A word which links or joins two equal words or groups of words:

The car is red (and, but, yet, so) Ted likes it.

Preposition   A word that signals a noun will follow and begins a prepositional phrase:

The bird flew (over, under, to, into) the tree.

Bob walked (across, beside, up, through) the bridge.

Original thoughts might be in kernel sentences, but in speaking or writing the thought we construct our form of language to fit the circumstances. "The dog is running" is a kernel sentence. The many possible transformations of it include:

Is the dog running?

The dog is not running.

The dog will run.

The dog has run.

By studying kernel and transformed sentences, and how they are generated, generative or transformational linguists have developed a system of explicit rules for properly formed sentences. Unlike the rules of traditional grammar, these rules do not describe how language *should be,* but the way it *is.* The rules are like formulas that explain the many ways kernel sentences can be transformed.

Generative or transformational linguists have helped us understand some important concepts of language. Their efforts have helped us see how speakers and writers form messages and how listeners and readers translate them. The relationships among words, sentences, and the larger context are now more thoroughly understood. Perhaps their most significant contribution to teachers has been the knowledge that every schoolchild has language competence, that children come to school with oral language already well developed.

Psycholinguistics

A third field of linguistics that has special significance for the classroom is psycholinguistics. Drawing from cognitive psychology and generative transformational linguistics, this field has in recent years developed a theory of how language is received by individuals. It explains how capable listeners process what they hear and how proficient readers process what they see in print. Much of the theory has been substantiated by research findings.

Both forms of receptive communication, according to this theory, are made up of a continuous series of hypothesis testings. The listener's or reader's attitudes, past experiences, and familiarity with language allow him or her to predict the upcoming message before it is actually received by the ears or eyes. Thus, both listening and reading depend upon the use of context, the language that surrounds the group of words under consideration at any given second. The prediction or hypothesis is either confirmed or modified when the group of words actually reaches the ears or is focused upon by the eyes. As one group of words is being confirmed and processed, hypotheses or predictions about the next group or groups are already being formed. This very rapid process might be diagrammed like this:

```
———————► confirm group of words W
        form prediction about group X ——► confirm group of words X
                                          form prediction about group Y ——►
```

As long as the message that is derived from this process continues to make sense and sound like familiar English, the listener or reader continues without interruption.

Psycholinguistic theory has several implications for the classroom, especially for reading. While it explains the process used by proficient readers rather than the process of learning to read, it clearly indicates the limited role of recognizing individual words while reading. Children need to be taught word recognition techniques, such as phonics, but these techniques are highly useful only in the beginning stages of learning to read. In addition, children need to develop their abilities to use context to make predictions. Weaver, Goodman, and others have written detailed accounts of activities that can be used to develop these abilities.[3]

HOW LINGUISTS HAVE HELPED
THE CLASSROOM TEACHER

Sometimes teachers cannot easily see the implications of linguistics for the classroom. Beyond the fact that an understanding of language broadens one's base of knowledge, there is little that they find obviously valuable in the study of linguistics. This is unfortunate, for the discoveries of linguists are needed in language arts teaching. Three of these discoveries especially should have an influence on the classroom: the function of oral language, the extent of language competence, and the nature of language.

Oral Language

Linguists have gathered evidence that oral language is the foundation of all other forms of communication. A systematic spoken language exists among every group of people on earth and each language includes an organized grammar. When languages include a written component of any type, it is based on the oral form. Learning to read and write, then, is based on an individual's ability to speak and listen.

The implication for the classroom is that oral language needs to be developed in the school. In the section that follows, we will see that children do not need to learn the basics of how English functions, but they do need to expand, refine, and apply the oral language they bring to school. When oral language is recognized as the first step in learning to read and write, kindergarten and first-grade programs do not limit readiness and beginning reading instruction to the study of letters and sounds. The importance of speaking and listening is so great in the language arts program that this text devotes three chapters to it.

Language Competence

By the time they enter school, children have usually developed a working knowledge of their home language. Linguists have discovered that, while they do not yet have full command of all adult grammar, children at this age do understand and use all of the basic structures of their oral language.[4] This understanding of how the rules of English work is acquired through trial and error, not through formal instruction.

There are at least two implications of this knowledge for language arts teachers. The first is that teachers do not need to instruct children about the facts of language and can therefore use their time to enrich and expand language. If the basic structures of English are already understood, they do not need to be taught. The second implication is that much language understanding can be acquired from trial and error in language use, through discovery and without formal instruction. Without question, certain mechanics of communication must be taught directly, but not all language growth is fostered in this way.

The Nature of Language

Linguists have helped us achieve a more thorough understanding of the nature of our language. Three characteristics of language are especially worth noting here: it is arbitrary, it changes continuously, and it has variations.

Language is arbitrary in that there is little relationship between the system of sounds or symbols we use and the objects or ideas they represent. The word *cat* does not look like an animal and its pronunciation is nothing like the cat's characteristics. The spellings, the words, and even the grammar of English were not designed scientifically. Every feature of a language is a result of gradual development and is, therefore, quite arbitrary.

Language changes continuously. Most of the change is slow enough that it largely goes unnoticed, but little by little standards and usage shift. Popular slang changes quickly. But even standards of "good" English are in a state of continuous movement.

Language has variations or dialects. After decades of national mass media, English today still varies from one part of the country, and from one cultural setting, to another. The word *greasy* rhymes with *easy* in some parts of the country and with *fleecy* in others; groceries may be packed in a poke or a bag or a sack in different places; and the pronunciations of words like *car* and *park* have many variations. As a result, standards of "good" English vary also.

The implication of these language characteristics is that the teacher must be accepting of nonstandard English. Eventually, of course, we want every child to be able to speak and write in a manner that is widely acceptable and that will not interfere with career potential. But first must come acceptance, so that the child can grow in confidence and motivation.

LINGUISTICS AND CHILDREN

The linguistic discoveries discussed above have had and should continue to have an influence on language arts instruction. The anticipated improvements in language arts programs cannot help but affect the children in school. As teachers recognize the importance of oral language, the role of experimentation in language growth, and all of the other implications discussed above, children should become better communicators. Linguistics, then, has given us a great deal that is of value.

One thing that linguistics has *not* given us very much of, however, is new body of content for the language arts curriculum. Without question, linguistic discoveries have pointed out the need for *change* in parts of the language arts curriculum. This text's chapter on grammar, for example, suggests a study of grammar that is quite different from traditional practices and those suggestions are based on linguistic discoveries. There are some exceptions of course, some linguistic concepts that can add interest and motivation to the language arts program. But linguistics has provided little new language arts content to teach to children.

The main point here is that children should not be forced to memorize the formulas, rules, or vocabulary of linguistics. They should not be required to analyze the deep and surface structure or the kernel and transformed sentences of written language. In other words, they should not be expected to become better communicators by learning *about* language. One implication of linguistic discoveries is that children learn to communicate by experimenting with language and practicing it in meaningful ways. It would seem a contradiction to the work of linguists if we made linguistics a major part of the language arts content.

There are some exceptions to the general rule about linguistics and language arts content. There are times when the study of language itself can be a valuable supplement to language arts activities. Sometimes the study of synonyms (carpet-rug, throw-pitch, fast-quick) and antonyms (wet-dry, increase-decrease) can help children see the importance of precise vocabulary. Study of regional dialects can build acceptance and understanding regarding speech differences in a classroom. The study of a few historical aspects of English or the comparison of English used in several countries can stimulate interest in language, if done in a challenging manner. As occasional supplements, such techniques can contribute to communication growth.

In addition, individuals who become interested in language study should be encouraged and supported by the teacher. Such an interest is extremely rare in a classroom where children are regularly forced to learn about language through memorization and analysis. Such an interest, however, might be common in a class characterized by discovery and meaningful practice. When such interests do develop, the teacher can help children find resources on language histories, foreign languages, word puzzles, or whatever type is needed. The teacher can also provide time for such activities and give recognition to the individuals who pursue language interests.

Linguistic content, however, should not become a major component in the language arts curriculum. As Chapter One described, the main purpose of language arts in school is to develop better communicators, not students who are better informed about their language. Thus, linguistics has contributed a great deal to language arts education, but it has not produced much content that can be transferred directly into the classroom.

SUMMARY

There are a number of fields of linguistics and each has made a contribution to our understanding of language. This understanding, in turn, can have an impact on the language arts program. Three of the fields of linguistics, however, have had a substantially larger influence on the classroom than the others: (1) descriptive or structural linguistics, (2) generative or transformational linguistics, and (3) psycholinguistics.

The influence of these fields is mainly in new insights into the way children learn or process language. Psycholinguistics has given us a theory about how individuals use context to understand what they hear and read. The other two fields have shown us the importance of oral language, the extent to which children have language competence when they enter school, and the changing and arbitrary nature of language.

Linguistics has not, however, given us a substantial body of new content to teach to children. In fact, it has demonstrated that most language is learned through *using* it rather than learning information *about* it.

Miss Kress, in Scene A at the beginning of this chapter, didn't seem to understand the contributions of linguistics very well. She seemed to view them simply as changes in the vocabulary used to describe language. Probably because she had been familiar with the old terminology for some time, she regarded linguistics as a nuisance.

Mr. Abdurian, on the other hand, understood at least one important implication of linguistic discoveries. He saw that the importance of oral language—speaking and listening—should influence the language arts program. He also saw that language is learned mainly through using it.

A teacher doesn't have to be an expert in linguistics to be a good language arts teacher. It may not be necessary to know a great deal more about language than the information contained in this chapter and the previous one. It is important, however, to apply the information that is described above to the instruction that takes place in the classroom. The remaining chapters in this text give many of the details that can make this possible.

NOTES

1. Wayne Harsh, *Grammar Instruction Today* (Davis, Calif.: Davis Publications in English, 1965), pp. 5–14.

2. Pose Lamb, "Linguistics and Language Arts," in *Resources in Reading-Language Instruction,* ed. Robert B. Ruddell and others (Englewood Cliffs, N.J.: Prentice-Hall, Inc., 1974) p. 76.

3. Constance Weaver, "Using Context: Before or After," *Language Arts,* 54 (Nov./Dec. 1977), 880–86; Yetta M. Goodman, "Reading Strategy Lessons: Expanding Reading Effectiveness," in *Help for the Reading Teacher,* ed. William Page (Urbana, Ill.: National Council for Research in English, 1975.)

4. Jean Malmstrom, *Understanding Language; A Primer for the Language Arts Teacher* (New York: St. Martin's Press, Inc., 1977), p. 4.

CHAPTER THREE
DEVELOPING VERBAL CONFIDENCE

Scene A

"Why was this gift so important to the people?" asked the teacher.
Alice answered, "They liked it."
"Why did they like it? Why was it important?" repeated the teacher.
"It was nice."
"Why was it nice? Did it help them?"
Alice shrugged her shoulders.
"Well," the teacher went on, "you remember how important water was to these people. Did the gift help them get water?"
Alice nodded.

Scene B

"Why was the captain afraid in this situation?" asked the teacher.
"He was a big chicken. Cluck, cluck!" said Tony.
"That's funny, Tony, but it doesn't help us answer the question. Can anyone tell me why the captain was frightened?"
"He was afraid that the enemy was just over the hill," said Mark.
"OK," smiled the teacher. "Now, why did—"
"My mom says my dad's over the hill," interrupted Tony.

In any classroom, there will be some learners who are outspoken and quite verbal, some who speak out part of the time, and some who join class discussions and verbal activities reluctantly if at all. There will be, in fact, a large range of verbal aggressiveness in a classroom. Children on both ends of the range may need help in adjusting to a society that rewards verbal confidence. A lack of verbal aggressiveness and an aggressiveness that is continually used to attract attention are two common indicators of low verbal confidence. Verbal or oral confidence, the willingness to speak out, is very important.

Many children (and adults) feel that they have nothing important to say or that they can't say it as well as others can. With few exceptions, this negative belief is not caused by physical speech defects. Nor is it very often caused by insufficient language ability. As Chapter One points out, almost all children have an oral language background by age five that would allow them to participate readily in classroom verbal activities. A lack of verbal confidence must have other causes.

As with other individual differences, this lack of confidence probably has a variety of causes. For some children, the cause may be an over protective parent who seldom allows them to speak or think for themselves. For others, it could be a dominating sibling who gives insufficient consequence to the things they say. Some children may have their confidence shattered by early experiences in school. Sometimes these factors are combined with others. In any event, the result is a poor self-evaluation or a low self-concept. Self-concept affects verbal confidence at two levels.

ORAL LANGUAGE AND SELF-CONCEPT

Some children whose verbal contributions are minimal, or who are aggressive but distracting, behave as they do because their overall self-concepts are poor. They do not view themselves as quite so important as most other people. When they are with others, they feel that whatever they might have to say is not very important or might sound "dumb."

Other children (and adults) suffer from a specific self-concept related to speaking. Evidence has been found that individuals have self-concepts specific to various personal abilities in addition to their overall self-concept. Thus, a person can evaluate himself or herself differently as an athlete, son or daughter, writer, or speaker. When children regard themselves highly but lack confidence as speakers, their oral behaviors are quite similar to the behaviors of those whose overall self-concept is low.

In both situations, individuals typically react to this lack of confidence in one of two ways. One way is to hide the feelings of inadequacy by remaining silent whenever there is any risk at hand. Those who use this mechanism speak out only when they are with an understanding parent, a small group of friends, or others with whom they feel safe. The other way to deal with inadequacy is to mask it behind attention-getting behaviors. Those who use this mechanism usually become the "class clowns" or cause other disturbances in the classroom.

How Self-Concepts Are Learned

Self-concepts are learned primarily from other people. We know how successful we are from the reactions others give to our efforts. We know how important we are from the amount of acceptance we receive from others. Personal feelings of success and importance make up our self-concepts.

The people from whom we learn self-concepts, however, are those who are important or significant to us. Parents are the most significant people for most young individuals. Purkey found a number of research studies which indicated that parents play an overpowering role in shaping self-concepts.[1] But teachers also have a large influence on self-concepts, or confidence.

Self-Concepts and the Teacher

It is possible that many classroom teachers contribute to the lack of confidence that is present in so many children. Sheldon claims that the large number of ineffective speakers and listeners can be traced to the lack of importance given to what children say in the classroom.[2] When the teacher is the chief speaker, translator, questioner, and information giver for the class, anything the children have to say receives little recognition. As we will see shortly, recognition is one important ingredient in an environment that builds confidence.

On the other hand, teachers can also be a positive factor in building children's oral confidence. Besides his findings regarding parents' roles, Purkey also reports a number of studies in which measured self-concepts have been changed in school programs.[3] It may be assumed that such change is also possible in self-concepts related to oral language.

After we have assumed that such self-concepts *can* be changed, however, we must still deal with the issue of whether they *should* be.

What is the role of the school here? This question can be answered only in the context of a larger issue, the role of oral language in the school program.

ORAL LANGUAGE IN SCHOOL

Speaking ability has an effect on many aspects of adult life. We have all seen individuals with extraordinary speaking abilities succeed in career and social situations even though their academic records have been less than extraordinary. Tiedt and Tiedt claim that the "ability to speak effectively can mean the difference between success in life and the lack of success."[4] Even in school, effective speakers tend to be more successful. Children who can express themselves well receive more recognition from their teachers, develop leadership qualities among their peers, and are better able to mask any academic deficiencies. Klein lists five additional functions of oral language that affect our lives:

1. Makes us reduce a collage of things and events into manageable categories so we can describe them to others

2. Allows us to deal with ideas and things without regard to distance in time or space

3. Increases our ability to preserve, accommodate, and assimilate our experiences

4. Makes language symbols a part of our personal reality

5. Forces us to abstract our experiences[5]

There are two reasons why lack of confidence affects speaking ability. First, individuals with low confidence are usually victims of self-fulfilling prophecy. It is a part of being human that people tend to do as well as they expect to do. Since children with a low self-concept see little hope of success as speakers, they tend to put little effort into effective oral communication. A second tie between self-concept and oral effectiveness is practice. Effective speech depends on practice.

In addition, oral practice is important in school because it leads to the improvement of other forms of communication, especially reading. Anastasiow points out several research studies which indicate that a well-developed language system is a prerequisite to good reading. Tiedt and Tiedt explain that the speaking vocabulary and an understanding of grammar, both of which are important for reading, are acquired through experience and practice. Loban and Chomsky have made similar claims.[6]

BUILDING VERBAL CONFIDENCE

Building someone's confidence in a classroom setting is not an easy task. For one reason, children's self-concepts are rather deeply ingrained by the time they enter school. For another, a teacher has less than thirty hours a week to interact with learners and sometimes counteract out-of-school influences. Often the aggressive children receive more of the teacher's attention than those with little verbal output simply because the aggressive ones are a threat to classroom orderliness.

Yet, there is much teachers can do. Even with their time limitations and other constraints, teachers can have a large impact on the child's confidence. The action they can take falls into two categories: setting up a learning environment and using teaching activities specifically designed to build verbal confidence.

The Environment

Learning is always influenced by the environment in which it takes place, but this is especially true when learning oral language. Because confidence is such an essential part of language development, the environment needs to be a healthy one. The conditions that prevail in the classroom are at least as important as the content that is taught there.

Classroom environment is determined by a number of factors. The furniture arrangement, the types of things on display, and the daily schedule play a part. The content that is taught and the materials that are used to teach it are important. Often the greatest influence on the learning environment, however, is the interaction between learners and teachers.

Much of what goes into human interaction cannot be described in a textbook. Since every human is an individual, it is impossible to set down guidelines that will produce good interaction in every situation. Furthermore, when we interact with other people, our personalities and our psychological needs enter the situation, as well as our knowledge of how to deal with people. In spite of these limitations, however, it is possible to describe four types of action that can be taken by teachers. Though it is impossible to describe how these actions fit every situation, we can examine the general way each contributes to the classroom environment.

Exploring Interests

Worthwhile speech occurs when there is something worth talking about. Individuals who hide their lack of confidence behind a barrage of verbiage need to find confidence in their ability to contribute to discussions in constructive ways. Individuals who do very little talking need to be able to talk about something with which they are familiar and comfortable. In these and other situations, motivation is provided by drawing learners into oral activities dealing with areas of interest to them.

Classroom activities like the following and like the ones described later in this chapter can quite easily be geared toward the interests of students. The purpose of these practice activities is not to teach skills, but to build confidence.

- *Personal experience sharing in small groups.* Often statements by the teacher remind children of personal experiences they've had, but there is seldom time to express them or reluctant speakers lack the confidence to do so. Small groups can provide an outlet for sharing experiences. Topics for this group activity must be selected carefully, because each individual must have had an experience to share. It is best if the topic can be tied to something of high interest that has recently occurred in the classroom. If a recent story in the reading text was about a child getting lost and the class showed an interest in it, for example, the small groups might discuss their experiences with getting lost. The procedure consists simply of dividing the class into compatible groups, saying enough about the topic to reactivate interest, and directing the groups to give each individual a turn. (See also "opinion trios" on page 46.)
- *Book discussion groups.* When a number of students have read the same book, they enjoy talking about it as much as we enjoy discussing a book with a friend. The discussions can be mildly directed if the teacher provides a number of discussion questions. Because the child who needs verbal practice most may also be the one who doesn't read independently, the activity works best in a structured setting where children are expected to read from a certain book list.

The interaction between learners and teacher has a great influence on the learning environment. (*Ken Karp*)

- *Literature groups.* Operating within the same format as above, learners are formed into groups to discuss a selection from children's literature that has been read to them. It is very helpful if copies of discussion questions are provided each group.

- *Discussion corner.* This is not an activity but a place in the classroom where a pair of children can go to talk. Rules for its use must, of course, fit the situation.

Proving Usefulness

A second aspect of the environment in which oral confidence grows is an awareness on the part of the learners that something useful is happening when language activities are used. When they see the purpose in their learning activities they experience language in the natural setting that Edelsky points out is so important for learning.[7] This establishes conditions similar to the ones they experienced while learning language as preschoolers. At home, children acquire most language without even being aware they are doing so, because the purpose is to accomplish something else. Adults or siblings do something with the child that also involves language, thereby setting up a natural learning environment from which both verbal ability and confidence can grow. The classroom can't usually equal the home in establishing a natural environment, but it can help children see that something useful is happening while they are involved in communication.

Obviously, this can happen only if a sufficient amount of the talking that learners do in school contributes to a recognized objective. Sometimes the discussions that take place in science, social studies, and other content subjects can be planned so that child-talk contributes to an objective in a given subject. In addition, activities can be

planned that are specifically designed to help learners see the usefulness of oral language, many of which can also be related to content
subject areas. The ones discussed here are several of the many possibilities.

- *Brainstorming.* When there is a problem, question, or situation for
  which there are many possible solutions or responses, small
  groups can be used to brainstorm. The purpose is not to reach
  the *right* answer, although this is often the next step, but to find
  as many alternatives as possible. Each small group may brainstorm the same issue or, in cases where it is appropriate, groups
  may deal with related issues. In order to promote the free flow
  of ideas, three rules are usually used: (1) don't criticize any ideas,
  (2) add or modify previous ideas as desired, and (3) list as many
  ideas as possible.
- *Problem solving.* This activity may follow brainstorming or, especially when lists of alternatives aren't important, may be used
  independently. Small groups explore a real problem and attempt
  to find a solution. The focus of the discussion in each group is
  on the likely outcome of each possible solution. The group attempts to reach an agreement on the best solution.
- *Session planning.* Small groups plan a real event. Class trips, dramatic productions, social studies or science projects, and class
  displays are among the many events that can be planned by
  groups of learners. Instructions and practice in group planning
  are usually necessary first. Students should understand that the
  following questions must be dealt with:

1. What exactly do we want to accomplish?
2. What would we have to have and do to accomplish it? (A flow
   chart or pert chart might be used with older students planning
   something that is complex.)
3. How can the prerequisite steps best be divided among subgroups
   or individuals, and how can they be coordinated?

All of these activities have a value in addition to that of building
a positive classroom environment. Problem solving and planning are
important life skills in and of themselves. If, however, these activities
are to help learners see the usefulness of oral language, they must deal
with useful topics. The students must have a genuine desire to solve
the problem or to plan, if these activities are to be fully effective.

Showing Recognition

A powerful tool that all teachers use to manipulate the classroom environment, whether or not they are aware of it, is recognition. Behaviors and attitudes that receive attention are encouraged and those that receive little attention are discouraged. Another way to encourage productive oral output in a classroom, then, is to give it recognition.

The first aspect of this process is to provide time and opportunity for children to speak. In classrooms where teachers do the vast majority of the speaking, there is little child-language to which recognition can be given. Opportunities must be given for learners to talk to each other as well as to the teacher. Learners must be given a chance to speak other than just answering the teacher's questions. Certainly there are times when everyone should be expected to listen to the teacher. But there must also be times when everyone is expected to listen to individual students.

The second part of recognition is allowing children to speak for themselves. Teachers are frequently tempted to interrupt their student speakers, translate their message to the other children, or repeat the message so that more students hear it. These behaviors, however, discourage children from listening to each other. When individuals are allowed to speak for themselves without interruption, interpretation, or repetition, they are more likely to feel that what they have to say is important. This recognition encourages other participants to express themselves.

Finally, the speakers must feel that what they have to say has some consequence, that it has merit. Teachers can contribute to this feeling by responding or reacting to what has been said. When learners see their teacher model this type of reaction to child-speech and when they have had guided practice in discussing, they frequently will also begin to react to each others' classroom talk in noncritical ways.

Choosing Acceptance or Criticism

It is often difficult to decide whether children's improperly worded statements should be accepted as they are or corrected. Most teachers have heard arguments for both sides. If "poor English" is left uncorrected, the child may never learn what is right. On the other hand, if a child's speech is criticized, he or she may stop speaking in the classroom altogether. In practice, there seems to be a time for accepting a child's speech and a time for correcting it.

Clearly, one of the times for accepting children's language without criticism is when it comes from those who lack confidence. Such

children need an environment in which it is safe to speak. Edelsky points out the fact that "during normal language acquisition in pre-school years, children are largely free from adult anxiety."[8] Parents expect errors in their young children's speech and react to the content of the message rather than the form. This practice should also be used in the classroom as long as verbal confidence is still developing. Marvin Klein claims that positive support for talk exercises is more likely to produce confidence, as well as oral skill, than correction of poor speaking habits.[9]

These four types of teacher action, then, combine to produce a classroom environment that encourages verbal confidence. When children are drawn into oral activities that deal with their interests and that they regard as useful and when teachers give recognition and acceptance to what is said, the conditions are ripe for building confidence. It is not easy to establish this type of classroom environment, but the outcomes make every effort by the teacher worthwhile.

Low-Risk Activities

The overall strategy for building verbal confidence is that of gradually introducing oral activities that involve low risks for the learners. Speaking to other people always involves some risks, for listeners might make unfavorable judgments about the speaker on the basis of what is said or how it's said. The confident speaker usually finds such risks are low and makes appropriate contributions to conversations, discussions, or whatever. Children who lack confidence, however, find many verbal classroom tasks risky and frightening. The program, therefore, should begin with low-risk practice activities and gradually expand into areas of greater risk.

There are basically three ways to reduce risk during verbal activities. The first, which should only be a temporary measure for children who have very low confidence, is to allow the speaker to displace some risk onto a character who is being role played or to speak as a part of a group. The second way is to reduce the size of the group that is

FIGURE 3–1 **Structuring the classroom for verbal confidence.**

listening. The third is to reduce the demand for correctness or for saying the right thing in the right way.

The activities that follow contain these low-risk elements. The first group contains activities that allow children to share their risk; the second, activities for small groups or for situations with reduced demands for precision. As participants increase in confidence, the group size and the demand for correctness can be increased using the same types of activities.

Although the activities are intended as practice rather than teaching activities, that is the teacher doesn't actually teach lessons, they are not merely supplementary. They are a part of language arts as much as are teaching activities that cover language skills.

For Very Low Confidence

These activities are especially useful for those children who have very little confidence in their oral language. Actually, they are of value for all children, but especially illustrate how to deal with those children who have the greatest need to build confidence. It is suggested, however, that these activities not be limited exclusively to low-confidence children, so they do not feel singled out or self-conscious.

- *Mime activities.* Especially at the beginning of efforts to help those with low confidence, activities that require no speaking at all can be helpful. With no audience, every individual in the class, including the teacher, performs very brief mime activities at the same time. The teacher announces each activity and then the teacher and every child perform it together for several minutes. Several of such activities can be used on a given day and a number of them can be done on several successive days: "Stand and act as if you were: a plant, a plant swaying in the breeze, a flower growing from seed, a soldier guarding something, a soldier marching, a skate board expert, an ice skater, a thief sneaking into a house, a frog, a burning candle."

- *Mime with a partner.* After children are comfortable with solo activities, similar types of creative dramatics can be done with pairs of children. Again, several brief activities can be done on one day and this can continue for several successive days. Pairs of children are asked to act as if they are: playing ping pong, pitching or catching a baseball, folding a blanket, turning a jump rope, carrying a large sheet of glass, swinging in a glider swing, and so on.

- *Choral speaking.* The advantages of membership in a choir without the requirements of singing are found in choral speaking. Selections of literature, often poetry, are practiced and read orally by the class or by groups of participants. As with a choir, some parts are read by everyone in unison, some by groups, and some occasionally solo. Variations in pitch and speed can also be included. It is most effective when the class has some choice about the literature used. The steps involved in using it are quite simple:

The class selects the piece of literature.

Unison, group, and solo parts are determined through experimentation.

Group and solo parts are assigned to children.

The selection is practiced.

Frequently, the selection is performed for an audience.

Children in all categories usually enjoy this activity, but it is especially beneficial to class members who lack verbal confidence. Once such children have become comfortable with performances before an audience, such as the mime activities just described, they should be ready for rehearsals and performances with choral speaking. They probably will become comfortable quite quickly, since their voices are blended in with all the others. Speaking in this way without being singled out is a good early step towards gaining verbal confidence.

- *Tape recording.* The person who has begun to gain some confidence but still needs much more can often make some progress by speaking privately into a tape recorder. In order for this practice to be effective, the child must be given the option of keeping the recording strictly private. With only a few minutes' training, most children can learn to record and erase, if they choose, on a cassette or other recorder. After they have had several such recording sessions, some children will want their teacher or close friends to hear the results. The recorder should be placed so that the child can sit with his or her back to the other children and be separate from them by enough distance that a feeling of privacy is maintained. Most teachers would want to allow other children to make recordings also, but the children who most need confidence must be given frequent opportunities with the recorder. One way to give the participants something to talk about is to post a question next to the recorder each day. Among the possible questions are:

How do I feel today?

What makes me the most happy?

What do I like about myself?

What do I do best?

- *Hidden voices.* At some point in the development of verbal confidence, many children are willing to speak in front of a small audience if they can pretend they are someone else. Opportunities for doing this are found in certain types of dramatics. The role playing that accompanies puppetry allows low-confidence learners to forget their own fears and limitations and become, in effect, the characters they are manipulating. Often the success of speaking for a character enables children to attempt speaking for themselves. The type or quality of the puppets themselves is quite unimportant; even paper-bag puppets or other homemade devices will allow children to "hide" behind their puppets (see Figure 3–2). When puppetry is first introduced, some reluctant speakers become comfortable more quickly if they can actually physically hide behind a puppet stage or curtain.

For All-Confidence Building

The remaining activities are designed to boost the oral confidence of anyone who needs it. Unlike the activities in the first group, these are based on the assumption that the participants are somewhat comfortable with oral activities when the audience is limited or the correctness demand is low. Activities such as the following, if repeated with variations over a period of time and if used in an environment such as the one described earlier, can build confidence to a positive level. The activities progress from least to most risk taking, but there is nothing mandatory in the sequence.

- *Opinion trios.* In this structured activity, the class is divided into groups of threes, and all individuals are given the opportunity to express their opinions to two listeners. After the activity is understood, the teacher announces an opinion question, and in each trio the individuals take turns responding. Limiting each individual's response to approximately one minute increases the attention level of the two listeners. Since the teacher is not listening to the responses, opinions tend to be given openly. After approximately three minutes, all trios are stopped, and the procedure is repeated with another question. Three questions in one ses-

Paper-bag Hand Puppet 1

With paint or crayon, a face is put on the bottom of the bag with the mouth extending under the flap. Without opening the bag, a hand is placed inside so that the fingers move the flap up and down.

Paper-bag Hand Puppet 2

A face is placed on the front of the bag and holes are cut in the sides for the thumb and the smallest finger.

Tongue Depressor Puppet

A paper face is glued to the top of the stick. It is held by the bottom.

Ring Puppet

A face is glued to a finger-sized paper ring. The puppet is used on the tip of a finger.

FIGURE 3–2 Easy-to-construct puppets.

sion might be appropriate. However, the success of this activity depends on the use of questions that are interesting to the participants. The first several times it is used, therefore, it is recommended that questions dealing with personal feelings be used. These might include:

Primary grades

Where is your favorite place to be and why?

What is the best thing you ever did for your parents?

How can you tell if a friend likes you?

If you could be anyone, who would you be? Why?

What is the worst thing anyone ever did to you?

Intermediate grades

What is the worst part of school? Why?

Of all the things you have to do at home, what do you hate most?

What is the best part of school? Why?

How can you tell if someone is your friend?

How could school lunches be made better?

Later, questions can be used that relate to content subjects, especially social studies and literature. However, they must always be of personal interest to the participants if the trio is to stay on the subject.

- *Personal partners.* This structured activity gives individuals the opportunity to share some of their feelings with a partner. After the class or group is divided into pairs, a list of questions is provided to everyone. If the children are beginning readers, the list will need to be limited and some pictorial representation of oral questions will need to be used. If the participants are already reading, a list of ten or twelve questions would be appropriate. The partners take turns asking each other questions from the list until time runs out. If an individual does not care to answer a certain question, he or she simply asks the partner to use a different question and that request must be honored. A partner may ask the same question she or he was asked or a new one. The teacher must stress confidentiality with this activity. The questions must be personal enough to draw children into the activity and yet not so personal that they encourage children to reveal more about themselves than they want to share. Such questions might include:

What thing have you done that's made you most proud?

What's the most unfair punishment you've ever received?

How do you feel about boys/girls (opposite sex)?

What thing or event could make you happy the most quickly?

What makes you the most angry?

How would you feel about more breaks in the school year and shorter summers?

- *Similarities and differences.* This activity gets individuals to compare themselves to someone else. It is done in a group of four to six people which may or may not include the teacher. The group sits in a circle, and individuals take turns making comparisons. The first person tells one way in which he or she is similar to and one way in which he or she is different from the person to the right. The similarity and difference may be as superficial or as personal as the speaker wishes. The next person in the circle then makes the same comparisons to the person on her or his right. After everyone has had a turn, the process may be repeated using the individuals to the left of the speakers.

- *Open-ended questioning.* Questioning is used by teachers at many times during a school day and is, therefore, not a separate activity in the same sense that the other suggestions in this list are. Rather, questioning is something that can be used to build oral confidence in nearly any context. It can be used in this way when the questions are open ended, when they have multiple answers. Single-answer questions do little to build confidence because only the learners who feel certain they know the right answer are encouraged to speak. In addition, only as much as is needed to answer the question will usually be spoken. Certainly, single-answer questions have their place in school, but it is the frequent use of open-ended questions that builds oral confidence. When children realize that there are many answers to a question and there is no negative result from "wrong" answers, they will be more prone to participate. Thousands of open-ended questions are available to teachers. A few examples are:

What are some ways people prove they are friends?

Did————do the right thing in this episode?

What are some reasons————did this?

What are some possible explanations for these chemicals behaving as they did?

- *Interest groups.* Students that have common interests can usually find a great deal to talk about in discussion groups. Interest groups can be organized around hobbies, sports, or other areas. Another very appropriate way to form the group is on the basis of reading interests. "Reading clubs" focused on such topics as mysteries, baseball stories, and horse stories, can be formed, and school time can be given for them to meet. This type of activity cannot be structured by the teacher as much as the activities described above. Only general directions or questions can be given to the groups and they must structure their own discussions from there. Independent discussion groups such as this, therefore, might be most appropriate for learners who have already gained a substantial amount of confidence. The general directions that are given to each group might be similar to the following:

1. Give each member of your club a 2–3 minute turn to tell about what he or she has ready in your topic area.
2. Questions may be asked of anyone at the end of his or her turn.
3. After each member has a turn, discuss and list as many things as you can that all of your books had in common.
4. Talk about why you like to read about your subject area.

- *Role playing.* A final boost to oral confidence might be a form of creative dramatics known as role playing. In this activity, the teacher or someone else describes a realistic situation involving a problem. Individuals take on the roles of people in the situation and behave as they believe the characters would behave. Nothing is planned except the situation, and nothing is rehearsed. Actions and conversations are spontaneous as the situation unfolds. While this activity requires that the participants already have some confidence, there is some safety in the fact that they are taking on the role of someone else rather than speaking for themselves.

The above activities and others like them can be used to build verbal confidence if other conditions are right. They can be used with variations as frequently as needed, but only if the environment is healthy will they help. It is worth pointing out again that an environment which is healthy for confidence building requires that oral activities be of interest to the participants, be seen as useful by them, and offer them recognition.

EVALUATING VERBAL CONFIDENCE

The purpose of evaluating oral confidence is to find the children who need special attention and help. Fortunately, schools do not ask teachers to give report card grades for this sensitive area, so evaluation is not confused with giving grades. Many of the activities suggested above involve the entire class, including those individuals who have adequate self-concepts related to speaking. However, even when confidence-building activities include everyone, the teacher needs to know which learners need the most involvement, the greatest attention, and the guarantee of adequate practice. It is true that such activities could simply be used with everyone, but individual needs might suffer. In spite of the fact that planned evaluation of verbal confidence is often neglected in actual practice, it is important.

Such evaluation is not possible with paper and pencil tests. Oral confidence can be evaluated only through interaction between teacher and child. During the beginning days of school in September, notes can be made about the quantity and quality of individual children's speech in various situations. The results of these observations cannot be tabulated or equated with scores the way that many skill-test results can, but there is no need to categorize confidence levels numerically. Even though the evaluation is quite subjective, then, teachers can determine a great deal about individual needs. Of course, some allowance must also be made for the fact that certain individuals need time to adjust to a new situation in school before they become verbal.

Some observations about oral confidence are very obvious, but others are more subtle. Children who have very low self-concepts and who are frightened even to answer routine questions in class are noticed during the first day or two of school. Other symptoms of low confidence may sometimes be overlooked, however. The child who answers a teacher's questions but never gives more information than necessary is one example. The child who speaks to the teacher but seldom to peers is another. Children who are outspoken but use their language to rebel against classroom activity or to become the class clown are seldom recognized as learners with low verbal confidence. In spite of the many other demands on a teacher's time, then, it is important to observe and evaluate every individual's oral confidence.

One of the best ways to structure the observation and evaluation of each individual is to develop a list of behaviors related to oral confidence. For practical purposes, the list can be rather short, but it should be applied to every child. Below is an example of such a list written in the form of questions:

Does the "quiet" child:

Answer questions in whole-class settings?

Verbalize more than answers in whole-class settings?

Speak loudly enough to be heard by the whole class?

Participate in group discussions?

Speak to me privately?

Participate in conversations during lunch and recess?

Join in family conversations at home?

Does the aggressive child:

Give serious answers to questions in whole-class settings?

Verbalize more than answers in whole-class settings?

Participate cooperatively in group discussions?

Speak to me privately in a friendly fashion?

Listen while others speak in lunch and recess conversations?

Join in family conversations at home?

The more positively these questions can be answered about an individual, the more confidence she or he is likely to have. Not only the number of questions to which an affirmative answer can be applied should be considered, but the degree to which they are true as well. While decisions about individual needs will be based on the teacher's judgment, a list such as this one can make the decisions more objective.

SUMMARY

Verbal or oral communication is important in nearly every aspect of life, so it deserves attention in school. But verbal confidence is a prerequisite to effective oral communication. The school must do its part in building confidence. By establishing a healthy environment and using appropriate teaching activities, the school can do much to develop confident, and then effective, users of oral language.

Lack of verbal confidence usually demonstrates itself in one of two forms. Some individuals, not willing to take the risk of saying something wrong or expressing it poorly, have little to say in the classroom and use "shy" behaviors. Other individuals hide their lack of confidence behind inappropriate comments and use attention-getting behaviors. Both types of behaviors are demonstrated in Scene A and Scene B at the chapter beginning. Both manifestations of low confidence can be improved through low-risk classroom activities and through a positive environment.

NOTES

1. William W. Purkey, *Self-Concept and School Achievement* (Englewood Cliffs, N.J.: Prentice-Hall, Inc., 1970), p. 37.
2. Harry J. Sheldon, "Wanted: More Effective Teaching of Oral Communication," *Language Arts,* 54 (September 1977), 665–67.
3. Purkey, *Self-Concept and School Achievement,* p. 44.
4. Iris M. Tiedt and Sidney W. Tiedt, *Contemporary English in the Elementary School,* 2nd ed. (Englewood Cliffs, N.J.: Prentice Hall, Inc., 1975), p. 256.
5. Marvin L. Klein, *Talk in the Language Arts Classroom* (Urbana, Ill.: National Council of Teachers of English, 1977), pp. 4–5.
6. Nicholas Anastasiow, *Oral Language: Expression of Thought* (Newark, Del.: International Reading Assoc., 1971), p. 14; Tiedt and Tiedt, *Contemporary English,* p. 257; Walter Loban, "Oral Langauge and Learning" in *Oral Language and Reading,* ed. James Walden (Urbana, Ill.: National Council of Teachers of English, 1969), pp. 101–12; Carol Chomsky, "Stages in Language Development and Reading Experience," *Harvard Education Review,* 42 (February 1972), 1–33.
7. Carole Edelsky, "Teaching Oral Language," *Language Arts,* 55 (March 1978), 291–96.
8. Ibid.
9. Klein, *Talk in the Language Arts Classroom,* p. 40.

CHAPTER FOUR
DEVELOPING VERBAL EXPRESSION

Scene A

"Are you tired of the same old games?" asked Rauf as the simulated television commercial began. "Then buy 'El Stick-o,' the exciting new toy," he said as he revealed an ordinary stick.

"With 'El Stick-o' you can play thousands of games. You can play tennis," Clare said as she raised the stick over her head.

"You can play pool," said Todd holding the stick as a pool cue.

"You can hunt elephants," said Rauf holding it like a spear.

"Or invent your own games," Clare added.

"So hurry to a nearby store and ask for 'El Stick-o.' Sold at leading stores everywhere for under twelve dollars," concluded Todd.

"Very good, Rauf, Clare, and Todd," reported Miss Franks. "Can anyone tell us what techniques were used to convince us in this commercial?"

Scene B

"Now, class, it's time to begin our speeches," announced Miss Nora. "You've had a week to get them ready, so I hope you're all prepared. I'll draw names from a hat—Jane, you're first."

"My speech is about sewing," Jane began nervously. "In order to sew, you have to have a needle, some thread, and something to sew . . ."

Once children have gained some confidence in themselves as speakers, they can begin to work on verbal expression. Verbal confidence is a prerequisite to the successful development of effective speaking, as Chapter Three explains, because self-expectations have a large influence on learning and because confident speakers get a larger quantity of productive practice. Although it is a prerequisite to expression, confidence should not be ignored after the emphasis on expression has begun.

Verbal expression is the ability that individuals develop to speak effectively. Individuals with good verbal expression abilities are more likely to accomplish their speaking objectives than are those with lesser abilities. The objectives of speech vary from one situation to another and the types of expression needed vary with them. Sometimes speakers need to give listeners some type of information. Sometimes speakers try to convince other people of something. At other times, speech is used to entertain listeners or to convey emotions. Verbal expression abilities are needed to inform, convince, entertain, or convey effectively.

Typically, teachers can begin to develop expression quite early in the school year if the first few weeks of their oral language programs produce a firm foundation of verbal confidence. The building of confidence need not and should not stop when teaching for expression begins. Most teaching activities that are designed to improve verbal expression can, in fact, also build confidence if they are given appropriate treatment.

The key to a continuation of confidence building after the emphasis on verbal expression has begun lies in the attention given to success. Children who experience repeated successes and recognition during their attempts to develop expression are likely to continue their growth in self-concept.

Especially for the learners who begin with low confidence, then, it is important to introduce verbal abilities at a pace they can readily absorb, and with low levels of criticism. Appropriate pacing prevents situations that overwhelm students and give them feelings of failure. In an environment with limited criticism at first, learners can recognize their successes and expand their abilities. Critical analysis can expand as abilities grow.

Verbal expression abilities can be classified into two categories. There are general abilities that are useful in nearly all situations. There are also specific abilities that are useful for specific types of verbal expression or in specific situations.

Verbal expression is built on verbal confidence. (*Chuck Iossi*)

GENERAL VERBAL ABILITIES

There are several categories of verbal abilities that influence the speaker's effectiveness regardless of his or her objective. Such specific objectives as informing, convincing, entertaining, and conveying emotions all make use of these general abilities. Among them are appropriate voice, descriptive vocabulary, and flexibility of word usage.

Appropriate Voice

One of the most obvious differences between an effective and ineffective speaker is the use of voice. Effective speakers seem to know when to increase or decrease their volume, raise or lower the pitch of their voices, and make pauses. These are the three types of control that we have over our voices.

Voice Controls

The volume variations that are used when we speak are often known as *stress*. This refers not only to such extremes as shouting or whispering during formal speeches, but to the emphasis placed on individual words or syllables in every oral communication. Sometimes stress determines the meaning of a word, as with *present* and *content,* because placing stress on different syllables changes the word. Sometimes stress changes the meaning of a sentence. For example, say this sentence with the boldface word stressed: **What** are you doing? What **are** you doing? What are **you** doing?

Pitch, the degree to which a voice uses high or low tones, is used along with volume to emphasize or deemphasize parts of the spoken message. Pitch and volume variations are found even in preschoolers' voices. The task of the school is to improve the effectiveness of their use through practice.

Pauses are a natural part of everyone's speech as well. They are lengthened when the phrases that precede or follow them deserve emphasis. As with volume and pitch, the effective use of pauses is not learned from classroom lessons but from guided practice.

Voice Activities

The practice that is needed to develop appropriate voice usage can be given through a variety of teaching activities. Much of the practice can be provided as learners discuss social studies, science, and other subject content. Some practice results from the reading instruction program. When teachers take advantage of these situations to guide appropriate use of voice, the learning is frequently very effective because it is in a meaningful setting. In addition, however, activities such as the following can be included in the language arts program to focus specifically on voice controls.

- *Expression plays.* The teacher gives a sentence that could be used in a variety of settings with a variety of voice tones. Volunteers tell who might say a sentence like this and then try to demonstrate how that person would say it. This not only gives the speaker practice in saying the sentence with appropriate expression, but gives all the listeners the opportunity to focus on differences in voice. For example, a teacher might write this sentence on the chalkboard: "What is that in your mouth?" A volunteer might suggest that it was said by a teacher and demonstrate an angry voice. Another volunteer might suggest the question was asked by a dentist and demonstrate a surprised voice. Examples of other sentences that can be used are:

You're wearing that perfume again.
There's another pile of clothes.

Have you done your homework?

I see one just around the corner.

One or two new sentences might be introduced each time the activity is used.

- *Voice imitation.* Children (and often adults) love to imitate other people. As long as it is done in a positive way, this natural activity can be used in the classroom to develop oral expression. The teacher provides the setting, the guidance, and the motivation. A favorite and useful source of imitations is television commercials, since nearly all children are exposed to them repeatedly. The class can be divided into small groups and each group can select a commercial to demonstrate to the class. Other people that can be imitated include television characters and announcers, politicians, and famous people. It is not wise to let children imitate each other since this can reinforce negative self-concepts or cause resentments.

- *Dramatics.* In order to play the role of a character in any form of dramatics involving dialogue, an individual must imitate the voice of that character. Not only does the child get practice in voice usage while performing the dramatization, but in any practice that precedes it as well. Dramatics are discussed later in this chapter.

- *Expression words.* Discuss with the class several familiar words that are used to tell how something is said. For example, the words *whispered, mumbled, gasped,* and *stuttered* might be discussed. Bring out the shades of difference in meaning. Then, introduce a sentence or short statement, for example, "Someone is at the door." Individuals may then speak the sentence in a way suggested by one of the words that has been discussed. When each word has been demonstrated once, a different sentence can be introduced.

- *Expression dialogue.* Divide the class into pairs and have each pair read a dialogue, such as the one in Box 4–1, with oral expression. Have each pair of learners prepare for the activity by deciding upon answers to the following questions:

1. Who are the characters (Person A and Person B)?
2. Where does the dialogue take place and when?
3. What are they doing? How do they feel?

Then have them read through the dialogue silently and decide upon an ending. Finally, have them read the dialogue orally with appropriate expression.

BOX 4–1   *SAMPLE DIALOGUE*

Person A: What do you have there?
Person B: Oh, nothing.
    A: So, you're keeping something from me again.
    B: Not really. It's just not important.
    A: I see. (pause) You know, though, lately you've been acting . . . well, different. I've been a little concerned about you.
    B: Different? I don't think I know what you mean.
    A: It's hard to describe. You seem to be keeping things to yourself. You're not telling me everything the way that you used to. Is something wrong?
    (finish the dialogue)

Descriptive Vocabulary

The broader the vocabulary base that is brought to a speaking situation, the more effective the speech is likely to be. Of course, the use of a lot of "big words" does not always make for effective speaking, but a good vocabulary allows the speaker the flexibility to draw upon the right words at the right time. The best type of language to use depends on relative formality, size of audience, purpose, and other factors in the situation. So that the appropriate language is available to the speaker, though, a broad vocabulary is useful in nearly every situation.

Vocabulary, however, is not acquired by simply memorizing words. Already in 1940, Glicksberg pointed out that words do not appear in isolation when they are used, but are part of an ongoing stream of thought.[1] The dependence of word meaning and word usage on context has been verified again and again through research. In fact, vocabulary growth, language acquisition, and child development are all entwined and interdependent.[2]

Petty and others and Vaughan, Crawley, and Mountain have shown that, according to accumulated research, direct instruction in vocabulary produces more vocabulary growth than does such informal techniques as listening and reading extensively.[3] While the research is convincing, three things qualify the results:

1. The research uses measuring techniques that are biased in favor of direct instructional techniques, namely vocabulary tests. Because such tests separate vocabulary from the context of communication, they force it into the difficult arena of abstraction.[4] The evidence that reading and listening are less effective in building vocabulary, therefore, may not be valid.

2. The research says nothing of the comparative value of learning words in isolation and learning words in context. Other types of research show an advantage for the latter.

3. Direct teaching of vocabulary is certainly not limited to practices that require memorization of words or definitions.

It seems safe to conclude, then, that listening and extensive reading, in conjunction with direct instruction in context, is best.

- One way that direct instruction can be used to teach vocabulary in context is through context sentences. The teacher duplicates and passes out or orally states sentences or short passages containing a word to be learned. The sentences are constructed so that the context gives strong clues about the word's meaning. The learners must tell what the approximate meaning of the word is. If this isn't possible, the dictionary is consulted. This use of dictionaries "as a last resort" is more in line with the way that adults use them. Since it is speaking vocabulary that is being emphasized, it is only appropriate that this be an oral activity rather than a written one. It can be done in groups and pairs as well as with the whole class. Of course, this activity requires more work from the teacher than does giving vocabulary lists to memorize or look up, but it is also more meaningful.

- Another direct teaching activity using context is the cloze technique. With this technique, words are deleted from a passage so that learners can use context to supply the missing words. It has a number of uses and its form varies from one to another. When it is used to build vocabulary, the teacher selects the words to be deleted on the basis of the ease with which they can be replaced by using context clues. Rather than guessing at the exact word that was omitted, learners list all of the single words that they can think of that would sensibly fill the blank. Cloze is usually a written activity, but for the purpose of building speaking vocabulary, it can be used orally. One way that teachers can implement this plan is to use a selection of children's literature. Words to be deleted are prechosen and the story is then read aloud to the class or group while illustrations are shown. When the prechosen word is reached, the teacher makes a designated noise, and the children respond with suggestions for the missing word. A short example using a familiar folktale follows.

Once upon a time, there were three _____ . They lived in a simple _____ in the woods. For breakfast one morning, Mama _____ porridge. When they tried to _____ it, they discovered it was too hot.

Enough time should be given for several suggestions to be offered, and these can be recorded on the chalkboard. However, the interruptions should not be so long as to destroy the story context. This activity does not allow the teacher to select words on the basis of a vocabulary list. In fact, the vocabulary that is learned will be that which learners share with each other. However, there is reason to believe that this technique does expand vocabulary, and it teaches children how to derive meaning from context.

- Vaughan, Crawley, and Mountain have explained still another technique for building vocabulary.[5] It involves sorting words into categories in an activity they call "vocabulary scavenger hunts." These are the steps to follow:

1. A group of students is given three or four categories, for example, *brass instruments, strings, woodwinds,* and *percussion.*
2. The same group is given a list of fifteen to twenty-five words including a few that are somewhat unfamiliar to the group, for example, the names of musical instruments.
3. The group classifies the words into the categories so that each word is placed once.
4. Individual members look for pictures to accompany the words, for example, pictures of the musical instruments in the list.
5. The activity proceeds like a Scavenger Hunt.

This activity lacks the context of an ongoing stream of language, but the categories may provide some contextual value. The activity also seems to be designed mainly for reading and writing vocabulary, but it would appear to aid speaking vocabulary when the learners are given the pronunciation of unrecognized words.

Synonyms and Multiple Meanings

In addition to generally adding more words to their oral vocabulary, learners need to increase their word flexibility. They need to develop an understanding that many words have more than one meaning, and a meaning can normally be expressed using more than one possible word (that is, there are synonyms). It is not possible to teach all of the countless combinations of words and meanings even on a basic word list, nor is it necessary. Learners who have developed word flexibility can learn specific word/meaning combinations as they encounter them.

The concept that words may have several meanings may be developed through activities like the following:

- *Saying four sentences.* Use all sentences that contain the same word. Plan the sentences so that two have approximately the same meaning for the word, and the other two have different meanings. For example:

I bought a set of dishes.
Please set the table.
This set of glasses is new.
I'll set the package on the chair.

The children listen and identify the two that are similar. Sometimes the other meanings may then be discussed. Because this is a listening activity, the number of sentences used must be limited.

- *Oral vocabulary cloze.* Prepare and read a paragraph to the students which uses the same two words in several ways, but leave out those words and replace them with pauses. For example:

watch   *run*

I went to the baseball stadium to _____ a game. I was in a hurry, but my dad told me not to _____ down the stairs. I was just in time to see a batter get the first _____ . After each inning I checked the time on my _____ . "I guess my _____ doesn't _____ very well," I said.

The listeners must decide which of the two words belongs in each blank. Afterwards, the various meanings can be discussed.

The concept that a similar meaning can be expressed with a variety of words may be developed through activities like the two discussed here.

- *Word brainstorming.* A sentence is given containing a common word such as *said, ran,* or *put.* For example, *Tom said his name.* The class is then challenged to find as many words as possible to replace the common word. For a word as common as *said,* they might be challenged to find as many as thirty or forty words. As the replacements are suggested, they are listed on the chalkboard.
- *Synonym ranking.* A list of familiar synonyms is placed on the chalkboard and read to the class. The participants then vote and reach a group decision about the word in the list that infers the greatest strength, intensity, size, or whatever. The other words in the list are then ranked in the same manner. Lists of words like the following might be used:

Exhausted	Huge	Admire
Tired	Large	Love
Weary	King-size	Like
Fatigued	Big	Adore
Beat	Giant	Tolerate

Combining Techniques

Although the research mentioned earlier gives some indication that direct instruction in vocabulary produces higher scores on vocabulary tests than informal techniques do, such informal techniques as reading and listening are far from useless. Children who do a great deal of reading have larger vocabularies than children who don't. Of course, such evidence doesn't show which factor caused which, but it does show some type of relationship. In all probability, motivating children to do extensive reading and listening *together with* direct instruction provides the best program for building speaking vocabulary.

Flexibility of Word Usage

Another important ingredient in effective speaking is flexibility. Speakers must adjust their voices and their language to fit their audiences and their purposes. Flexibility must be applied to the two areas already discussed, voice and vocabulary. It must also be applied to a third area, word usage.

Flexibility in Voice and Vocabulary

In order for speakers to adjust their voices and vocabulary to their audiences and purposes, they must first develop the abilities described earlier. They must learn the range of effective voice tones and volume. They must build up a substantial speaking vocabulary. As these abilities increase, learners can begin to be aware of the various purposes for speech, and begin to learn how to match voice and vocabulary to the situation. Such learning occurs through guided practice, following the same strategies that have already been described.

Flexibility in Word Usage

Speakers also need to adjust their word usage to fit their audiences. The audience or the listeners vary from the formal situation of a public address to the intimate situation of two friends chatting. Quite obviously, children speak in informal situations much more frequently than in formal situations. During informal conversations agreement of subject and verb, proper use of plural word forms, consistency of person and tense, and other "good" English is usually not necessary. Few children have difficulty adjusting their language to the informal peer group situation. It is to the more formal situations that most school-age learners have difficulty adjusting.

There are two probable causes of this difficulty. One is a lack of knowledge about the word usage required for formal situations. The other is a lack of motivation to use what is known.

The amount that speakers need to know about word usage is relatively small. It normally includes:

A few generalizations about, and several exceptions for, making singular words into plurals

Generalizations for keeping the subject and verb of a sentence in agreement on person (first person: I, me, we, us, myself, and so on; second person: you, your, yourselves; third person: he, she, it, they, them, themselves, and so on), on singular and plural forms, and on tense (past, past perfect, present, and so on)

A few generalizations on how to make words possessive

The acceptable forms of contractions and certain troublesome verbs

The quantity of this knowledge is not so small that it should be regarded lightly. On the other hand, it is not so great that it should take ten years of concentrated study to master, as the practices in some schools would seem to indicate. Students who see a need for this knowledge could learn it with relative ease under normal conditions.

The reason so many learners never fully master this knowledge is that they are not motivated to do so. Since most children do not experience many situations which call for more formal or "standard" usage, they see little need for it. When teachers demand "correct" usage in the classroom, they usually do not increase this motivation because the need is not perceived by the learners. An artificial need set up by teachers, based strictly on their demands, is far different from needs which the learners see as "real." In fact, artificial demands for correct usage can often build resistance and resentment in students which interferes with learning the principles of usage.

There are three types of strategies teachers can use to improve flexibility in word usage, including usage in more formal situations. They can create a realistic environment for word usage, provide activities that practice good usage, and develop situations in which formal usage is really required.

The ideal environment for encouraging usage flexibility is much easier to describe than to create. Creating an environment involves a different process of group interaction for every teacher, but some generalities can be made. Learners should be challenged to continuously work toward a fuller understanding of usage, but not commanded to speak a certain way. Learners should be expected to apply the more formal usage at appropriate times, but be allowed to use less formal English when that is appropriate. Policies such as "we only speak good English in this classroom" are frequently counterproductive. The teacher's main tool should be modeling. As learners experience appropriate but flexible usage in the real language of their teachers, they adopt it more than when they are forced to use it unwillingly. A classroom environment that largely adheres to these standards is likely to improve usage flexibility.

A second strategy that is sometimes necessary to build students' flexibility is providing practice in correct word usage. Correct usage must be understood before it can be used. Understanding isn't acquired by memorizing rules or by choosing the correct words to fill in blanks on written exercises. Usage is an *oral* skill on which written usage is based. School activities that develop correct usage must also be oral. Children should orally experiment with and listen to standard patterns of English until these patterns sound normal and natural to them. The following paragraphs discuss activities that might be used for this.

- Using language generated by students, sentences are written and divided so that the desired element of usage must be practiced in putting the sentences back together. For example, if agreement in number is the element to be practiced, the sentences are divided between subject and verb. (The boy/goes to school. The boys/go to the park.) Students then match any sentence beginning with any sentence ending that agrees in number. The sentences need to be written on strips of paper to allow such matching, but as they are reconstructed they are spoken a number of times.

- Using language suggested by students, sentences are written on strips of paper and read to the learners. They then decide which of the models provided by the teacher contains the element of usage in the same form as the sentence in question. For example, if past and present tense are being studied, learners categorize each sentence using the teacher's model of past tense or of present tense. Again, the activity stresses oral language, as each sentence is spoken several times while the decision is made.

- Short oral skits which contain the needed correct forms of usage are used. More than one element of usage may be stressed in a given skit. Learners practice and present the skits, thereby reinforcing the correct forms. Further practice in hearing correct usage can be given if the skits are tape recorded.

The other available strategy for meeting this objective is establishing real needs for more formal types of usage. Such activities as interviewing school personnel, questioning classroom visitors, speaking to small groups of parents, making announcements, and making tape recordings for younger children are examples of situations that call for formal word usage. Certain role plays such as giving TV news or being radio announcers are also useful. Such activities can be used periodically to give learners occasional real need for the formal types of usage. With a full range of word usage levels available to speakers, then, flexibility will be possible.

SPECIFIC VERBAL ABILITIES

In addition to the general verbal abilities that effective speakers need to draw upon, there are abilities that are specific to certain objectives. When an individual is attempting to convince a friend to go with him to a party, for example, appropriate voice, vocabulary, and word usage are not enough. Some ability to convince is also needed. In addition to the abilities specific to convincing others, speaking objectives that require specific abilities include giving information, expressing emotions, and entertaining.

Giving Information

There are several types of speaking that fall within the category of information. Describing things or events, giving directions, summarizing, and asking questions are all forms of information giving. All four types of speaking are somewhat similar in that their objectives all include clarity of meaning. Yet, each requires its own set of abilities.

Describing

The ability to "paint a verbal picture," to inform others about a person, place, thing, or event, can be called describing. It involves the ability to explain what it is that distinguishes whatever is being described from everything that is not being described. Frequently, it is a process of naming smaller and smaller categories to which the person, place, or other thing belongs. It is an ability that is necessary at many times as an adult as well as during childhood.

The ability to describe is learned through practice and through feedback or reactions from others. Reactions of listeners are quite apparent when descriptions are not understood. When descriptions are understood, listeners follow along and look pleased or relaxed. On the other hand, sharp criticism of descriptions tends to inhibit growth in describing. The classroom provides an environment in which teachers can give learners guided practice and feedback that is honest but helpful. There are many opportunities to practice descriptions during the daily learning experiences that occur in a classroom. In addition, activities such as the following can be used to work specifically on this ability.

- Four familiar types of food are placed within view of the listeners. The student selected to give the description is given a taste of one of the foods without the listeners' seeing which one. The selected person then describes the taste, completing the description before receiving any feedback. None of the foods can be named during the description. The listeners then vote to show which one they believe was described. As the participants become more skilled, the foods can be made more similar. This activity can be used in a number of ways, by varying the senses used. The feel, smell, sound, and sight of objects can also be described.

- A collection of familiar objects can be placed in a bag. The student selected to give the description reaches in the bag and selects one object. After allowing a moment for thought, the individual describes all the characteristics of the object without naming it (appearance, use, texture, and so forth). Each listener then writes what he or she believes it is, and all answers are shared before the object is shown.

- An enjoyable way to practice descriptions, but one that lacks clear feedback, is a "doodle-scription." The teacher provides a few simple lines on the chalkboard that might be part of a drawing. For example:

Volunteers then describe additional details, perhaps while pointing to their location on the "drawing."

- A collection of large photographs or portraits of known people can be displayed (not people personally known). The student selected to give the description secretly selects one of the pictures and describes the person's physical features to the listeners. As with the first activity above, the listeners can then vote on the person they believe was described. The activity can also be done with unknown people, with photographs of landscapes, and any number of categories.

- Keeping events in order is an important part of a description that deals with events. It is doubtful if there exists a separate skill for telling events in sequence, but practice can point out the *importance* of sequencing. Such practice can be given by relating the steps of a well-known event in a scrambled order and asking individuals to sequence them correctly. At first, the number of steps should be small; difficulty can gradually be increased as the activity is repeated, by increasing the number of steps.

- In order to combine sequencing with other aspects of describing, a large picture from a magazine is displayed to the class. An action picture is usually best. First the class discusses what probably happened prior to the scene in the picture, with individual volunteers giving specific details. Then, the class members describe what probably happened after the picture was taken.

Giving Directions

The ability to give directions is one that is called upon again and again in life. When we give directions, our listeners expect clarity, efficiency, and accuracy. They expect steps to be given in logical sequence. We expect the same when others tell us how to get to a designated place or how to do something. Giving directions clearly, efficiently, and accurately without losing the sequence of necessary steps is evidently quite difficult. The ability to do so is, again, acquired through experience and feedback. The most effective teaching technique, therefore, is to provide guided practice. The practice should begin at a simple level and gradually become more complex.

The following activities are especially useful for providing practice in a classroom. Each activity can be varied in difficulty, beginning at very simple levels. Each includes feedback so that direction givers can see immediately how well the directions are being received.

- The teacher builds a very simple structure from three or four building blocks or other toy building materials while the class watches. An individual volunteer then gives step-by-step directions for repeating the same construction. As the directions are given by the child, the teacher follows them exactly. Other volunteers are called upon, if the first one isn't successful, until the structure is identical to the one first demonstrated. When several successes have been achieved at this level, more difficult structures may be demonstrated.

- After a teacher's demonstration, one child gives another directions on where to walk within the classroom. At first, the directions could have only two steps, such as, "Go to the pencil sharpener and go left three steps." The child following the directions listens to both steps before beginning the first. Then the steps can be increased to three and more. If it is manageable, several pairs of students can work at one time. This activity is also useful for building listening comprehension.

- Copies of a simple map and a small movable object are distributed to everyone. The person selected to give the directions moves to a place where his map and object cannot be seen. He places his object on the map and describes to the others where he has placed it. The others listen to the directions and attempt to place their objects on the same position. After a check to see how many listeners were able to locate the correct position, the individual makes a two-step move with his object and gives directions to the others. The listeners follow the directions, using their own maps. As with the first activity, the number of steps in the directions can be varied and the size of the group can be adjusted. The value for listening comprehension is evident. This activity is also valuable for map-reading practice.

- Each individual is given identical sheets of inexpensive or scrap paper. A selected person stands where his or her hands are hidden and makes one simple fold while giving directions to the others. After everyone has had an opportunity to follow the directions, the individual holds up the folded paper and checks to see how many people were able to follow the directions (if given well, directions for even one fold involve several steps). The same variations are possible here as in the two activities described earlier. If it is possible to have simple origami (Japanese paper folding) demonstrated, this would provide an excellent follow up.

- Several identical sets of building materials are assembled. Each set may have only three or four items such as a tack, a wooden block, a drinking straw, and a popcycle stick, but each set must be exactly the same. In a hidden place, the teacher builds an abstract design using all of the materials in one set. The class is then divided into groups and each group selects one direction giver. The selected individuals may view the hidden construction as often as needed, but the other members of the groups may not see it. Using a set of building materials, each group follows the directions of their selected individual in constructing a design identical to the one hidden from their view.

Activities such as the five above can be used any number of times with variations. One way to use them is to devote several language arts class periods early in the year to introducing direction giving. After that, the activities can be used from time to time throughout the school year.

Summarizing

Individuals need summarizing abilities whenever they must give a shorter version of something that has already been said or written. Spoken summaries, unlike their written counterparts, usually need to be spontaneous. Nevertheless, children can learn to develop summarizing abilities in school. Like the other specific uses of oral language, summarizing can best be learned through practice and feedback, beginning with easy tasks and working toward the more difficult. The following activities are examples of those that can provide such practice and can be varied in difficulty:

- A current daily newspaper is divided and given to a number of individuals. Each person summarizes one or more articles and presents them to the remainder of the class. A little flair is added if the participants imitate a local television newscast. Since most such productions now use a team to report news, the use of several students should seem quite normal. (Caution: This activity can be repeated frequently, but using it daily throughout the year would probably overdo its usefulness and make it counterproductive.)

- Each individual constructs a simple personal time line, a line with dots to represent the important events in his or her life. Example:

1974	1975	1977	1979
Born	Learned to walk	Picture in newspaper	Started school

Over a period of several days, individuals use their personal time lines to give brief summaries of their lives.

- One of the most difficult things to summarize seems to be a story, especially if it was viewed on television. Perhaps a few minutes can be used two or three times a week to give a student an opportunity to summarize a favorite show. Limit the summary to three minutes and insist on the limitation. To help the summarizer prepare, ask him or her to think about the four or five most important events and how they tie together. These events can then form the framework for the brief summary.

Questioning

Although questioning is not usually regarded as a method of giving information to others, it has some similarities with other types of information giving. In one sense, in fact, it does inform the listener, "There is something I want to know."

Children do not need to be taught to ask questions. Unless their normal curiosities have been terribly suppressed, they have asked thousands of them before they ever entered school. But they do need to learn to ask questions effectively. Good questions let listeners know precisely what the individual wants to find out. Asking precise questions is as important to effective communication as is the skilled use of other information-giving techniques. Learning to ask questions effectively, like the other types of oral language, comes through meaningful practice. The activities described below encourage learners to improve their questioning strategies:

- Variations of the "Twenty Questions" game lead learners to develop questions that narrow the field. The person who is "it" selects an object, concept, or category, and the participants ask questions that can be answered only with "yes" or "no." The object of the game is to identify what has been selected, using the least number of questions possible. Since this activity tends to focus on the attributes of objects and concepts, it also provides useful practice with various skills and helps in the development of science and social studies concepts.

- After students have been exposed to a relatively brief set of information, they are asked to list questions that could be answered with the information. This procedure is somewhat the opposite of the typical situation in which the teacher asks questions about the information. Because the information must be understood before appropriate questions can be based on it, this strategy can be used frequently in any situation that normally calls for discussion of information.

- Simple forms of interviewing can be used in a classroom. After listening to several model interviews by viewing together a television news show or listening to a tape recording, learners role play short interviews. Real interviews can then be arranged in a variety of ways. One useful method is to give each child the opportunity to ask one prepared question of a forwarned and invited classroom guest.

Convincing

The ability to convince others is useful at any stage of life. Salespeople, advertising agents, defense attorneys, political candidates, and many other people depend on their ability to convince for career success. In all walks of life, however, individuals who are able to convince are active in decision making, self-fulfillment, and possibly leadership. A leader at any level is simply one who has convinced others to follow. The vast majority of convincing strategies seem to be applied through the spoken word rather than through writing.

Some children in elementary school acquire abilities to convince others without any intentional training in school. A large part of the credit for such abilities can probably be attributed to verbal confidence. Any attempt to convince involves risk taking, so children who have more confidence will take greater risks and be more convincing.

Much of the development of convincing abilities, then, is dependent upon strategies like those discussed in Chapter Three. The goal of building confidence is not to make everyone a leader, but to give every individual the opportunity to be recognized and to develop oral effectiveness.

Confidence, however, isn't the total picture. Strategies for convincing others need to be acquired. Children can be given some general guidelines such as, "Try to imagine what would convince *you* in this area." Primarily, however, strategies are acquired through practice. Activities such as the following can be used for practice without weakening confidence:

- Nominations and campaigns can be made within a classroom. Classroom colors, motto, flag, flower, animal, and so on can be nominated and actually voted upon. The book of the month can be the object of a campaign. Limiting nominations and campaigns to objects eliminates the comparisons of individual children that is typical in the election of people.
- Television commercials have such an appeal for children that they provide a good basis for practicing the ability to convince. Small groups can be allowed to create and present their own commercials for products that are not normally advertised. Elementary-school children especially enjoy making commercials for "worthless" objects such as rocks, sticks, and strings. Emphasis should be placed on convincing rather than entertaining (see the opening scene of this chapter).
- In preparation for the above activities or as a separate activity, groups or the class can think of and list as many arguments for a certain position as possible. As discussed in Chapter Three, listing as many alternatives as possible is sometimes called *brainstorming*. In this activity a special adaptation is used that encourages learners to think of and sort through points which might be convincing to listeners. Examples of questions that could be used include:

What are some reasons for going to a movie that you might use to convince your parents?
What are some reasons you might give your friend to buy the rock collection you want to sell?

After the reasons or arguments have been listed, the participants can discuss which ones would be most effective.

- A very motivating activity is an invention contest. Small groups or individuals decide what each thinks would be the best new invention the world could use at this time. (Examples: bubblegum-flavored spinach, a homework machine, an automatic dog walker.) Then arguments that might convince the class that this is the best invention are planned. Each invention is then "sold" to the class in the most convincing manner possible. If competition is not a negative factor, the class can turn the activity into a contest by voting for the best inventions. (Naturally, no one is allowed to vote for his or her own.)

Entertaining

Another use of oral language is to entertain others. This category includes the use of humor, storytelling, and dramatics.

Humor

Although we all seem to need a certain amount of humor in our lives, not everyone needs to be a comedian. The school, therefore, may not need to give high priority to the development of comedic abilities, but it should give every individual an opportunity to "try one's hand" at comedy. Joke telling is probably the most practical way to do this. Each individual takes a turn telling a prepared (and perhaps monitored) joke to the class or a group. The teacher will have to have a ready supply of jokes for those individuals who remember none of their own. Of course, humor may be included in storytelling and dramatics as well.

Storytelling

The art of telling a story requires somewhat different abilities from those needed to summarize or describe. Expert storytelling requires both of those abilities—appropriate voice and an audience relationship—which it is difficult to describe. Children in an elementary school should not be expected to become expert, but they should be guided to grow in such abilities. Storytelling is a valuable classroom activity because, as children prepare a story, they are practicing reading skills and various oral language abilities. In addition, storytelling activities help the child develop storytelling abilities themselves.

Unless children have already been exposed to storytelling at home, the teaching process begins with modeling. As children listen to the teacher or to recorded stories, they acquire some of the techniques used in this art. Practice in telling stories should begin with very short episodes and should involve only small audiences. Length of the stories and size of the audience can then be gradually increased. John Stewig describes three things that the teacher provides whenever children prepare for and tell a story: a time and place to practice, feedback before the "performance," and an audience.[6] Storytelling should receive attention from time to time throughout the school year.

Dramatics

One of the purposes of dramatics is to entertain others. Dramatics also has several other important functions, however. Therefore a complete discussion of this form of oral language is included later in the chapter.

Expressing Emotions

A final specific use of verbal language that can be fostered by the school is that of expressing emotions. The school's purpose in encouraging such expression, however, is quite different from that of other language training. The school need not be concerned about the *ability* to express emotions as much as about the child's willingness to do so. Individuals whose only outlet for emotions is aggressive or withdrawn behavior frequently have developed this pattern because they are reluctant to express emotions verbally. Our society seems to discourage such expression, as if emotions were a sign of immaturity. The school typically is even more discouraging. In their extensive studies of teacher-pupil interactions, Flanders and Amidon found that acceptance of feelings accounted for only .005 percent of the verbal interaction in the many classrooms they observed.[7]

The role of the classroom teacher should be to encourage the expression of emotions in socially acceptable ways. Children begin to express themselves when they discover it is safe to do so. Since many children have already learned that talking about feelings is not acceptable, the message that such expression is now approved must be conveyed in a conspicuous manner. One way to do this is to discuss the emotions of story characters and let the discussion develop into one about personal emotions. In addition, some of the activities suggested in Chapter Three can be adjusted to intentionally deal with students' emotions. When children reveal their emotions in a classroom, however, two precautions must be taken:

1. A strong point must be made, and periodically reinforced, that statements made during such discussions must remain confidential. Children who violate this confidentiality must be held accountable. Only then will individuals feel safe.
2. No child should ever be forced or pressured to reveal emotions. Such pressure would not only encourage individuals to lie about their feelings but would be counterproductive.

When children feel that openness is safe, they will tend to reveal their emotions. Then, the need to express frustration, anger, and other emotions will not be released through aggressive or withdrawn behavior, but through verbal expression.

Summary of Verbal Abilities

A number of verbal abilities are discussed in this chapter. They have been placed into two categories: those that are general and are used in nearly every verbal situation, and those that serve a more specific purpose. The various abilities have been diagrammed in Figure 4–1 in the same order as they appear in the text.

DRAMATICS

Dramatics can have an important function in the language arts program. A specific type of oral language ability is certainly involved in dramatization, but dramatics is also different in one important way from the specific oral language abilities discussed earlier. The purpose

FIGURE 4–1 Categorizing verbal abilities.

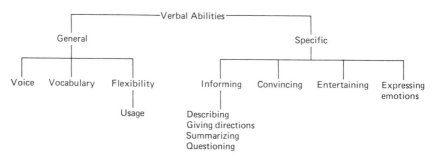

of dramatics is in the process not in the product. With the exception of a tiny minority of students who will become professional actors, the purpose is not to improve dramatization abilities for future use but to draw from the experience a variety of benefits at the present. The types of benefits depend on the type of drama. Two very broad types are discussed next.

Creative Dramatics

Creative dramatics is a term used to describe any form of improvised drama. Children act spontaneously in reaction to any of many possible stimuli. Its purposes in the classroom are to stimulate creativity and to give children the opportunity to express themselves freely. Sometimes these dramatics are performed in front of a classroom audience, but performance is not related to their objectives. The emotional benefits of free expression are an end in themselves, and creativity needs no defense.

There are, however, several secondary benefits that are derived from creative dramatics at least part of the time. As Chapter Three describes, some of the simpler types can help learners overcome their lack of verbal confidence. Dramatics provide practice in voice control development and may even aid in developing vocabulary. Listening may also be improved. But all of these are secondary to the primary objectives related to expression and creativity.

The number of dramatic activities that can be used is almost endless. Most children have already engaged in hundreds of types of dramatic play before they ever begin school. The list of creative dramatic activities below simply gives examples of what is possible; no evidence exists that there is a proper sequence for such activities, but they are listed in a simple to complex order:

- *Nonverbal individual.* All individuals in the classroom do the same activity independently but simultaneously, thereby eliminating any audience and any threat. The activity is usually a pantomime or a similar nonverbal dramatization of a simple nature. Since they are usually very short, a number of activities are done in one session. Among the many possibilities that can be acted out are: a thief tiptoeing through a house, a plant growing, a tree swaying in the wind, a person peeling and eating a banana, a person making a sandwich.
- *Nonverbal with partners.* Pantomime can be extended to pairs or small groups of participants. All groups work simultaneously so

that again there is no audience. Pantomime activities for small groups include: playing tennis, carrying a heavy table, carrying a huge pane of glass, jumping rope, having a snowball fight.

*   *Puppet dialogs.* One of the least threatening ways to initiate verbal drama is through some form of puppetry. Short creative dramatics with partners may be the best way to introduce it. Finger puppets made by painting faces on fingers, homemade hand puppets made from small paper bags or old socks, or commercially made puppets can all be used effectively. Children may respond creatively to literature they have just heard or read, to a realistic problem situation, or to a real event in their lives.

*   *Role playing.* In role playing, children creatively react to situations in the same manner that they do with puppetry. The chief difference is that they use themselves to fill the roles instead of using puppets. At first, groups of two or three children can react to situations or events that are quite prestructured by the teacher and should be rather short. As confidence grows, the group size and length of the role play can grow and the teacher's role can decrease. Children usually have little problem becoming involved in role playing, unless the school has led them to be uncomfortable with it. They have had years of practice in creative play before entering school.

Formal Dramatics

Formal dramatics are those activities in which the participants interpret and dramatize a prepared script. However, the difference between creative and formal dramatics is a continuum ranging from completely spontaneous creativity to total commitment to a prepared script. Obviously, many activities fall between the two extremes.

Formal dramatics has a more limited function in the elementary school than does creative dramatics. The opportunities for self-expression and creativity are reduced as the activity moves closer to the formal end of the continuum, so the objectives are necessarily different as well. Certainly, dramatic performers can gain a feeling of accomplishment and can develop oral expression abilities through drama, but only after a good deal of practice and work. Elementary teachers should use formal dramatics, then, only when they believe that it is an efficient way to meet clear objectives. The rehearsal and public performance of a full-length play by elementary children is probably not appropriate in the average situation.

Some activities that fall between creative and formal dramatics, however, might be very useful. Among these are:

- Charades that use preset signals for such factors as number of words or syllables. Individuals nonverbally dramatize a statement (book or movie title, famous quotation, and so on). The audience must guess the statement in the shortest time possible. Gerbrandt has described in detail how to use charades in the classroom.[8]

- Dramatizing a story that has been read in the reading texts, but doing so without using the texts as a script and without rehearsal.

- Letting small groups of children write and dramatize their own short plays.

DIALECT

In the discussion of word usage earlier in this chapter, no mention was made of dialect. It was intentionally omitted, although it includes word usage, because the use of a dialect deserves separate attention. Several important issues have been raised about dialect in the classroom.

Dialect is nothing more than a variation in a language. Every individual uses variations of speech that are slightly different from those of other people but that closely resemble the speech of those in the nearby environment. A dialect may be unique in the way vowels are pronounced, in the extent to which consonants are pronounced, in pitch, and in stress. In many cases, it may even contain unique rules of grammar. Many dialects develop among people who have lived as a relatively stable group for several generations in one geographic area. Thus, various dialects characterize various parts of our country.

Regional dialects, however, seldom stir as much controversy as do socioeconomic or racial dialects. Speech varies from one socioeconomic level to another just as it does from one region to another. Some dialects are commonly associated with certain racial or ethnic groups. "Black English," which is in reality a range of English variations not limited to blacks, is an example of this type of dialect. The English produced by several Spanish-speaking groups and by American Indians are others. The dialects that seem to be commonly noticed are those associated with minority groups.

Minority-Group Dialects

If all dialects were regarded as equal with no status implications involved, they would simply be interesting. Most regional dialects come quite close to this neutral description. The language that is associated with minority groups, however, is quite the opposite. The degree to which a member of a minority group has adopted "standard English" is regarded as an indicator of status by the white middle class and sometimes by the minority group itself. Conversely, the stronger the dialect of such people, the more they are likely to be the objects of prejudice and discrimination. The fact that nonstandard dialects are unrelated to any deficiency in thought or mental development is often ignored.[9] All of this is true in spite of the lack of a common definition of standard English.

To complicate the situation, speakers of minority dialects frequently have difficulty in school. Their oral language and writing abilities often seem deficient, especially to teachers who do not understand the minority culture, and their reading test scores tend to fall below national norms for their age. Early theories about the correlation between dialect and school difficulties were based on cause and effect. Minority dialects were blamed for much of the difficulty that these youngsters have in acquiring school language skills.

Nicholas Anastasiow and Michael Hanes, however, have explained in detail how differences in school success are related to socioeconomic status rather than to the variation of English spoken.[10] Their extensive research has shown that parents of poverty children and of middle-class children tend to differ in values related to school, in the form of communication used during parent-child interaction, and in the amount of playing with language that children are encouraged to do. Parents of middle-class status tend to expect that education will prepare their children for a good adult life and that their children will do well in school, while parents of poverty status have lower expectations. Middle-class parents tend to interact with their children in generalized ways such as, "Good boys don't do that," while lower-class parents tend to give specific commands. Middle-class parents tend to encourage more play with words and to repeat and expand childrens' statements. Of course, these are tendencies, not universal differences. The differences were found, however, between socioeconomic groups and not between racial or ethnic groups. The researchers found consistency in the two socioeconomic groups regardless of ethnic background.

These differences in child-rearing practices appear to be a more important factor in preparing children for school than is dialect. The reduced experience with language in poor homes may reduce the rate of cognitive (thinking) development because cognition and language develop together. However, dialect differences are unrelated. Anastasiow and Hanes examined the results of their language performance studies after statistically equalizing the differences in cognitive development of the children.[11] When white middle-class and black inner-city children were compared using this technique, both groups performed equally on language tasks. The implication is that the lag in cognitive development resulting from poor parents' child-rearing practices is responsible for much of the difficulty that these children tend to have with language tasks in school, while differences in dialect seem to make little difference.

We shouldn't expect differences in dialect to interfere with learning, because there is nothing inferior about minority-group dialects. Every English dialect has its own consistent and effective grammar rules, most of which are identical or similar to those of "standard" dialects. Every dialect has a vocabulary and a pronunciation system which allows for communication as fully as any other. While there are differences between printed English and minority group dialects, there are differences between "standard" oral language and written English as well.

Speaking a minority-group dialect may not interfere with learning, but it has social consequences. Because we live in a society that continues to be prejudiced about and to discriminate against minority groups, membership in those groups has economic and social disadvantages. Because dialect is associated with such membership, individuals who can speak in standard forms of English lose some of these disadvantages in the job market. The only long-range cure for this sad state of affairs is a change in the attitudes of our society, but in the meantime the individual with a minority-group dialect must learn a different variant of English if he or she wishes a wider range of career opportunities.

The School and Dialect

Elaine Fowler has identified three basic ways that the school can deal with black dialect. Perhaps her scheme can be applied to other minority dialects as well.[12] One way to deal with dialect is to eradicate it. Another is to accept it but teach standard English along with it. The third is to appreciate it and expand on it.

The first of these, eradicating the dialect, is totally unacceptable. Children who are forced to learn standard English and forbidden to use their dialect in the classroom are led to believe the language their families use, and with which they do their thinking, is inferior. Because it is damaging to verbal confidence and to self-concepts, then, this practice would not be acceptable even if it were successful. In addition, however, there is a clear lack of evidence that attempts at eradication have ever been effective.

Developing bidialectal students, those with two dialects, is another way of dealing with the problem. Children are told that their minority dialect is all right on the playground or in the streets, but another dialect is used in the classroom and when speaking to people of higher prestige. Advocates of this plan usually support the teaching of standard English in the same way that a second language is taught. While this method eliminates some of the negative implications for speakers of minority dialects, the message is still clear that their form of speech is inferior to middle-class white English. Furthermore, it has been pointed out that this method has not produced people who have succeeded in careers that they otherwise would have been denied.[13]

The third way to deal with dialect is to accept it, appreciate it, and expand on it. In this way, minority dialects would be treated the way that regional dialects normally are. No attempt is made to teach standard English or to change the speech of the minority members. Dialect is not ignored but actually appreciated. It is discussed in the classroom and the children's language is actually used during instruction. This approach appears to be best for building verbal confidence and can be used to help learners become effective in oral language, but it does little to help minority members cope with the realities of a prejudiced society.

Perhaps the best answer lies somewhere between the last two approaches. If this is true, then the discussion in Chapter Two about verbal confidence applies to this area as well. Speakers of minority dialects need to build their confidence as speakers before they begin to expand their language to include more standard forms. They should come to recognize that there are acceptable alternatives to their language, but should not be asked to reject the system of communication and thought through which they identify themselves. The suggestions listed below should be helpful in expanding language toward standard forms once learners have some confidence. It should not be expected, however, that an elementary-school child grounded in one dialect will master a standard dialect before he or she leaves. Such mastery occurs only when an individual, usually a young adult, makes a decision to acquire it.

1. Learn to understand the dialect of the children you teach. Recent court action may require this, but required or not, an understanding is necessary for acceptance, especially while verbal confidence is being established.

2. On the other hand, be a model of standard English in your own speech. This will help the dialect speakers in your classroom appreciate this alternative.

3. In the primary grades, use experience stories as part of the instruction. After discussing a common experience, allow individuals to dictate statements as you copy them on large chart paper exactly as they are given but in standard spelling. Then use the charts for instruction in sight words, grammar, and so on.

4. Use the suggestions for building grammar that are given in Chapter Eight, but build slowly from dialect forms into more standard forms. This should be done through expansion of the children's language rather than replacement.

EVALUATING ORAL LANGUAGE

There are no standardized or other formal tests that evaluate verbal expression. Some attempts have been made to develop informal measures of oral language that have consistency from one setting to the next. Carol Dixon, for example, has developed a system for evaluating children's language as it is dictated to the teacher for language experience stories.[14] However, such measures are usually developed to evaluate one or two aspects of oral language. No paper-and-pencil test could ever evaluate verbal expression as it has been discussed in this chapter.

Such evaluations have to, by their very nature, be subjective. A teacher's judgment must be used to determine if progress is being made in the various general and specific abilities of oral language. Because few individuals can remember every detail of each child's progress, however, some recording system must normally be used to keep track of oral abilities. A number of systems are possible including checklists and record sheets for teachers' comments. The checklist shown in Figure 4–2 is one effective tool for recording individual oral progress. As a child progresses, the appropriate column is checked off in any given area of ability.

The specific oral abilities to entertain and to express emotions and the area of dramatics are not included in the checklist because these aspects cannot and should not be evaluated. Also to be noted is the fact that prepared speeches are not included in the evaluation. Uninformed teachers who want to evaluate oral language frequently

LEVELS OF ABILITY					
	Beginning	Some	Substantial Amount	Advanced	Highly Developed
General Abilities					
Voice tone					
Vocabulary					
Word usage					
Specific Abilities					
Describing					
Giving directions					
Summarizing					
Asking questions					
Convincing					

FIGURE 4–2 Checklist for recording individual oral progress.

assign speeches and award each speaker a letter grade. Prepared formal speeches are usually too threatening and of too little value to be useful in the elementary classroom. They also, therefore, are not effective as evaluation tools in an elementary school. Evaluation needs to be appropriate for the grade level and developmental stage of the child and it needs to deal with the aspects of language that have been designated by the objectives.

SUMMARY

One of the most neglected areas of language arts is that of oral language. Perhaps because children come to school already speaking or perhaps because writing mechanics and reading are stressed so highly, verbal effectiveness often receives little attention. Yet, verbal communication is the type that is used most often in life's situations.

The role of the school should be that of taking the child's language as it is, building confidence as discussed in Chapter Three, and then developing it to its fullest. There are a number of general and specific oral abilities, which have been identified in this chapter, for which the school should take on the responsibility. The most effective method for developing these abilities is through guided practice.

Miss Franks, in Scene A at the opening of this chapter, evidently provided practice in using oral expression, practice that was both guided and based on the development of confidence. We can't tell from this scene just what led up to the simulation of television commercials, but we do know that the class had previously discussed techniques of convincing. There is also evidence that the group had planned the oral activity and felt confident about it. This is a good example of a language activity that has a purpose, the kind that leads to language learning.

Miss Nora, in Scene B, also provided her class with oral language practice. The contrast, however, is quite sharp. The practice that her class received was evidently unguided, for her comments lead us to believe that any preparation was "homework." More importantly, the activity was apparently also without a meaningful purpose. The students gave "speeches" because they were told to do so. Perhaps assigned speeches are somewhat better than drill on facts *about* language, but there is seldom much language learning when there is no purpose for it.

The school needs to concentrate on oral language as certainly as it does on that which is written. It can do a great deal to produce citizens who have something to say and know how to say it.

NOTES

1. Charles I. Glicksberg, "The Dynamics of Vocabulary Building," *English Journal,* 29 (March 1940), 197–201.

2. Nicholas Anastasiow, *Oral Language: Expression of Thought* (Newark, Del.: International Reading Association, 1971).

3. Walter J. Petty, and others, *The State of Knowledge about the Teaching of Vocabulary* (Champaign, Ill.: National Council of Teachers of English, 1968), 84; Sally Vaughan, Sharon Crawley, and Lee Mountain, "A Multiple-Modality Approach to Word Study: Vocabulary Scavenger Hunts," *Reading Teacher,* 32 (January 1979), 434.

4. Kenneth S. Goodman, "Do You Have to Be Smart to Read? Do You Have to Read to Be Smart?" *Reading Teacher,* 28 (April 1975), 625–32.

5. Vaughan, Crawley, and Mountain, "A Multiple-Modality Approach," pp. 435–37.

6. John Stewig, "Storyteller: Endangered Species?" *Language Arts,* 55 (March 1978), 344–45.

7. N. A. Flanders and E. J. Amidon, *The Role of the Teacher in the Classroom* (Minneapolis: Minneapolis Association for Productive Teaching, 1967).

8. Gary L. Gerbrandt, *An Idea Book for Acting Out and Writing Language, K–8* (Urbana, Ill.: National Council of Teachers of English, 1974), pp. 36–37.

9. John B. Carroll, "Language and Cognition," in *Language Differences: Do They Interfere,* ed. James L. Laffey and Roger Shuy (Newark, Del.: International Reading Association, 1973), p. 184.

10. Nicholas J. Anastasiow and Michael L. Hanes, *Language Patterns of Poverty Children* (Springfield, Ill.: Charles C. Thomas, Publisher, 1976), pp. 54–56.

11. Ibid., p. 118.

12. Elaine D. Fowler, "Black Dialect in the Classroom," *Language Arts,* 53 (March 1976), 276–80.

13. James Sledd, "Doublespeak: Dialectology in the Service of Big Brother," *College English,* 33 (January 1972), 441.

14. Carol N. Dixon, "Language Experience Stories as a Diagnostic Tool," *Language Arts,* 54 (May 1977), 501–5.

CHAPTER FIVE
IMPROVING LISTENING

Scene A

"Now pay attention, class," said Mr. Roberts. "Are you listening, Charles? How about you, Amy? Now here's how you do this page. Look at the example sentence on top. Notice that all of the words we've been talking about are underlined. Maria and Cheryl, pay attention! Do you see which words are underlined? Your assignment is to do the same thing with sentences One through Twelve down here. Charles, did you hear me? Are there any questions?"

"What page did you say?" asked Carla.

Scene B

"What are some reasons so many people think Abraham Lincoln was a good president?" asked Mr. Rodriguez.

"He kept the North and South together," said Carol.

"He freed the slaves," said Jerome.

"He was shot," said Rafael.

"That doesn't have anything to do with why people like him," Carol said.

"Yes, it does," Rafael answered. "The other presidents who were shot are famous too."

Mr. Rodriguez interrupted, "Not all of them, Rafael, but you have a good point. So do you, Carol and Jerome. Now, before we try to find more answers about Mr. Lincoln's popularity, I would like to read you a letter by a modern author written to President Lincoln as if he were still alive. Listen to see if you can tell what the writer's main idea is."

The most common form of communication is listening. Everyone who is free of a severe hearing impairment knows how to do it. Even if we do a great deal of talking and we love to read and write, most of us listen more than we engage in any other type of communication.

Furthermore, listening is the "primary" form of communication. It is through listening that the infant first becomes aware of and first begins to understand language. Because it seems to appear in the development of language before speaking, reading, and writing appear, it is often called the primary or first form. Listening is also regarded as the foundation of the other forms of language, although it is difficult to separate the preliminary steps of learning to speak from those of learning to listen.

In addition to its extensive use and its role as an introducer of language, listening is important because of its application to life. Many careers depend upon "good listening." In a number of human service professions listening is actually part of the work load, but in nearly all jobs listening to directions and to information is needed to at least some extent. Personal relations with other people at school or work, in social situations, and at home also depend upon "good listening." One of the best indicators of closeness in a relationship is the willingness of its members to truly listen to each other. Even success in school seems to be related to one's ability to listen.

The importance of listening, then, is quite clear. This view is so unanimous that in all of the literature about communication it is nearly impossible to find claims for its lack of importance. It should follow, then, that listening should occupy an important position in the language arts curriculum.

LANGUAGE ARTS AND LISTENING

In spite of its acknowledged importance, listening as an area of study is largely ignored by the school. It was true in 1954 when H. A. Anderson wrote, "Listening, at all educational levels, has been the forgotten language art for generations."[1] It is still true today. While teachers may frequently remind learners to "listen up," "pay attention," or "listen carefully," they are seldom able to offer them any advice about *how* to listen. Clearly, there is a discrepancy between what is said and what is done about listening. There are a number of possible explanations for the lack of attention given to listening in the language arts program.

Mastery Before School

One possible explanation is that whatever skills are involved in listening are already mastered by the time the child enters school and no instruction is therefore needed. There is a great deal of logic to this argument. As we saw in Chapter One, the amount of linguistic knowledge that the child brings to school is massive. Certainly he or she must know how to listen or such oral abilities could never have been learned. Even the common belief that as children grow older they expand their attention spans—the amount of continuous time they can listen—has been challenged. Sometimes even very young children can listen for long periods of time when they are engrossed with something of high interest.

If the reason listening is omitted from the language arts is because educators feel that children have already mastered it, however, why is it a source of concern and frustration for so many teachers? Why is it necessary for them to remind their young charges to listen, and why do they find themselves repeating directions and instructions so frequently? Obviously, something about the children's listening isn't complete in such situations.

Listening Can't Be Taught

A second possible explanation for the lack of attention given to listening instruction is that listening is not teachable. Whatever it is that goes into the ability to listen, according to this argument, it must be learned naturally. Children learn to listen by interacting with their environment, not through instruction. If this is true, it would be foolish for the school to use time and resources on listening instruction.

Yet, there is substantial research evidence that listening can be taught. Thomas Devine, in summarizing listening research over a fifty year period, says hundreds of research studies have found that listening comprehension (the ability to answer questions about what has been heard) can be improved through classroom activities.[2] If listening consists of the process that research has studied, it is difficult to argue that it isn't teachable. Of course, it is possible that research has explored only *part* of the listening process.

Lack of Knowledge

Finally, it is possible that listening is taught so little in school because no one really understands what to teach or how to teach it. Certainly the research that was just described is not limited to the examination of one technique for improving listening comprehension, but deals with a confusion of techniques. Furthermore, that research does not deal with listening in its totality, as we will see shortly, but with one aspect of it. A survey of the professional *opinion* about listening shows even more confusion than the research techniques do.

Conclusion

Without question, we still have a great deal to learn about listening, and it is difficult to expand our knowledge. Even though we use listening nearly every waking hour of every day, we can learn about the listening of other people only indirectly. It is a mental process that does not produce consistent overt behaviors. We cannot easily tell when someone is paying attention to, understanding, or remembering what is being said. We do not even know if the research results that have been described can be applied to "normal" situations or if such results occur only under research conditions.

It is small wonder, then, that schools and teachers do not understand what to do about listening. There is confusion about what children need to learn about listening, about how much of listening can be taught, and about how and what to teach. Assuming that lack of knowledge is at least a part of the reason listening receives so little attention in the classroom, then, the sections that follow attempt to eliminate some of the confusion.

THE PROCESS OF LISTENING

If we are ever to develop a way to improve listening, we must first understand the process involved. Techniques of teaching that do not deal with the listening process have little chance of making improvements. Unfortunately, as noted, the process can't be observed directly. Research and experience, however, have given us enough information to make possible several logical theories or models about listening. Two models, each with several levels or steps, are especially appropriate.

John Stammer has described three levels of auditory intake. The first level is *hearing* and consists of physical activation of the ear apparatus. The second is *listening*, which is equivalent to paying attention or to concentrating on the message. The third level is *auding*, which is understanding the message and relating it to previous experiences and concepts.[3]

Of these three levels, the one that is the object of most concern is auding. There are times when the purpose of the sound produced is only that of hearing, such as the background music provided in department stores or the noise of an alarm clock going off. There are also times when the listening level is appropriate, a typical situation being listening to recorded music or practicing one's speech before delivering it. But most messages involving oral language require auding. Certainly, in a classroom it is not usually hearing or listening that teachers expect, but auding. Without auding, directions cannot be followed, action cannot be taken, and very little can be remembered.

Yet, auding can't take place unless two lower levels of auditory action also take place. The individual must hear and listen to the message before it can be translated into something meaningful. This fact is illustrated by the following simple model:

Sound ———▶ Hearing ———▶ Listening ———▶ Auding

In order for sound to enter the level of hearing, to pass into the level of listening, and to move on to the level of auding, it must first activate the ear, then be regarded as important by the listener, and finally make sense in the light of past experiences. Therefore, the school must be concerned with all three levels.

Another useful type of listening model is built on steps of the listening process. Such a model is an explanation of how sound is translated into meaning. Sara Lundsteen has developed a logical model of this type.[4]

Lundsteen's model recognizes two outside factors present before or during the time the ear is activated, namely previous knowledge of the listener and the listening material. It then describes ten steps proficient listeners use to derive meaning from the message:

1. Hear the speech sound or other message and distinguish it from other voices or sounds.
2. Hold the sounds in memory in order to combine units of speech into a meaningful message in the subsequent steps.
3. Attend to the message. This step includes focusing or concentrating on the message and selecting context clues that can be used to derive meaning with efficiency.
4. Form tentative images from the sound cues. Using background knowledge, listeners translate the message into internal speech and form tentative "pictures" of the actions, objects, or concepts being described.

5. Search the past store of ideas in long-term memory so that experiences, values, and concepts can be related to what is being heard.
6. Compare what has been heard with what has been found in the long-term memory.
7. Test the cues. The listener makes a hypothesis about the meaning of the message. If the hypothesis makes sense in context, this step ends. If not, the listener may question the speaker or may search the short-term memory for more cues.
8. Recode. This step is optional. If the hypothesis in Step 7, however, doesn't make sense to the listener, a new hypothesis will need to be established.
9. Get the literal meaning of the message from the steps above.
10. Intellectualize or apply what has been heard by correlating the message with the existing store of knowledge and experience.

Implications from the Models

In examining both models, we can see the following implications:

1. Only part of the sound that reaches the ear is brought to the level of conscious awareness. Listening and auding require an active, intentional process of interacting with the spoken message.
2. Individuals use an internal sorting process to determine whether something is worthy of hearing, listening, or auding. The process is based on the individual's background experiences and personal values. Sounds not worthy of any of these conscious levels are ignored.
3. Listeners make great use of context as they try to understand the message. Individuals pick out meaningful clues from the context in order to make hypotheses about the speaker's meaning. They do not string together a series of individual word meanings, but use overall context and past experience to interpret the message.
4. There is a distinct difference between the upper two levels. Paying attention occurs only when the listener perceives that it is important to do so. Comprehending can occur only with sufficient background knowledge. The effects of this distinction in the classroom will be discussed next.

The terms used in the above models may cause us some confusion, especially the use of the word *listening* to refer to one level as well as to the overall auditory intake process. Therefore, the remainder of this chapter will refer to the listening level as *paying attention*. Auding will be called *comprehending*.

PAYING ATTENTION

One of the worst misconceptions in classroom teaching is the notion that children who *do* not listen well, *can* not listen well. This idea is so wrong because, as we have seen, even the best listeners don't process all that they hear. Unfortunately, this misconception has led to many wasted hours teaching children *how* to listen when the cause of the concern is that they *do not* listen. In terms of the listening levels described earlier, such teaching practices work on the improvement of comprehension, when the problem in the classroom is related to paying attention.

This is not to say that training children to improve their comprehension is bad. Evidently children can be taught to better comprehend what they hear and listen to. The research summarized by Devine that was mentioned earlier clearly shows that students can answer questions about what they've heard more accurately after training than they can before training.[5] The area of improving listening comprehension is discussed in detail later in this chapter.

The point here is that paying attention and understanding are two separate levels of listening, and the latter cannot function without the former. If teachers want children to follow directions and give other evidence of understanding what has been said, they must first lead their pupils to a level of paying attention. Regardless of how highly proficient we become in listening comprehension, we always ignore a great deal of what we hear. This is not only normal but necessary. Therefore, the school must focus on techniques that help learners pay attention as much as it does on techniques for developing listening comprehension.

Making Sense

We have seen that the sorting process an individual uses to determine which sounds should be brought to the awareness level is, in part, based on the hearer's value system. Only those sounds to which some value or importance is attached by the individual receive some attention. It is the individual hearer who makes the determination. Perhaps it will be useful at this time to examine how an individual uses that sorting process or makes that determination.

Frank Smith has explained that listening, like other forms of communication, is a matter of making sense.[6] All of us have a natural desire to make sense of our world, including our communication. We learn the language that we need to obtain information and meet our needs, we translate our experiences, and we interpret what we hear and read in ways that make sense. When new language, new needs, or new experiences come our way, we try to fit them into the scheme we have already developed to make sense of our world.

In the same way, we only pay attention to the sounds that make sense to us and ignore the rest. Making sense in this case includes having some purpose. As Smith says, "Where language does not make sense, where it has no apparent purpose, not only will children fail to learn from it but they will actively ignore it."[7]

The conclusion that can be drawn from all of this is that the classroom must make use of teaching strategies and learning activities that steer learners toward paying attention. Paying attention is not a skill, at least not in the usual sense of the word. It cannot be taught in the way skills usually can. Children can be shown how to compute, decode words, and comprehend what they hear, but they can't be shown how to pay attention. Rather, they must be given learning experiences that make sense, that have some apparent purpose.

This is not to say that the spoken language to which individuals will pay attention remains unchanged as they mature. Studies have shown that children improve with age in their ability to focus attention on selected presentations and to resist certain distractions while listening.[8] In addition, interests and values about what is important change as experience accumulates and maturation occurs. Attention paying does seem to change.

However, there is no evidence to date that children can be taught or coerced to pay attention with any long-lasting effects. Lessons and practice in attention paying seem to produce no results once the lessons and practice have ended. Reminding learners to "pay attention" can call everyone's attention to something important, but unless the *children* regard it as important the reminder will have an extremely short effect. Furthermore, when such reminders are overused, children begin to ignore them and they become totally ineffective.

Evidently, force has some effect on attention. When a teacher punishes or criticizes children each time they are caught not paying attention, some level of fear prevails in the classroom. The fear leads children to try to pay attention, but because no one can pay attention all of the time, this technique is not highly effective. Furthermore, there is reason to suspect that such fear tactics have negative psychological effects. Even from the teacher's standpoint such tactics are less than desirable, for they often send frustrated, head-shaking teachers to the teacher's lounge mumbling that "kids today just won't listen."

Even more ineffective than lessons and force is the practice of sermonizing about paying attention. Even when children become convinced by lectures that extoll the virtues of listening, it doesn't increase their attention greatly. Listening in order to fulfill a duty probably can't be sustained for a very long time. Furthermore, such lectures usually aren't very convincing.

The most effective way to help children pay attention is to provide them with something that is worth paying attention to. Children are no different from adults in this respect; if there is something being said that has a purpose, that has personal relevance, that makes sense, it will receive attention unless something demanding even more attention is happening nearby.

Teaching That Gets Attention

It should be clear by now that the teacher's objective in dealing with attention should not be that of teaching children *how,* or of coercing them, but should be that of getting their attention when it is needed. There are a number of conditions that can be established and a number of strategies that can be used to gain such attention, to lead learners to listen.

Classroom Atmosphere

One of the most important steps that can be taken to improve the level of attention in a classroom is to set up a listening environment. Such an environment is one in which all members of the class have opportunities to speak and where the things members say are accepted and respected. While it is certainly much easier to describe the need for a listening environment than it is to establish one, there are several suggestions that can help make it possible.

1. The teacher is the key. Because the teacher serves as a model for elementary-school children and because the teacher controls the reward system (which behaviors are recognized, praised, rejected, and so forth), he or she greatly influences the amount that children are willing to pay attention. If the teacher gives individuals the opportunity to speak, and then gives them uninterrupted attention when they do, the learners will gradually come to do the same. Furthermore, the teacher's expectations about what is im-

A good listening environment helps children pay attention. (*Ken Karp*)

portant to listen to, how much attention should be given, and other factors influence the atmosphere of the classroom.

2. In order for teachers to provide children with opportunities to speak to a listening audience, however, the amount of teacher talk typically needs to be reduced. Harry Sheldon points out that when the teacher is the chief speaker, translator, questioner, and even listener and information filter for the class, learners have little need to speak or listen themselves. Daniel Tutolo claims that the best way to help children select important input for close attention is to keep teacher talk down. Not only is there no time for child-talk and for teacher-listening when teachers dominate the oral language, but also too much teacher talk works against a listening environment in other ways.[9]

3. A classroom organization and teaching style must be established that gives learners the opportunity to speak to each other. The most common way to do this is through discussion groups, although any of the activities suggested in Chapters Three and Four can also serve this purpose. Paul Burns and Leo Schell see the use of group discussions for functional purposes as useful in

developing such listening habits as respecting the opinions of others, waiting one's turn, and responding appropriately.[10] Such speaking and listening activities can be as formal or informal, as structured or unstructured, as the teacher desires, so this suggestion has little to do with classroom control or "discipline." It is not surprising that speaking and listening can best be developed together in a classroom, for this is the way they are developed naturally in children from birth.

4. The listening environment should not be limited to the part of the day labeled "language arts," but should extend to all parts of the curriculum. Children should see that paying attention is not just another topic to cover in school, but something that is put to use in many aspects of school and life. So, the teacher's modeling example and the opportunities to speak should be present throughout the day. This may not be as difficult as it first seems, for discussion groups and other oral language activities fit well into the science class, the literature program, and especially the social studies curriculum.

5. Encourage learners to ask questions. Charlotte Patterson has reported research which shows that children remember answers to questions they have asked better than they remember certain other information.[11] She also suggests that getting satisfying answers to their questions seems to encourage children to ask more questions. Question-answer interactions are still another piece of the listening environment.

Establishing a classroom environment, however, is a personal matter. These five suggestions should serve as a guideline for teachers who wish to set up a listening environment. However, the interaction that exists between learners and the individual teacher is both essential and impossible to adequately describe. Teachers who can develop a positive relationship with children and follow these five suggestions will have a listening environment that is healthy and useful.

Purposes of Listening

It was stated earlier that part of the "making sense" process that we use when we listen is listening for a purpose. In fact, when there is no apparent purpose for paying attention, we stop operating at this level and drop back to only hearing. It is not enough to give children a purpose that encourages listening as a duty, that says they should listen because it is generally good for them. The purpose needs to be one with which the listeners can relate at the present time.

Every individual has a desire and a need to receive attention. Even teachers fall prey to this human tendency. The statements that most teachers want their students to listen to above all else are their own. And, of course, most teachers *do* have more information to give than any of their pupils. What is so frequently overlooked, however, is that those who hear don't usually attach the same importance to a message as do those who speak.

Most of the difficulty that teachers experience with children's listening is related to the importance or pertinence of what they say. If the children see some meaningful purpose for understanding the teacher's words, they will move them from the hearing level to the conscious level of attention. If they don't see it, they won't.

In dealing with purposes for listening, then, the teacher needs to examine two things. First, her or his own purposes must be clarified. Then the match between teacher and student purposes must be examined.

It isn't practical or realistic to suggest that teachers should stop to examine the purpose of everything they say during the day. But the purposes of key statements, the ones that are frequently introduced with announcements such as "now pay attention," should be clear. Examples of key statements might be directions and the introduction of new concepts.

But it isn't enough that teachers simply know what their purposes are. They must also consider how well their purposes match those of the learners. It is the hearers who will determine if the message is worth listening to. If they discover, for example, that what is now being said is similar to previous statements that had no immediate meaning or consequence for them, they will quickly tune out.

The task of providing purposes for listening, then, is a difficult and complex one. It involves an overall approach to teaching that gives learners a reason for being in school, a reason that is visible to, and accepted by, them. It involves teaching in a way that goes beyond simply covering content, and it delves into areas about which the learners have real concerns. Sometimes this is accomplished by demonstrating to the class how a given piece of content affects their lives ("You can use this math concept to save money at the store"). Sometimes it means expanding or shifting the content to include student concerns ("Would Abraham Lincoln be a good student if he were young now and went to this school?"). Providing purposes for listening goes well beyond the times when the teacher is talking.

Two types of classroom practices that seem especially promising for bringing the purposes of the teacher and of the learners together are decision making and open-ended tasks. Decision making is developed by offering children choices, beginning with options between two similar tasks and slowly building toward multiple, wide-ranging choices. Open-ended tasks are questions that have a number of acceptable answers or problems that can properly be solved in more than one way. The use of choices and open-ended tasks helps to bring the purposes of teacher and learners together, because the teacher continues to set up the guidelines and the topic area, but the individual child is an active participant in determining the specific objective of the task. The use of these two practices also frequently contributes to the listening environment described earlier.

The difficult part of offering children choices is not in identifying tasks from which they can choose, but in overcoming the fear that such a practice will reduce classroom control. Finding tasks from which children can choose is as easy as finding two practice activities for a skill instead of one, and letting each individual choose. Of course, the type and amount of choice should advance as the participants learn how to make choices, but most teachers find this easier than changing their beliefs about who should make the decisions. Even though giving up some decision making power is frightening to some teachers, the rewards are greater. Children who learn to make decisions of their own about learning, even though small at first, make some commitment to their choice. The result is a more purposeful experience. Furthermore, little change is usually required in classroom management techniques.

Likewise, the difficult part of providing open-ended tasks in school is breaking away from the belief that every question and problem has one right answer. When there is only one answer, it is easier to evaluate pupil progress, but far too often the children's purpose becomes to find the easiest way to get right answers. When many answers or solutions are acceptable, discovery, personal involvement, and learning are more likely to occur. Once this belief about answers has been accepted by the teacher, open-ended questions such as, "What are some other ways the princess could have taken care of her problem in this story?" or "What are some reasons George Washington had for staying at Valley Forge?" can replace one-answer questions about the princess, George Washington, and countless other situations.

Decision making, open-ended tasks, and other activities that are meaningful to learners are directly related to listening. When students have a sufficient number of purposeful learning experiences, they have a personal reason for going to school. Then they also have a purpose for paying attention to what is spoken in the classroom. A classroom that is filled with purposeful learning experiences does not require a curriculum of fun and games. Games have their place in school, but the main emphasis should be on lessons and activities that have meaning and a purpose that the learners can clearly see.

COMPREHENDING

Comprehension is the aspect of listening in which schools have been able to demonstrate decided student improvement. Devine reports that dozens of research studies every year show listening can be improved through instruction, and his examples indicate that he is speaking of listening comprehension.[12] When learners receive training in responding to what they have heard, they become better able to respond in appropriate ways.

For all of the reasons listed earlier, however, training in listening comprehension does *not* improve learners' ability or tendency to pay attention. When learners have been *led* to pay attention, on the other hand, their abilities to comprehend what they hear are extremely important. The whole purpose in listening is to understand, to make sense of what is being said. Of course, every child who can hear has some listening comprehension ability, usually a great deal. The school's role in developing this ability, then, is to refine and sharpen it so that learners understand more of what they hear and appreciate it more fully.

Influences on Listening

The necessity of paying attention in order to understand a spoken message has already been discussed at length. All of the factors that have an effect on attention paying also have an effect on listening comprehension, then, because the amount of comprehension is limited to the amount of attention being given. However, there are also a number of other influences on the quantity and quality of comprehension.

Confidence

In every area of communication, the individual's confidence is an important factor. The person with confidence tends to speak, read, and write more, and to do so more effectively. In this text, the importance of confidence is recognized to the extent that two chapters are devoted to it.

Even in listening, confidence is an important influence. There is reason to believe that listeners who expect to understand what is said to them are more successful in comprehension than listeners who don't expect to understand much. Such expectations or self-concepts are a result of previous experiences with listening and have usually developed over a long period of time.

The school is in a position to modify listening expectations or self-concepts to some extent and thereby to improve listening comprehension. This can be done by giving learners experiences with listening in which they experience repeated success. The procedures and activities that build confidence in speaking usually build confidence in listening as well. Because the chapter on building verbal confidence gives detailed suggestions for such teaching strategies, they are not included here.

Using Context

In describing the process of listening, Lundsteen has pointed out how listeners make use of context to derive meaning from spoken messages.[13] Rather than stringing together the meanings of isolated words, they use meaning from the overall message and their understanding of the rules of English to understand the meanings of specific statements. This is done by picking up cues from the speaker and making hypotheses about how given statements fit in with the main idea and the purpose of the speaker. The hypotheses are then tested to see if they make sense when compared with things the speaker says later and with the listener's background of experiences. In a two-way conversation, a listener sometimes asks the speaker for clarification. More often, however, hypothesis testing is the way that listeners make sense of what they hear.

The school can help learners develop a better understanding of the rules of language and of how to use context in listening. Both of these understandings are best learned through meaningful practice. It is true that the practice that children receive through normal conversation is very helpful also, but the school is in the unique position of having at its disposal a wide variety of listening experiences.

Background Knowledge

When individuals listen to a topic with which they are familiar or when they are exposed to a concept they have already learned, their comprehension is obviously better than when they are listening to the unfamiliar. One way to improve comprehension, then, is to provide learners with more background knowledge. Unfortunately, it is impossible to determine in advance just what knowledge each individual should be given. Furthermore, the concepts that any two individuals form from the same knowledge or experience will be different, because new concepts are based on and interact with previous concepts. The school cannot possibly provide every student with every bit of background knowledge that will ever be needed. It can, however, expand and extend previous knowledge to some degree, especially in areas of concern to the school.

Outside Factors

In addition to the confidence, understanding of language, and background knowledge that listeners bring to the situation, there are outside factors that influence their comprehension. These factors include other noises, the volume of the speaker, room temperature, and so forth. While some of these are uncontrollable, the teacher has more control over them in a classroom than anyone else does. Many of the factors that make up a good listening environment, as described earlier in this chapter, not only invite students' attention but increase their comprehension when attention is maintained.

Improving Comprehension

The role of the teacher in developing listening comprehension, as is evident in the points just discussed, is not one of teaching lessons on "how to listen," but one of structuring guided practice. The practice activities that are provided, however, must not ignore the factors that influence listening. Any activities that are selected, then, must do the following:

1. Contribute to the confidence of the students
2. Deal with meaningful language context
3. Use the students' existing store of knowledge and, if possible, extend it somewhat
4. Minimize outside distractions

The activities described next are designed to largely meet these criteria; however, a teacher would have to follow some flexible directions:

1. Adjust the activity so that it is at an appropriate level of difficulty, is interesting to learners, and includes ways that allow students who have low confidence to openly succeed.
2. Gear the topic and sequence of the activity to deal with knowledge the students already have.
3. Minimize outside distractions.

Although the process of listening is similar regardless of its purpose, it is possible to discuss listening activities of several types. For the sake of convenience, then, the following activities are divided into three categories, listening for directions, listening for information, and analytical and critical listening.

Listening for Directions

One of the greatest concerns of teachers is their students' ability to follow directions. This is probably true because so often children seem unable to follow directions on class assignments and in classroom or playground behavior. It is very likely that the majority of this seeming inability isn't inability at all, but refusal to pay attention to directions or intentional noncompliance. If the suggestions for gaining attention that are described in the first part of this chapter are followed, directions will usually be followed reasonably well.

Listening for directions, however, does require skill in noting details and placing them in sequence. This skill is developed through practice. The best way to make practice meaningful is to use it in a setting that already has a purpose. Art, math, physical education, social studies, and science lend themselves to listening activities. Among many possibilities for meaningful practice are:

- *Placing events or steps in order.* In any subject area, there are times when events or steps are told out of sequence and the listener is expected to know the proper order. Some general practice in this ability can be helpful. Prepare paragraphs that include a sequence of events told out of order, read them to the listeners, and have them decide on the correct order. The events or steps should be limited in number at first. An example of such a paragraph is:

  Every four years our nation elects a president. Before the election, however, the candidates for president conduct big campaigns. Even before the campaigns, the candidates must be selected by their political parties. Several months after the election, the president takes office.

- *Treasure hunting from verbal instructions.* The treasure hunt party game, in which children hunt for a note which leads them to the next note, and so on, can be adapted to the classroom and used as a listening activity. Using a textbook (so everyone has a copy), children follow the verbal directions of the teacher as they find clues on one page that lead them to another page. Examples of directions that can be given a step at a time might be:

  Begin on page 47. Find the ninth word on the page. Near the bottom of the page, find exactly the same word. Right after the word is a numeral. Add that number to the page number you are on. The sum is a new page number. Find it. In the picture on this page, find a white animal.

- *Following a map.* Part of the skill of map reading can be learned at the same time that listening is practiced. Using copies of simple classroom maps at beginning stages, or more complex maps for advanced map readers, the learners follow directions given orally by their teacher. The directions take them from one place to another on the map. The various stops along the way can be discussed by the class, noted by individuals directly on their map copies, or used in some other way. As learners improve, more than one step at a time can be given.

- *Doing science experiments.* Directions for doing a science experiment or activity can frequently be given orally. As the learners discover science concepts, they can also practice listening to follow directions. As with the activities above, directions should be given one step at a time at first. After experiencing success in listening to a single step and following it, however, children should be led to listen to two steps at a time before following them, and eventually to three and four.

- *Using a number line or ruler.* Among the many possible oral directions that can be given during math instruction are those in the use of a number line or ruler. Once each child is supplied with such an instrument, the teacher directs various moves up and down or left and right, telling the participants how many numbers, centimeters, or inches to move. The object is to end at the same numeral as other members of the class.

Listening for Information

Except for listening for entertainment and for social purposes, the majority of our listening has as its purpose to gain information. We listen to gain information useful in our careers, to keep abreast of current events, to better meet our individual needs, and simply to learn for the sake of learning. Most people learn how to listen for information reasonably well on their own, but the school can sharpen this ability through guided listening activities.

It may be possible to categorize informational listening into types as well as into purposes. Some language arts authorities speak of listening for details, for the main idea, for sequence, and for other items. In fact, listening for directions could easily be regarded as a type of information gaining. Since there is very little evidence that listening for details involves a different process than listening for the main idea or for sequence, this text does not treat each type separately. The area related to directions is separated from other informational listening simply because it is of great concern to many teachers.

Of the many activities that could logically be expected to sharpen comprehension during listening for information, the following examples are typical. They have been selected because they seem to be purposeful and easily adapted to many situations.

- *Missing persons.* Individuals pass a verbal description from one person to the next while trying to keep all of the details unchanged. Arrangements must be made so that each individual listens to the description only once before repeating it for the next person. This can be done by isolating a group of children, bringing back one to hear the description, asking that child to relate the description to the next child who is brought back, and so on until the last child relates it to the class. It can also be done by having individuals listen to the previous child's taped description through earphones and then relating the description into the tape recorder. One type of description that can be used is of a fictitious person being described as if he or she were being reported to a Missing Persons Bureau. The number of details could be small at first, increasing as the activity is reused. Other descriptions might include minor traffic accidents, historical events, sports events, and missing objects.

- *Summarizing the day.* An activity that has double value and can be repeated often is a class summary, just before school closes for the day, of what happened in the classroom during the day. One value, especially for primary-grade children, is to provide them with something to tell at home. The other value is that it provides good practice in listening for information. The activity consists simply of calling on individuals to summarize some of the highlights of the school day.

- *Echoing a partner.* Each student takes turns sharing an event, feeling, or opinion with a partner. After the class has been paired off, each pair receives a list of questions from which to select. After hearing his or her partner's response, each individual summarizes it. Questions could include: What is the scariest thing that ever happened to me? What irritates me the most? What is most important to me?

- *Listening to partners.* Near the beginning of the school year, students can be assigned partners that they do not know well and given time to ask their partners questions. The activity will be more effective if time is spent beforehand discussing what questions to ask. After the conversations, each individual can tell a few important, positive things about his or her partner.

- *Naming that object.* Three similar objects are placed in front of the class or group. Without being overly obvious, the teacher describes one of them. At the end of the description, the learners vote for the object they think was described. The more similar the objects, the more careful listening is required. The objects might include bunches of flowers, sets of rocks, art pieces, samples of cloth, pictures of unfamiliar animals (for example, birds or insects), toys, or tools. The activity can also be used to review social studies events or famous people (for example, "name this war" or "name this president") or to review science principles or elements. Because it is easy to make such descriptions too difficult and because success is important in listening, it is wise to use a multiple-choice format in letting listeners respond.

Analytical and Critical Listening

Listening is not really completed until the message that has been heard is applied to previous experiences. Listeners must make sense of what is heard by fitting it in with what they already know. This can only be done by analyzing and evaluating the message. Everyone knows how to analyze and evaluate messages, therefore, and the school does not need to introduce this concept. The school does, however, need to help most learners refine and broaden their bases for making such judgments.

There are three strategies that can be used in a classroom to build better bases for analytical and critical listening:

1. *Exchange of ideas.* Learners need to become aware of the manner
    in which their peers analyze and evaluate what they hear. Discus-
    sions in groups and in class can be used to bring out these types
    of thinking after the oral presentation of material that lends itself
    to discussion. To be effective, such discussions must clearly allow
    individuals to express their views.

2. *Exposure to outside ideas.* Learners must also be exposed to the
    analytical and critical thinking of people outside their peer
    group. Literature, outside speakers, and various types of media
    can be used to show learners a variety of viewpoints on issues of
    concern to them.

3. *Development of expectations.* The greatest influence on learners' use
    of analytical and critical thinking is the environment in which the
    thinking takes place. If the classroom is a place where such think-
    ing is expected, the members of the class are more likely to
    develop expectations for themselves as analysts and evaluators.
    The discussions mentioned in the first item can promote these
    expectations. Repeated acceptance by the teacher of analytical
    and critical ideas throughout the several content subjects of the
    school day can have a powerful impact. In addition, listening
    activities specifically designed to foster these types of thinking
    can be a great help.

Many teaching activities can be adjusted to include the use of
student analysis and evaluation. Some examples follow. Unlike the
activities in the earlier parts of the chapter, these actively involve the
teacher, because analytical and critical listening are not easily learned
through practice alone. The role of the teacher in each teaching activity is pointed out.

*   *Identifying the main idea.* After listening to a selection, students are
    asked to summarize the point of the author's message or the main
    idea. This task requires analytical thinking. More often than not,
    there is more than one possible interpretation of the main idea,
    and all logical responses should be encouraged. More important
    than correctly identifying the point is the thinking that went into
    it, so learners might be asked to tell what clues about the main
    idea they used while listening. The teacher's role in this activity
    is to ask probing questions.

*   *Judging story characters.* Children listen to a short story and then
    discuss specific qualities of main characters. This can be espe-
    cially effective if they jot down brief ideas as they listen. The first

few times that this activity is used, the story should be read to the class twice. During one reading, the listeners focus on the actions and statements of the characters. During the other reading, they note and jot down words which the author uses to describe the characters. At some point, the role that these two devices play in giving us impressions of characters can also be discussed. The teacher must read the story, guide the note-taking, and lead the discussion.

- *Recognizing points of view.* The teacher reads two descriptions of the same event or two statements about the same issue that have somewhat differing viewpoints. Editorials or news reports from two newspapers which take differing stances can be used with middle-grade children. Materials for younger children may need to be written by the teacher. The children listen and discuss the differences between the two articles. The first several times this activity is used, specific questions that point to the differences must be asked, because the listeners will probably not know on what types of differences to focus their attention.

- *Analyzing television favorites.* It would be an ideal situation if a popular television show could be shown in school, followed immediately by a discussion of what was seen and especially what was heard. Since this is usually impossible, reasonable substitutes must be used such as discussions of what has been viewed at home. Attention should be called not only to the characters and plots, but to the various effects that are used to make impressions. Since so many people have difficulty identifying *why* they enjoy a particular show, this ability is evidently very useful. With the help of the teacher's probing questions, children can be asked to list good and poor qualities of a given series, to watch a certain show as homework and take specified notes on it, or to make individual charts of the general qualities they enjoy in their favorite shows.

- *Understanding propaganda techniques.* Children can be led to a better understanding of advertising as well as a gain in critical listening ability through the study of propaganda or sales techniques. Primary-grade children can simply listen to the verbal parts of a favorite television commercial, which has been carefully copied and brought to school by a teacher, and talk about the honesty and the intent of each line. Older children can learn about and find examples of the five widely used propaganda techniques: glittering generalities (overstated generalizations), bandwagon effects (suggestions that "everyone" uses a product), testimonials (statements of support from famous or knowledgeable people), stacking the deck (presenting only one viewpoint), and positive associations (implying a relationship between a product and pleasant events or circumstances). The techniques can be introduced by the teacher through pictured advertisements in magazines and newspapers, and students can then categorize other preselected advertisements. Finally, the practice can be extended to examination of television commercials at home.

EVALUATING LISTENING

It is just as important to measure the performance of learners in listening as it is, for example, their performance in reading and math. Because listening is the primary form of language, it is only logical that we need to find out how well students are able to do it. With knowledge of the performance level of a group of children, a teacher can better design a listening program.

Unfortunately, the measurement of listening is associated with a number of difficulties. The idea that listening can be easily tested is as naive as the idea that it can be easily taught. To understand why measurement is difficult, let us return to the concept that listening has three levels. Early in the chapter, the model of John Stammer is discussed in which the "hearing," "listening," and "auding" levels are described. To avoid confusion over the double use of terms, the levels are called "hearing," "paying attention," and "comprehending" in this text. Measurement of listening must consider all three levels.

Hearing and Paying Attention

The measurement of hearing ability has been perfected for some time. Not only is it possible to obtain test results on an individual's hearing capacity, but the results can largely be trusted. Such information is highly important because paying attention and comprehending are certainly dependent upon hearing. Learners with minor hearing impairments who are part of a regular class, as well as children with more severe impairments who are mainstreamed into the regular classroom, need special attention to provide them with the greatest opportunities possible to hear. The measurement of hearing impairment, however, is normally administered by the medical staff rather than the classroom teacher.

While measures of hearing have been perfected, measures of paying attention haven't been invented. It is doubtful that they ever will be. In light of what is said earlier in this chapter about attention paying, it is not logical to expect that this level of listening can be measured.

All listeners must sort what they hear into two categories—that which deserves attention and that which does not. The decisions that go into this sorting process are evidently unconscious (the listener is not even aware of them) and are based on individual and personal values. This is what makes attention paying so difficult to study.

Measurement of attention paying is outside the scope of tests. We have become quite good at testing certain types of skills, but attention seems to be quite unrelated to skills. To some extent, we have begun to succeed in testing general attitudes and self-concepts, but the attitudes involved in attention seem to be anything but general, and often are not stable even from one moment to the next. While paying attention affects one's score on a test of listening comprehension, this level of listening can't be tested by itself.

Nor does it need to be. The real question in the classroom is not, "How well can these learners pay attention"? It is, "*Are* these learners paying attention"? Teachers usually know the answer to this question before they ask it. To be sure, frequent errors are made about individuals who look like they're not paying attention but give surprisingly perceptive responses. Errors are also made about those who look like they're attentive and aren't. Box 5–1 lists some typical behaviors of children who are paying attention. By observing such behaviors, teachers usually have enough information about their class to judge the degree to which they must adopt the suggestions given earlier in this chapter.

BOX 5–1 *TYPICAL BEHAVIORS OF PAYING ATTENTION*

While behaviors vary from individual to individual, the following are typical of the listener who is interested and paying attention:

1. Looks at the speaker a large percentage of the time
2. Sits relatively still in a "normal" position
3. Responds to humor with smiles or laughter and to other emotional content with facial expressions
4. Limits any comments to those appropriate to the content
5. Refrains from disturbing those around him or her

Comprehending

Tests of listening comprehension have certainly been invented. Lundsteen has described several published listening comprehension tests. In a 1968 publication, Duker found sixty-five unpublished listening tests, mostly in dissertations, that had already been developed. Standardized tests related to listening are listed in Box 5–2.[14]

Just as certainly, these tests have not been perfected. It is the difficulty involved in measuring comprehension that is to blame, however, not the test developers. There are two problems that especially make testing difficult.

One problem is the lack of clarity over what to measure. If listeners are asked to answer questions about what they have heard, should the questions ask strictly for factual (literal) responses or should they

BOX 5–2 *STANDARDIZED TESTS RELATED TO LISTENING*

Brown-Carken Listening Comprehension Test Five types of listening comprehension are tested in seventy-eight items: (1) immediate recall, (2) following directions, (3) recognizing functions of sentences, (4) vocabulary, and (5) comprehension of a twelve-minute lecture.

Cooperative Primary Tests (Educational Testing Service) The listening subtests included require the examinee to remember, interpret, and draw inferences from the material that is heard. The teacher reads excerpts of various lengths and the children mark the appropriate picture.

Durrell-Sullivan Reading Capacity Test (Harcourt) Designed for preschool and primary-grade children, this instrument provides estimates of individual potential for learning to read through the testing of listening comprehension.

Illinois Test of Psycholinguistic Abilities (University of Illinois) Several subtests are related to listening: Auditory Decoding, Auditory-Vocal Association, Auditory-Vocal Automatic Ability, and Auditory-Vocal Sequencing. It is designed for ages two and one-half to nine.

The *STEP Listening Test (Educational Testing Services)* Available at levels ranging from fourth grade to college, it measures various responses to material read to or by the examinees.

Wepman Auditory Discrimination Test Children ages five to nine are individually presented words in pairs and asked if the two words are the same or different.

Names of Individuals						
Follows spoken directions						
Understands spoken information						
Uses analytical and critical listening powers						

FIGURE 5–1 Checklist for listening comprehension.

ask for critical and analytical responses? If only factual questions are used, it can be argued, the test is not measuring the total listening process. If critical and analytical questions are used, the individual's experiences and values affect the results. In addition to this dilemma, the length and interest level of the message to which the listeners are exposed influences the test results.

The other problem is one that is common to all standardized tests, that of reliability. The published tests are useful in measuring groups the size of an entire class because the overperformers balance out the underperformers on the test. For individual results, however, the test error is too great. Individual scores should be regarded as clues, not as facts.

This does not mean that listening comprehension tests should be avoided. They provide general indicators about the performance of the whole class and clues about individuals. What it does mean is that teachers' observation must be used along with test results. During daily interaction with individual children, teachers usually learn a great deal about their listening comprehension. Figure 5–1 shows a checklist which teachers might use to keep records of the listening comprehension they observe. These observations should be used in combination with test results to determine the best course of action in building listening comprehension.

SUMMARY

The actions that a teacher can take to improve listening in the classroom fall into three categories: (1) making it possible for every individual to hear, (2) providing learning experiences that gain the learners' attention, and (3) improving listening comprehension. Mr. Rodriguez, the teacher in Scene B at the beginning of the chapter, displayed some evidence that he uses all three types of action. The children had learned to take turns in speaking, and they and the teacher seemed to have no difficulty in hearing each other. The learning activities in which the students in this scene were involved certainly gained their attention. The short scene gives us two clues about why this was so. First, the discussion was open ended so that there were many possible right answers, thereby making it easy for the learners to become involved and see the purpose of the activity. Second, this classroom seemed to have a "listening environment," one in which people were free to speak out without fear of criticism. In addition to the evidence that children in this classroom could hear and were led to pay attention, there was at least one indication that Mr. Rodriguez dealt with listening comprehension. Listening for the main idea in relevant material is a valuable technique for this purpose.

In contrast, Mr. Roberts in Scene A seemed to ignore all three types of constructive action. Instead of gaining attention through teaching activities for which the learners saw a purpose, he attempted to demand it through constant reminders. His lack of success may be typical for this strategy and for others that ignore the fact that attention is given by any listener only to that which seems valuable. There was no evidence during this short scene that listening comprehension was dealt with in this classroom. Even the students' ability to hear seemed to be disregarded. The directions weren't very clear, other student activities were evidently occurring at the same time, and at least one child was totally lost upon completion of the directions.

Listening is an important part of the language arts, but its importance is not limited to the language arts period. When the setting is one in which learners *can* hear, they will. When there is a purpose for paying attention to the spoken messages in a classroom, the individuals who recognize the purpose will largely pay attention. When listening comprehension is refined and sharpened through a variety of activities, more of what is said in the classroom will be understood.

NOTES

1. Harold A. Anderson, "Needed Research in Listening," *Elementary English* (April 1954), 215–24.
2. Thomas G. Devine, "Listening: What Do We Know after Fifty Years of Research and Theorizing?" *Journal of Reading,* 21 (January 1978), 298.

3. John D. Stammer, "Target: The Basics of Listening," *Language Arts,* 54 (September 1977), 661–64.

4. Sara W. Lundsteen, *Listening,* 2nd ed. (Urbana, Ill.: ERIC Clearinghouse on Reading and Communication Skills and National Council of Teachers of English, 1979), pp. 17–48.

5. Devine, "Listening," p. 298.

6. Frank Smith, "The Language Arts and the Learner's Mind," *Language Arts,* 56 (February 1979), 118–25.

7. Ibid., p. 119.

8. Anna-Beth Doyle, "Listening to Distraction: A Developmental Study of Selective Attention," *Journal of Experimental Child Psychology,* 15 (1973), 100–115.

9. Harry J. Sheldon, "Wanted: More Effective Teaching of Oral Communication," *Language Arts,* 54 (September 1977), 666; Daniel Tutolo, "Attention: Necessary Aspect of Listening," *Language Arts,* 56 (January 1979), 35.

10. Paul Burns and Leo Schell, *Elementary School Language Arts: Selected Readings,* 2nd ed. (Chicago: Rand McNally & Company, 1973).

11. Charlotte J. Patterson, "Teaching Children to Listen," *Today's Education,* 67 (April/May 1978), 52–53.

12. Devine, "Listening," p. 298.

13. Lundsteen, *Listening,* pp. 34–39.

14. Lundsteen, *Listening,* pp. 83–87; S. Duker, *Listening Bibliography,* 2nd ed. (Metuchen, N.J.: Scarecrow Press, Inc., 1968).

CHAPTER SIX
BUILDING
WRITING CONFIDENCE

Scene A

"OK, boys and girls. Put away everything else. It's time for writing, now," said Mrs. Todd. "Today we're going to write a story about Halloween. Get out your paper. Before you start, can anyone tell me why we should be careful to write neatly and spell everything correctly?"

"So other people can read it," said Anita.

"So we don't get a lot of red marks on our paper," said Brad.

"So we get a good grade," said Beth.

Mrs. Todd continued, "What do we do if we don't know how to spell a word?"

"Look in the dictionary," recited the class together.

After a few minutes of quiet, except for pencils scratching and Mrs. Todd's footsteps, she said, "Loreen, why aren't you writing? And what about you, Tae-Ho?"

"I can't think of anything," Loreen replied.

"I can't write," pouted Tae-Ho.

Scene B

"I have an idea about how we can raise money for our trip," said Mr. Larsen. "We could write and sell a book of short stories. With all of the good writing you've been doing lately, it shouldn't be that difficult."

"Do you think anybody would buy it?" asked Mike.

"Well, we could start with all of your parents," replied Mr. Larsen. "But I think if you each write a good story, lots of people will want to buy it."

"I could use that story I wrote last week and make it longer," said Al.

"Could the book have poems in it too?" asked Debra.

"Could someone write more than one story if they wanted?" asked Dan.

What does it mean when a person says, "I can't write"? For a few individuals, it means that they have a physical condition which actually prevents them from moving a pencil. There are also some totally illiterate individuals who have not learned to read or write even the simplest message. A confession about writing inabilities, however, usually comes from someone who can write words and phrases but who expects nothing of consequence to happen when he or she sits down with a blank sheet of paper and writing equipment.

While some people admit that they can't write, there are probably many more poor writers who don't admit it. While their expectations about their writing products are as negative as those who admit it, their awareness of the importance of literacy in society leads them to cover up their assumed inability. For them, life is often filled with one scheme after another to hide their secret. Since such people can usually write their names, make lists, and fill out forms, it is only such lengthy pieces as letters, reports, and discourses that they feel they must avoid. Many of them have reached high positions and can hide behind secretaries. Others rely on spouses, friends, and their own craftiness to conceal their writing problem.

It is likely that there are even more people who can produce full-length written products when they need to, but avoid them when possible. Putting thoughts on paper is such a painful process and filled with so many uncertainties for these people that other means of communication are always preferred. Letters are usually avoided, and such documents as term papers are major obstacles.

The people who fall into or between these categories usually have one thing in common. They lack confidence in their writing abilities or, to say it another way, they have low self-concepts. Their view of themselves as nonwriters or poor writers keeps them from becoming better.

Of course, it could be argued that the real problem of such individuals is their lack of ability and that their low confidence is only a by-product. Research has been unable to determine if lack of confidence causes low writing ability or vice versa. Regardless of whether it is a product or cause, however, low confidence or self-concept is a deterrent to improvement.

In Chapter Three, we saw that individuals have a global self-concept, but they also have specific self-concepts such as those related to speaking. The school influences specific self-concepts and they, in turn, influence abilities. This is as true with writing as it is with such areas as talking. The school has, in fact, a greater impact on self-concepts related to writing than it does on those related to speaking,

because speaking confidence is often largely already established when the child enters school. Confidence in one's writing ability, however, is learned mostly in school because that is where the majority of the ability is learned. Thus, the impact of the school on writing confidence is even greater than it is on speaking confidence.

It is clear that the school has this impact on confidence whether it acknowledges it or not and whether it does something about it or not. Every learning experience is laced with attitudes and self-evaluations.[1] If a school or a specific teacher pretends that self-concept does not exist or that it is unimportant, its influence on writing ability will not be lessened in any way.

It is appropriate, then, that we look at what the school can and should do about writing confidence. The school's role in this specific area, however, can be understood only in the larger context of its role in the overall writing program. The entire discussion of writing in this chapter and in subsequent chapters is tied to an understanding of the school's role.

THE ROLE OF THE SCHOOL

There is little question that the school should teach children to write. From the beginning of education history, writing has been one of the "three Rs" and is considered basic for an education. Writing is a vital tool at every level of a school career and in the majority of occupations and professions that follow. It is also very important for the routines and pleasures of personal living. Furthermore, it is generally acknowledged that it is in school that one should develop writing abilities.

It is also generally acknowledged that the responsibility for teaching writing goes far beyond lessons in copying words. Learners should gain the ability to construct proper sentences with correct spelling and punctuation, but even this is not enough. The school is expected to produce good writers, those who can logically put together and develop letters and reports, those who can write stories with a plot and theme, those who can communicate through writing.

Choosing an Emphasis

There is enormous agreement that the school should produce such writers, but there is much confusion about how it should go about producing them. A pull in three different directions has left many teachers and school authorities uncertain about what to emphasize in the writing program. The three seemingly contradictory goals are:

1. Learners should be encouraged to be creative.
2. They should write properly and correctly.
3. Writing should be done with expression.

As society's expectations of the school fluctuate, the relative importance of these three areas changes. Unfortunately, teachers often find themselves forced to choose which of the three will be emphasized, because it is difficult to give appropriate attention to creativity, correctness, and expression simultaneously.

A major cause of the difficulty in achieving these three goals of writing instruction is the disregard of yet a fourth goal, writing confidence. We have already seen that lack of confidence is an obstacle which prevents improvement for problem writers. But confidence evidently functions in the opposite direction also. When learners view themselves as capable writers, it is much easier to foster their creativity, develop their expression, and teach them the mechanics of correct writing.

If writing confidence is this important, the school should deal with it. If its presence makes the teaching of creativity, expression, and mechanics easier, and if its absence deters writing improvement, it can't be ignored. Classroom teachers should make planned and intentional efforts to build writing confidence.

But doesn't the additional responsibility of developing confidence only add to the dilemma of the teacher? If it is difficult to determine the relative priorities for creativity, expression, and mechanics, won't the addition of a fourth area only add to the confusion?

It is true that attempts to emphasize all four areas of writing instruction simultaneously can be very frustrating for teachers. But there is no need to emphasize all of them at once. Rather, there is a logical sequence that a writing program should follow.

An Emphasis Sequence

The emphasis of a writing program should change as writers advance in their creativity and writing confidence. Figure 6–1 shows this sequence.

FIGURE 6–1   A sequence of emphases for writing.

Before examination of the details of this sequence, it should be pointed out that this is not a lockstep teaching sequence or a hierarchy of skills. It is only a sequence of what should be *emphasized* in the writing program. In other words, mechanics and expression should be included in the program from the beginning, but they should not be stressed until the learners have developed a reasonable measure of confidence and extended their creativity.

Oral Language

The first emphasis in a writing program should be on speaking, and speaking should continue to play a role in the development of writing. As we saw in Chapter Four, oral language is the foundation of all other forms of communication. Writing ability is based on speaking ability, so the expansion and development of oral language is the most logical first step in writing. Even after this initial emphasis, oral language should be a part of writing activities. Weaver has described the advantages listed by a number of writing authorities for letting children talk about their thoughts before putting them on paper.[2] The spoken word is a natural bridge from thoughts to written products.

Confidence and Creativity

In moving from one emphasis to another, the second part of a writing program should concentrate on developing creativity and confidence. Although an individual's creative abilities and writing confidence are in two quite different categories, they can readily be emphasized at the same time. The fact that both flourish when attention is given to feelings of success rather than to correctness makes them logical candidates for the part of the program that precedes the emphasis on mechanics and expression. After oral language has received adequate attention, then, the emphasis should shift to creative writing and writing confidence. Creativity is discussed in more detail in the next chapter, while confidence-building techniques are described in the latter part of this chapter.

Mechanics and Expression

When it is clear that an individual has confidence in his or her ability to write, it is time to begin emphasizing the correct forms of writing mechanics and written expression. Certainly, the attention to confidence should never stop, but the time comes when it no longer needs top priority. Writing mechanics include such techniques as handwriting, spelling, punctuating, and capitalizing. Written expression not only includes the skills of sentence construction and paragraphing but the more abstract ability to communicate effectively and efficiently. Both areas of the writing program can be emphasized simultaneously, and both are discussed in the chapters that follow.

BUILDING WRITING CONFIDENCE

As the preceding section suggests, the school's goal of producing able writers is more likely to be met if confidence can be established in the learners before an emphasis on mechanics and expression is begun. This is not to say that confidence is the most important aspect of writing. Indeed, many teachers feel that the sequence suggested above is wrong. They believe mechanics need to be stressed from the beginning so that children never fall into being "sloppy" about their writing. But the overwhelming impact that confidence has upon writing ability cannot be ignored.

Ideally, children should be past a need for oral language emphasis by the middle of first grade, should spend the remainder of their primary years in an atmosphere that encourages creativity and confidence, and should be ready to concentrate heavily on mechanics and written expression by the time they begin the fourth grade. In reality, however, the program seldom works that way. Teachers at every grade level encounter children who lack confidence, some of whom have such negative self-concepts that efforts to teach writing lead to frustration. Some of these children are passed on by teachers who never emphasize confidence. Therefore, nearly every teacher needs to organize the *yearly* writing program to follow the sequence described above.

Nearly every writing teacher, then, has a need to build confidence. Fortunately, there are specific teaching techniques that usually are capable of raising such confidence. The techniques are all related to providing the learners with a sense of success, the essential ingredient in a program to build confidence or self-concept. Purkey, in his thorough review of self-concept research, concluded, "Perhaps the single most important step that teachers can take in the classroom is to provide an educational atmosphere of success rather than failure."[3]

Success-building techniques are part of an ongoing teaching process. As they relate to writing, however, it seems appropriate to divide them into three categories: establishing a writing environment, dealing with students' written products, and using activities specifically geared toward success.

A Writing Environment

Before a person can be successful at doing anything, he or she has to try it. People can become convinced they *might* succeed before trying, but only after something has been completed can its success be determined. Nor is trying one time, even if it is successful, enough to have a substantial impact on self-concept. Many successes are needed to establish confidence, so many attempts need to be made.

Getting children to try, to put adequate effort into their writing, can be a challenge. Only when adequate effort is made can there be a successful product. Of course, learners who have experienced a number of writing successes will be more eager to try again, but arranging for those first successes can be difficult. The most certain way to call forth the initial writing effort and to keep children trying is to establish a writing environment in the classroom.

A writing environment is not easy to define. As its name suggests, it includes everything in the children's surroundings. In a sense, the discussions later in the chapter about dealing with the learners' products and about specific teaching activities are also part of the environment. At this point, however, it seems logical to look at the parts of the learners' environment that motivate them to try, to put their energy into writing in the first place. Six aspects of that environment have been described by various authorities.

Teacher Personality

The most important teaching tool in a classroom is the teacher. The teacher's influence on the writing environment is greater than any other factor. Petty and Bowen have described the ideal writing teacher as one who is flexible, honest, patient, interested in the learners, relaxed, friendly, and confident, as well as one who can bring logic and sequence into the classroom.[4] It is doubtful that substantial changes in personality can be brought about by simply making decisions to change. Teachers can, however, bend their personalities in a positive direction and sometimes make gradual changes over time. It is especially important that the teacher use his or her personality to the fullest to make writing activities pleasant and free from tension.

Writing Opportunities

A writing environment also includes time for students to write. As obvious as this may seem, it is sometimes difficult to schedule time for writing when there are so many other demands for time in school. Yet, the importance of an activity is usually indicated by the amount of time allotted for it. An essential part of a writing environment is the continuous implication that writing is important. Some of the time can be carved from subject areas outside the language arts, because writing is a natural supplement to such areas as social studies and science. If suggestions for the teaching of skills, offered in later chapters, are followed, more language arts time can also be used. Regardless of the method, writing time should be provided almost daily.

Appropriate Expectations

Another aspect of the environment is an appropriate set of expectations about each individual's writing products. The child's level of writing ability as well as her or his level of confidence must be considered if success is to be attained. If the teacher expects too little, a lack of importance is attached to writing, or the child is led to underestimate his or her own ability. If the teacher expects too much, frustration is aroused and success is unlikely. The difficult task of finding the appropriate level is aided by the evaluation techniques described at the end of this and the next chapters.

Writing Purposes

When students write something only because they are expected to write, they usually have little commitment to the task. In other words, there is little motivation to put forth much effort. Teacher approval or report card grades stimulate some children, but the best writing is done when there is some personal reason for doing it. A writing environment, then, includes many authentic purposes for writing. Teachers can create, facilitate, or help learners discover many such purposes; for example:

Place an article in the classroom newspaper

Exchange letters with a "pen pal" in another school

Contribute to a class book

Develop part of a science or social studies project

Answer an editorial in a newspaper

Advertise something the class is doing or selling

Share with other members of the class

Involvement

In order to write, anyone has to have something to write about. A writing environment, therefore, has to include an overall belief that everyone has something important to say. This may be the very core of writing confidence—the individual's belief that he or she has something worthwhile to write. Calkins has explained that this belief is created when children are allowed and expected to write about their own feelings and life experiences. When children write about their vacation plans, injuries, aspirations, personal triumphs, and similar concerns, they become personally involved in their writing.[5] Personal involvement in any activity gives individuals a purpose and leads them to put forth sincere effort.

Social Interaction

Rubin has claimed that writing ability is blocked when learners are not allowed to talk and interact with each other as a part of the writing activity.[6] Perhaps the type of social interaction should fit the nature and type of writing, but this claim is in line with two concepts already mentioned in this text. One is that oral language is important in developing writing. The other is that a writing environment should include a degree of flexibility. Therefore, social interaction may often contribute to a positive writing environment.

Dealing with Written Products

It is essential that student writers feel a degree of success associated with their written products, especially during the part of the writing program which emphasizes confidence. Writers who are already confident can deal with a certain amount of failure because they see themselves as writers who have periodic challenges. Children lacking confidence can't deal with very much failure because they have not yet seen themselves as writers or, if they have previously had mainly unsuccessful writing experiences, they see themselves as nonwriters. The writing environment described above can lead learners to attempt their own writing, but that isn't enough to make them continue their efforts if their products aren't successful. When the emphasis is on confidence building, and to some extent even when it isn't, success is very important.

Providing learners with writing successes is difficult, however, if certain common teaching practices are used. Most of these practices take place after the writers finish their papers. By looking at these negative practices, perhaps we can learn what to avoid in building success.

As was said, the practices begin by having the students turn in their writing assignments. The teacher then begins the long process of finding errors and marking them on the papers. Often this consists of a shorthand system for indicating spelling and punctuation errors, poor wording, improper grammar, unclear ideas, and the like. Sometimes these errors are marked in red, giving the paper a "bleeding" effect. The next negative practice is to return the papers to the students with instructions to correct them. Finally, the recopied papers are often given a grade which influences the report card. Variations of these practices are common, such as requiring writers to find their own errors on their papers before recopying them.

Many writing authorities have criticized these negative teaching practices pointing out a number of problems with them. First of all, such techniques are not based on what we have come to know about learning to write. Not only is the emphasis placed on the mechanical skills of writing at the expense of written expression and confidence, but only the simplest and narrowest skills are taught because they can be evaluated most easily.[7] The evaluation, or letter grade, therefore, isn't fair because it also is based on the mechanical skills of spelling, handwriting, and punctuation much more than on the overall art of writing. Even if such practices are limited to the teaching of skills, they aren't sound. There is no actual teaching of skills involved; the teacher's role is limited to that of an error hunter and the child is expected to learn from the errors with little guidance.

Secondly, the teaching practices described above are more likely to destroy writing confidence than to build it. This is because attention is drawn only to what student writers do wrong. They receive little recognition for what is good or right about their papers; most of the marks on the paper are for specific errors. In a very real sense, then, every time a paper is given back by a teacher using these practices the child is criticized. Not only have a number of research studies shown that praise is far more effective in teaching children to write than is criticism,[8] but we have seen that confidence is dependent upon success and criticism is an indication of failure.

Finally, the teaching practices described above have been criticized for the results they produce, namely children who write less and more poorly. In summarizing recent research, Hillerich has pointed out that children who regularly received such criticism wrote less, had fewer creative ideas, enjoyed writing less, and even made more mechanical errors than children who received praise without criticism.[9] It is easy to see why this happens. Children learn that if they write little in the first place, they will have little to rewrite or recopy when they reach this step. They also discover that if they use simple sentences, words that they know they can spell, and traditional ideas, they will receive less criticism from the teacher's red pencil. Experimenting with new sentence forms, expressive wording, and creative ideas involves a risk that isn't rewarded. In fact, the more advanced or brighter students discover these strategies earlier and may well have the shortest and dullest writing products.

The teaching practices described above, therefore, should be avoided. Does this mean, however, that writing shouldn't be assigned, that writing mechanics should be ignored, or that children should never be expected to rewrite what they have written? Certainly not. At appropriate times writing should be assigned, and at other times it should be voluntary. Writing mechanics should certainly not be ignored, but they should be emphasized only when confidence has been established. Rewriting is an important part of a writing program, again after confidence is established.

What is being stressed here is that these components of writing should be used in a positive manner. An important part of this positive use is timing. It has already been said throughout this chapter that the emphasis on mechanics should come *after* the emphasis on confidence. Another part is dealing with mechanics and rewriting in ways that build rather than destroy. In the chapters that follow, we will look at positive, constructive methods of dealing with these components of writing.

Confidence-Building Activities

In addition to establishing a writing environment and avoiding negative practices with writing products, there are certain teaching activities that a teacher can use to build writing confidence. These activities give children some practice with written expression and writing mechanics, but they strongly emphasize success. The impression should not be made that such techniques are only supplementary, for they are as essential as those for skills. The activities are especially useful during the part of the writing program in which confidence is receiving the greatest attention.

Getting Started

There are two types of beginners in writing, those who have never written and those who virtually need to begin again. The first group is very susceptible to the effects of success or failure as a specific writing self-concept begins to form. The group that needs to start again almost always has a negative self-concept quite firmly established from previous writing experiences. Both groups, therefore, need repeated successes from the very beginning, although they have almost no writing ability on which to build the success.

Writing at this early stage consists of dictating language so that someone, usually the teacher, can write it down. In the teaching of reading, the products of such dictation are known as *experience stories* and the approach as the *language experience approach.* It is an effective way to get children started in reading, but it is just as effective as a beginning writing technique. If the teacher refers to the activity as "writing," explains to the learners that they are the real authors, and accepts exactly what they say, these beginners see the products as their own. They begin to realize that they have something to say, something worth writing. As a result, feelings of success and confidence receive a firm boost. The technique is also useful with more advanced writers.

Continuing the Confidence

When children begin to write their own ideas, they usually need help in getting the words on paper. One of the most difficult tasks seems to be remembering an idea long enough to put it all down. If

Confidence in one's writing ability is largely learned in school. (*Carmine L. Galasso*)

each word must be spelled correctly as it is written, the task becomes impossible. A shorthand system allows writers to keep going when a word gives them trouble. A common system is to simply write the first letter of the word, which is usually known, and draw a pencil line to form a blank for the remainder of it. This allows the child to get thoughts onto paper before they are lost. Later, after the thoughts are written, the spellings of the missing words can be sought from the teacher or other sources. This practice helps to prepare learners for proofreading when it is introduced several months later. It does so by demonstrating that one should not expect to write perfectly on the first draft. It also continues the confidence that was established earlier through the dictation of stories, because learners continue to see that they have something to say that can be written down.

When the time comes that children can be expected to proofread and rewrite their first drafts, care must again be taken so that the confidence which has been established is not shattered. This should not be a dramatic occasion when suddenly the pleasure of writing must give way to correctness. The introduction of proofreading can be handled positively in several ways. One is to introduce it gradually with a few skills at a time being added to the list of those for which correctness is expected. An alternative is to begin with *parts* of the first draft which must be rewritten. Another positive way to introduce proofreading is with small groups. After a first draft is written, several learners work together on all of their papers. The use of proofreading groups is discussed in detail in the chapters dealing with writing skills.

Recognition as an Author

Part of a writing self-concept is the perception of oneself as an author. The more that a teacher can do to instill this sense of authorship, the easier it should be to build confidence. Children should come to see that it isn't necessary for their writings to appear in national publications in order for them to be considered authors. Part of the sense of authorship comes from frequent mention and discussion of it in the classroom. The study of selected authors or even a visit from a recognized author might be one way to initiate this authorship climate.

Gonzales has described a plan for making children feel like authors through bookmaking. After learners write a lengthy work over a period of days, they use the "author center" to simulate some of the steps in editing and publishing a book of their own. Typed manuscript, homemade hard covers, and an author party when the book "comes out" all contribute to the feeling of authorship.[10]

Personal Feedback

In an earlier part of this chapter, negative methods for dealing with students' written products were criticized. Not only should the negative practices be avoided, but positive activities should be substituted. Developing writers *do* need guidance and feedback from teachers, but it must be given in ways that build confidence rather than destroy it.

Probably the best method for meeting this criterion is through the use of personal feedback. Instead of marking errors on a student's paper, the teacher communicates overall reactions, specific satisfaction and pleasures derived from reading it, questions, and suggestions. The communication is more like a friendly discussion than a critique. There are at least two ways to do this.

Individual conferences are one effective method of communication. By sitting down with the child's written product, it is possible to have a two-way interaction instead of one-way teacher comments. The child's purpose and technique can be clarified, the teacher's reaction can be clearly expressed, and the discussion can be friendly. If the tone of the conference is positive, this activity can contribute to confidence building. Of course, individual conferences are time consuming, but this fact is balanced by the gain in afterschool hours that are frequently spent in marking students' errors. In addition, conferences can be brief, scheduled so that only a few are held each day, and sometimes conducted outside the language arts part of the day.

The communication can also be done in writing. Staton has described a system in which students write to the teacher in a journal each day and the teacher writes back briefly each night.[11] Time consuming as this activity would be, it allows the teacher to go beyond responses to children's writing into areas of classroom interaction and personal growth. Other forms of written reaction to written products are possible, but they must have a different function than the red pencil error hunting that is so common. If written communication is to be as effective as individual conferences, it must give overall reactions and show interest in the student's message. Regardless of the form, feedback from the teacher must be personal and mainly positive during the part of the writing program that emphasizes confidence.

Specific Activities

Sometimes even more is needed to get writing confidence started, especially with children who have already had some unsuccessful experiences with writing. In such cases, activities that involve writing for the sake of writing can be used at first. When reluctant writers see that they can succeed in these activities, they are frequently encouraged to attempt the more meaningful writing projects that follow. Some examples of activities that can serve this function are discussed next.

- *Pass-along writing.* A general topic for a story is announced to the class or group, for example a story of a bear cub or a nervous baseball player. Each participant then writes a one sentence beginning to the story on the top line of her or his paper. Without sharing the writing with anyone, each individual then folds the top of the paper down to cover the sentence and passes the product to the student behind or to the right of him or her. Without looking at the first sentence that was just received, each writer then adds another statement or sentence just below the fold. The paper is folded a second time and passed in the same direction, and the procedure is repeated until four or five parts, including an ending, have been added. The children then open the paper and share their rather disjointed and often humorous "stories."

- *Poetry writing.* Many teachers avoid poetry because they are uncomfortable with it or they feel it is too difficult for elementary pupils. However, if used properly, it can have the opposite effect. Because many children view poetry writing as difficult, initial successes with it can instill a great deal of confidence, not only in writing poetry but in all writing. The activity must use poetry that is relatively structured and easy to write. Haiku and Cinquain usually meet this criteria best. The teacher shares a number of examples from the selected type of poetry with the class. This needs to be done with enthusiasm. Then, he or she explains the format or directions for writing this type of poetry and challenges the students to try writing a poem. After a few minutes, volunteers read their poems to the class. If the teacher greets the results with enthusiasm and praise, many children will volunteer, usually even the reluctant writers. Details about Haiku and Cinquain, including their writing formats, are found on page 156.

- *Caption writing for photographs.* Especially for upper elementary students who have many humorous verbal statements but low writing confidence, labeling photographs can start building confidence. Humorous one-line captions for pictures are often easy for such individuals to write, especially if the true circumstances of the photographs are known. Familiar magazine pictures are useful, but action photographs are better. If photos of classroom peers are not available, individuals might be able to bring and use pictures from home.

EVALUATING WRITING CONFIDENCE

If the sequence for writing instruction is made to resemble the one suggested in this chapter, it is important to know when a reasonable level of writing confidence has been attained. The emphasis of any individual's writing program should continue to be on confidence building until that level is established. Although every individual gains confidence at a different rate, it is not difficult to adjust a writing program so that the stress for some learners is on confidence while for others it is on writing ability. Various levels of confidence can be dealt with in this way even when everyone is involved in the same writing activity, because it is in the teacher's reaction to written products that most individualization occurs.

A teacher must have a method, then, for determining when the emphasis for each individual can be gradually changed from confidence to writing abilities. It would be ideal if a test could simply be given to determine when confidence is adequate. By their very nature, however, paper-and-pencil tests do not measure intangibles such as confidence. Furthermore, there is no agreement about how much confidence is needed to give children a foundation for writing ability. Writing confidence can be evaluated only through the teacher's observation of and interaction with the child.

Judgments on the basis of observation and interaction, however, should not be arbitrary. The confidence of each child should be considered carefully on the basis of predetermined criteria. One of the most effective ways to structure such decision making is through the use of a checklist containing the behaviors which best seem to exemplify confidence. The checklist in Box 6–1 is an example. The more positively the questions on a checklist can be answered about an individual, the more writing confidence that person evidently has. Not only should the number of affirmative answers be considered, but the degree to which they are true as well. Checklists such as the one shown in Box 6–1 reduce the arbitrariness of decisions related to confidence.

BOX 6–1   *SAMPLE CHECKLIST OF BEHAVIORS EXPRESSING CONFIDENCE*

Does the child:

Give indications of pleasure at the prospect of writing?

Appear to be free from excessive tension when writing?

Continue writing when "stuck" on individual words?

Put sincere effort into his or her writing?

Usually find a topic for writing rather easily?

Usually produce a quantity that matches individual ability?*

Take pride in his or her written products?

Frequently share his or her written ideas with others when given the opportunity?

Respond positively to suggestions and feedback?

*When the majority of the class writes minimal amounts, the teacher should also evaluate the amount of confidence building that the classroom provides.

SUMMARY

Writing self-concept, or confidence, is essential for growth in writing ability. Children who view themselves as writers usually develop better writing skills and written expression than those who lack such confidence. For this reason, it is important to emphasize confidence before mechanical skills and expression are emphasized.

There are three types of classroom practices that build writing self-concepts or confidence. A writing environment in the classroom can encourage learners to get started. The teacher's method for dealing with written products has a great impact on the children's feelings of success. Finally, there are a number of specific activities that build confidence.

In Scene B at the beginning of this chapter, Mr. Larsen seemed to understand many of these concepts of writing instruction. Evidence that a writing environment existed is seen in the children's enthusiasm for writing, the teacher's positive comments, the apparent plentiful opportunities for writing, and the involvement of the learners in this activity. We can't tell from this short episode how Mr. Larsen dealt with their written products, but Al's comment makes us suspect that more happened than assigning a grade or identifying errors. Perhaps most outstanding of all was this teacher's emphasis on authorship, the specific activity being a form of bookmaking. Mr. Larsen did a great deal of confidence building.

Mrs. Todd, on the other hand, seemed to ignore the effects of confidence. The children's obvious purpose in writing was to please their teacher and avoid any extra writing. This is contrary to a positive writing environment. Mrs. Todd's method for dealing with written products was one of error hunting and grading. She seemed much more concerned with correctness than with confidence.

Ignoring writing confidence is self-defeating for a teacher. The role of the school to produce good writers is fulfilled more effectively when confidence is emphasized before writing ability. Not only is writing instruction easier when learners are confident, but the instruction has a more permanent and positive effect on the lives of the children.

NOTES

1. William W. Purkey, *Self-Concept and School Achievement* (Englewood Cliffs, N.J.: Prentice-Hall, Inc., 1970).
2. Gail Cohen Weaver, "ERIC/RCS Report: Integrating Written Composition with Other Language Arts Activities," *Language Arts,* 55 (October 1978), 874.
3. Purkey, *Self-Concept and School Achievement,* p. 55.
4. Walter J. Petty and Mary Bowen, *Slithery Snakes and Other Aids to Children's Writing* (New York: Meredith Publishing Co., 1967), p. 9.
5. Lucy McCormick Calkins, "Children Write—and Their Writing Becomes Their Textbook," *Language Arts,* 55 (October 1978), 804.
6. Andee Rubin, "Making Stories, Making Sense," *Language Arts,* 57 (March 1980), 285–86.
7. Kenneth J. Kantor, "Appreciating Children's Writing," *Language Arts,* 56 (October 1979), 743.
8. Robert L. Hillerich, "Developing Written Expression: How to Raise—Not Raze—Writers," *Language Arts,* 56 (October 1979), 669–70.
9. Ibid.
10. Dolores Gonzales, "An Author Center for Children," *Language Arts,* 57 (March 1980), 280–84.
11. Jana Staton, "Writing and Counseling: Using a Dialogue Journal," *Language Arts,* 57 (May 1980), 514–18.

CHAPTER SEVEN
MOTIVATING CREATIVE WRITING

Scene A

"Our creative writing assignment for today," said Mr. Compau, "is to write about January. I'm sure everyone can find something interesting to write about January. Now remember, you must use each of this week's spelling words at least once in the story."

Rhona, James, Pat, and Erick began writing immediately. Tyrone, Chuck, and Heidi stared out the window. Four other children stared at their papers. Wayne and Linda whispered continuously in the back of the room. Myrna headed for the drinking fountain, and Hector asked permission to use the restroom.

Scene B

"How is the popcorn different now than it was before?" asked Ms. Snyder after making popcorn in class.

"When you put it in your mouth it doesn't hurt," said Elaine.

"It tastes better," said Ming.

"It's much bigger and it's white," said Jerome.

"It exploded," said Mary Ann.

"If popcorn had any feelings, how do you think it would feel to be popped?" Ms. Snyder asked.

Even more responses followed.

"Have any of you ever felt like the popcorn?"

Again, pupil responses followed.

"Let's write down some things about popcorn," the teacher finally said. "You may write a report about it, a story, or a poem. Remember, if you need any kind of help, I'll be happy to give it."

Anyone who has ever written anything that is not copied from someone else has been involved in creative writing. The writing may or may not have had original content, have been of excellent quality, or have been extensive. But if the writing represented the writer's own thoughts, it was creative.

There has been continuing debate among writing authorities about what is and isn't creative writing. One common way to classify writing, especially in school, is to speak of creative and practical writing. Creative writing is regarded as that which is imaginative, narrative (as in story writing), or both. Practical writing is seen as that which fulfills life's needs, such as letter writing, report writing, and form completion.

To make a distinction between imaginative and practical writing can be valuable. To think of the first type as creative and the second as noncreative is, however, not a very realistic distinction. While it is true that imaginative writing probably lends itself to creativity more easily, it is misleading to presume that the writing of letters, forms, and other practical documents requires no creativity.

Lewis defines creative writing as the written formulation of ideas anytime the writer is thinking for himself.[1] Therefore, creative writing is a process, not a product. It makes sense to define it in this way because no artificial lines separate written products according to their literary style or function. Thinking for oneself is a process that is as important in practical writing as it is in imaginative writing.

When we think for ourselves, our thinking is partly original and partly based on our previous experiences. To be original, our ideas or solutions do not need to be completely new to the world, but they do need to be new to us. Since creativity is only partly original, then, we may speak of the *degree* to which a written product is original.

Using previous experiences related to the topic being written and related to the language patterns being used is also an important aspect of creative writing. Selecting ideas, solutions, and language that have been used before but are appropriate for the writing at hand plays a major role in creative expression. It is the use of the writer's own thinking, rather than the use of learned responses, that makes writing creative.

Of course not all writing is creative. There are times when writing someone else's thinking or writing predetermined responses is appropriate. The school should encourage creative writing in practical settings as well as in imaginative ones.

WHY CREATIVE WRITING?

There are four types of benefits attributed to a writing program which encourages creativity: (1) it has overall intellectual value for the child, (2) it encourages creativity as a trait, (3) it aids in the development of confidence and positive attitudes toward writing, and (4) it provides part of the foundation needed to produce effective writers. All four are important, but the last two are especially related to this chapter.

Intellectual Value and Creativity

While intellectual endeavors and creativity are sometimes thought of as opposites, this need not be true. Petty and Bowen report that "children engaged in creative writing are likely to be using more of their mental capabilities than they do for many other kinds of school activity."[2] In addition, creativity is a human trait that has value for its own sake. A creative writing program can stimulate both the intellectual and creative levels of the learner.

Building Confidence and Attitudes

In the previous chapter, we saw the importance of confidence in learning to write. Not only is creative writing a logical emphasis to accompany confidence building, it can assist in the attainment of that goal. The key ingredient in confidence building is success, and a sense of success is a likely outcome of creative writing, especially when it is handled in a manner similar to the one described in this chapter. During the early part of a writing program, a time when confidence and creativity usually need to be emphasized, it is difficult for writers to achieve recognition and satisfaction on the basis of their writing mechanics or written expression. Those two types of ability are not usually mastered this early in the program, whether we are speaking of children just entering school or older learners who lack confidence. But when the products are judged on the basis of independent thinking, recognition and satisfaction can rather easily be achieved. Therefore, creative writing is an impetus for feelings of success and confidence.

In a similar manner, creative writing usually builds positive attitudes about writing. The success and satisfaction that flow from such independent writing lead students to enjoy it. When we examine our own interests, we find that most of the activities which we enjoy are those which we do well. Since creative writing is more likely to provide success than other types, it builds more positive attitudes. Such attitudes have a great influence on an individual's writing productivity throughout her or his lifetime.

Foundations for Writing

Finally, creative writing is valuable because it builds foundations for the writing abilities which are emphasized later in the writing program. This is true largely as a result of the factors described above. Because learners use their individual thinking powers to the fullest, and develop confidence and enjoyment from it, they tend to do two things that are very useful for the expansion of abilities.

First, they tend to write much more. One of the results of writing success found by Hillerich in his summary of research was that children who felt successful wrote more and enjoyed it more.[3] Assuming that practice is important in the development of abilities, creative writing builds foundations for writing by motivating a great deal of practice.

Second, these factors tend to free writers to take more risks. Their confidence and freedom from fear of criticism leads them to experiment with words, ideas, and methods for expressing them. When this experimentation is reinforced through a teacher's recognition, learners are likely to adopt a larger vocabulary, a larger bank of sentence patterns, and an attitude favorable to even more experimentation. Later in the writing program, when the emphasis changes to writing mechanics and written expression, risk-taking writers can more easily deal with these abilities because they see new skills as additions rather than threats to their writing effectiveness.

SEQUENCE OF INSTRUCTION

The previous chapter suggested a sequence for teaching writing. A writing program should be composed of four general thrusts: building confidence, motivating creativity, teaching the mechanics of writing, and developing written expression. All four of these areas should be present throughout a writing program, but not all of them should be emphasized at the same time. Rather, a certain sequence in the emphasis is logical. The suggested sequence, once an oral language background has been established, emphasizes first confidence and creativity and then gradually mechanics and expression.

Now that we have examined the benefits of creative writing, the logic of this sequence should be more clear. Creative writing and confidence are natural partners because they both thrive in the same type of writing environment. They both depend on success and yet they both perpetuate success. The emphasis on confidence and creativity needs to precede that on mechanics and expression, because too much attention to the latter stifles creativity and breaks down confidence. On the other hand, mechanical and expressive abilities are more easily learned when the results of confidence and creative writing are already evident.

TECHNIQUES FOR MOTIVATING CREATIVE WRITING

There is general agreement among educators that creativity cannot be taught. Developing children's creativity is not a matter of teaching a certain series of lessons or providing practice in certain skills. If creativity is defined as thinking for oneself, it is obvious why lessons and skills aren't helpful.

The role of the teacher in fostering creativity, on the other hand, is a very important one. Since nearly every child has some ability to think for himself or herself, it is the teacher's role to bring this creativity out and onto paper. Creativity can be encouraged and nourished by establishing appropriate conditions of freedom in the classroom.

A substantial part of this freedom, a freedom from too many mechanical writing restrictions and from a fear of making mistakes, has already been discussed in the previous chapter. In addition, however, there are two other types of freedom that stimulate creativity. While these freedoms overlap with the ones already discussed, they also merit separate attention. Freedom to express ideas and freedom to experiment with words are especially important for developing writers, so that they will use and expand their abilities to think for themselves.

Freedom to Express Ideas

Living in a society that legally supports freedom of speech, we expect that individuals have the right to speak and write what they believe so long as it isn't harmful to others. We expect the school system to support that freedom as well, and to a large extent it does. Freedom to express ideas, however, involves more than the basic right to freedom of speech.

The most important ingredient in the learners' freedom to express ideas is a withholding of the teacher's criticism. If creativity is to be encouraged, children must feel that they have true freedom to think for themselves rather than that they must write what they believe the teacher wants them to say. They need to believe that they have selected the specific writing topic, that they have developed the content in their own way, and that they have been successful in doing so. This can only happen when the teacher eliminates most restrictions on what they write and avoids criticism of the topic or content once the writing product is completed. Written expression is important but, as with writing mechanics, emphasis on it must be delayed.

Some authorities on writing contend that this freedom should be extended to include the manner in which the writing is undertaken. Smith, Goodman, and Meredith, for example, explain that the writer should not have the writing too well planned before beginning the story or composition.[4] Rather, she or he should be allowed to let the writing develop as it progresses, much as an artist does with her or his medium. Of course, organization is important in writing also and should be encouraged. But outlining and other forms of detailed planning can be postponed like the other areas of writing mechanics and expression and should never be overemphasized in imaginative writing.

Giving students freedom to express their ideas, however, does *not* mean that they can be left to write on their own. It is not enough to assign writing and tell them to "write about anything you want." Most children flounder aimlessly under such directions. It is just as ridiculous to expect that they need no directions and will write whenever they feel like it. Writing requires much more effort than speaking does, and there is frequently little natural inclination or ability to pick up a pencil and write.

Children need to be stimulated or motivated to write creatively. This can best be done as a class or group activity. The form of the stimulus will vary with every situation, but it will usually involve a real or vicarious experience or a discussion about previous experiences the learners have had. The sequence for initiating writing might be:

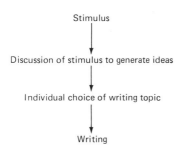

We can see that this approach reduces the apparent contradiction between the need for a stimulus and the need for freedom to express ideas. By talking about their experiences with peers and the teacher, children generate many writing ideas. If individuals feel confident to speak out about their ideas, they will add areas of their own interest to the discussion. From the array of ideas that are brought out during the discussion, the individual can then choose the one that best meets the purpose of the writing as he or she sees it.

Gerbrandt suggests that the use of small groups is another important step in this sequence. Once children have been taught how to learn in groups, peer interaction can stimulate more ideas and help individuals refine them.[5] After the class discussion has ended, the learners are divided into groups. In the small groups, individuals share their ideas for writing, give feedback to the other group members about their ideas, and thereby test their plans against those of others. A teacher who has used groups a number of times before can usually feel sufficiently confident to stay out of the groups unless help is requested. When the group interaction is ended, individuals begin their writing. The groups can also be used to aid with proofreading after the first drafts are written. Proofreading groups are discussed in the chapters that follow.

The ideal stimulus for writing is one that relates to some other activity for which the learners already see a purpose. Writing a letter to obtain information about an upcoming class trip or writing a script for a dramatic presentation the class will give are excellent examples. Sometimes, however, the writing contains its own purpose if it is about an interesting topic. In this case, the stimulus must be very appealing. The following list may provide some interesting stimuli for young children:

Observing a pet or caged animal

Taking short walking tours

Preparing and eating various foods

Executing an unusual art project

Learning to play a tune on a musical instrument

Dramatizing a favorite story

Discussing emotions or emotional experiences

Discussing favorite leisure activities

For older children, the following should be helpful:

Conducting a science experiment

Inviting a guest to describe an interesting hobby or experience

Taking apart a light switch or simple appliance

Tape-recording (or video taping)

Role playing

Constructing a project (pinhole camera, diorama, relief map, or other)

Discussing personal values

Discussing favorite television stars

Some teachers attempt to deal with interests on an individual basis. One common method of doing this is to randomly distribute magazine pictures and assign each individual to write about her or his picture. Another method is to provide a list of "story starters" and let each individual select an appealing one to use as the beginning of a story. Story starters are beginning sentences such as, "John had been curious about the old trunk in his attic for years" or "Pam and Sue were walking home one dark night when they heard strange footsteps." While these methods often interest children who are already motivated to write, they usually provide less stimulus than activities that allow the class or group to interact and share ideas.

Freedom to Choose Words

Individuals who can write with variety and expression usually have larger vocabularies than those who are less able. This well-established assumption has led well-intended educators to attempt to improve their students' writing by forcing words upon them. Such devices as vocabulary tests, word drills, and practice sheets have often been used to work toward this objective. These devices, however, have usually been ineffective and sometimes counter-productive.

Words are learned when they are used in meaningful contexts. A study by Gipe suggests that the meanings of words are remembered only when they appear in context a number of times and when that context makes the meaning clear.[6] Adding to one's writing vocabulary results from many meaningful exposures to words in listening and reading, usually in natural settings such as conversation and independent reading. Words and definitions can be memorized for a short time even when the purpose for doing so is unclear, but they are quickly forgotten when the test or exercise is over.

Forcing words upon children and then expecting or even requiring them to use the words in their writing is a double evil. Not only are learners required to memorize words they aren't likely to remember, they are losing some of their freedom to express their own ideas.

When children are engaged in creative writing, they should have the freedom to use words of their own choosing. Encouraging them to use "flower" language or to use a vocabulary that is inappropriate for their level of development only leads to unnatural writing products. It is better for them to use a small vocabulary effectively than it is to use a large one ineffectively. Freedom to express ideas is crippled by requirements to include a list of words determined by the teacher. If the writing is to be creative, words that have been learned should be used by individuals in their own natural way.

IMAGINATIVE WRITING

In this text, the position is taken that creative writing can and should be used for practical as well as imaginative purposes. Because creative writing is defined as writing one's own ideas, it is useful in many settings. It is logical, however, that imaginative writing offers a greater amount and a wider range of opportunity to practice creativity than do the other types of writing. As learners develop characters, settings, moods, and plots, they can express their ideas in multiple ways.

Imaginative writing is any writing that makes no effort to report or represent factual information. The majority of it is narrative writing, including various types of fiction, myths, fables, tall tales, and legends. A large part of poetry is also imaginative writing, but that is treated separately later in the chapter.

Imaginative Writing for Young Children

Young children of preschool and beginning school ages are usually filled with rich and varied imaginations. Perhaps one of the reasons this is true is that the school, the family, and society have not yet robbed them of this precious gift. By carefully nourishing their use of fantasy and by giving it a new outlet, namely writing, the school can prolong and expand children's imaginations. Teachers of young children, then, are faced with the opportunity to have a long-lasting effect upon imaginative writing.

The distinction between realistic and imaginative writing is not as clear and not as important when working with young children.

Everyone needs to learn how to separate fantasy from reality, but normal children need little help in doing so when they are ready. In addition, even young children need to become aware of the need for accuracy when the occasion calls for it. However, the egocentric view of the world that these children have and their mushrooming need for independence almost demand that imagination and their own lives be intertwined.

When young children put themselves and their own experiences into imaginary stories, they are taking significant steps in gaining control over their environment.[7] The same is true when they put fantasy into stories about their own experiences. Preschoolers test their world and gain a sense of control over it through dramatic play, acting out scene after scene of life as they want or expect it to be. Children with beginning writing abilities can and should do the same with words. Thus, it is not only true that mental maturation and development promote writing, but that writing promotes mental maturation and development.

Dictating Stories

If children are allowed to mix their own experiences with imagination, both can be called "stories" in the primary grades classroom. But how can children who barely write or don't write at all "write" a story? The answer is obvious if we don't limit our definition of *writer* to the person who holds the pencil.

Beginning writers can perform every step and deal with every aspect of imaginative writing except for handwriting. If the school can provide someone who will take dictation, young children can write. The person who usually takes dictation is the teacher, but the task can be performed by aides, parents, or any other willing adults or older children.

The procedure for stimulating dictated stories is similar to the one for stimulating all other creative writing. The children are provided with an experience, or a common experience is discussed. If an experience is provided (see "Freedom to Express Ideas" above), it is followed by a discussion. In either event, the discussion stimulates factual or imaginative ideas. Especially with young children, the discussion also forms a bridge between oral and written language.

The children then dictate their "stories" in one of two ways. A group chart may be constructed by giving each of several volunteers a turn at dictating a sentence. The teacher adds the sentence, with a felt pen, to the developing story on large chart paper. Individual expe-

By giving dictation to someone who can put down their words, even young children can write. (*Leslie Deeb*)

rience stories may be dictated one at a time to the teacher while the other children are occupied with illustrating the experience that was discussed minutes earlier. The group chart lends itself better to easy classroom management and the individual story lends itself to a greater feeling of authorship, but both are valuable.

Once the dictation is completed, the products can be used in a number of ways. One way is to use them as supplements to or substitutes for reading texts in the reading program. They can also be used to encourage progress in writing. Giving children the opportunity to share their dictated stories with others and giving them recognition are strong encouragements to write again and to do so more independently.

Beginning Independent Writing

Once children begin to regard themselves as writers, they are anxious to get on with writing independently. They want to gain complete control over their own writing and move away from dictated stories. They should be encouraged to do so. The transition from dictating to handwriting can be gradual, as children write what they are able and the teacher helps them with the rest. The more advanced writers sometimes become impatient with waiting for someone to take dictation and begin to pick up the pencil themselves. The less advanced writers may need to continue dictating and need to continue experiencing success until they also see their own need to do the handwriting. While independent writing should be encouraged as early as possible, pushing the children who are not ready too early can destroy the confidence that was discussed in the previous chapter.

The procedure for stimulating writing when children are just beginning to write independently is like the procedure at other times. In fact, the same experiences and procedures can be used in a classroom even when some children are still dictating their stories and others are writing them independently. The class discusses an experience to stimulate ideas, and then individuals write on their own, the teacher takes dictation, or provides help to those who can do only some of their own writing. The example related next shows how well this can work in a classroom.

Miss Prinski's first-grade class had been studying family life in various parts of the world. Included in one of the discussions was the importance of rice in some cultures. On this particular day, therefore, language and social studies were combined while experience stories were constructed about cooking rice. A few kernels of uncooked rice were distributed to each child to feel, smell, and taste. Then the teacher cooked a quantity of rice in a transparent pot while the children watched and discussed the behavior of the boiling kernels. After the rice cooled, the children again felt, smelled, and tasted it. They were led to see the food value of rice.

Miss Prinski then read them part of a story about a child and his rice ball. They then discussed what it would be like to have rice as a main diet. It was at this point that the writing began. Miss Prinski had stimulated many ideas, but her only suggestion for writing was, "Write a story about someone who eats rice or about rice itself." The independent writers were given their own paper and allowed to move to any part of the room. The children who needed some help were given the same directions, but they knew the procedure for coming to Miss Prinski whenever they were stuck. The others, who still needed to dictate their stories, attempted a few written words or illustrated the experience while waiting for their turn with the teacher. To avoid feelings of stigma toward the less advanced children, the teacher treated the written products of all children with equal pride and acceptance.

Imaginative Writing for Older Children

Learners who have confidence in their writing abilities and whose creativity and imagination have continued to expand in school need very little stimulation or encouragement to write imaginatively. Unfortunately, these ideal conditions do not simply develop with age. On the contrary, in many school situations children have less confidence, creativity, and willingness to express their imaginations by the time they reach third or fourth grade than they did when they first entered school.

On the one hand, then, developing imaginative writing with older children is similar to developing it with younger children. It is similar in that teachers of upper elementary grades often have to begin the school year by emphasizing confidence building and creative writing and delaying emphasis on writing skills, just as primary teachers do. It is similar because older children who have had their confidence and creativity diminished need the same writing procedures as younger children do: experiencing, talking through the experience, and writing with little fear of criticism. In some extreme cases, it may even be necessary to use dictation instead of independent writing.

On the other hand, developing imaginative writing can be quite different with older children. The difference may be in one of two directions. If the budding writers have had the freedom and stimulation that is needed to encourage imagination, the teacher no longer needs to concentrate so highly on selecting the best experiences, carefully developing a motivating discussion, and helping individuals with their writing. These procedures continue to be important, but more of the teacher's energy can be expended on other aspects of writing. If the learners' imaginations have been throttled in previous school years, however, the task of rebuilding imaginative expression is much more difficult than is the task of nurturing it in children who are just beginning. It is likely that within the same classroom will be individuals who can and do write imaginatively with little guidance and those who need a great deal of support in rebuilding imaginative expression.

It is necessary, therefore, to individualize the writing program, but this can be done without using individual writing activities or assignments. The individualization can occur within the expectations and guidance of individuals while the class works together. The same stimulus is provided for everyone and everyone enters into discussion of it, but each individual responds at his or her own level and in his or her own way. More teacher attention, recognition, and guidance is given to the learners with the least imaginative expression.

Providing older children with a stimulus that is motivating is often a great challenge to teachers. Whether it is a discussion about common experience or an in-class experience followed by a discussion, it needs to draw in both eager and reluctant writers. Because the teacher does not need to concentrate as much effort on stimulating the children who already write imaginatively, the stimulus can be geared more toward the interest areas of those who need the most help.

Earlier in this chapter, a short list of experiences was provided to illustrate the type of stimulus that often helps older as well as younger children. Such experiences are one excellent way to get writing started. Another way, one that might lend itself even better to writing that is imaginative, is to use various types of literature. Myths, fables, tall tales, legends, mysteries, animal stories, and science fiction all provide potential writing stimuli and encourage growing writers to adapt their writing to these forms. The literature is read to the class, it is discussed, other literature examples are often given, and the writing is then begun—as in the next paragraph.

Mr. O'Brien read a version of the legend of John Henry to his class, stopping at one or two places for reaction from the class. After the reading, the fifth graders were asked if they thought there ever was a real John Henry and a discussion followed. The teacher briefly explained the manner in which legends originate and grow. He then asked students to speculate on what types of workers would create a John Henry and under what condition they would do so. Students then named and briefly described other legendary characters they knew. Finally, Mr. O'Brien announced that each person would have the opportunity to write a legend of his or her own. After sharing more ideas, the learners began to write.

WRITING POETRY

Once children learn that poetry is an acceptable form of communication and discover that they are capable of writing it, a whole new form of writing is open to them. Poetry has every bit of communication power that other forms of writing have. In fact, it often fosters the ability to write ideas concisely and expressively more easily than does prose. In addition, poetry has an aesthetic value that is difficult to match in other types of writing.

Poetry is also valuable in helping students learn about their language. Because poetry lends itself to expressing ideas concisely, writers are encouraged to experiment with words and with relationships among words. The growth of language through discovery is a likely result. When children learn to write something that they previously regarded as difficult, their confidence is frequently boosted.

Motivating children to write poetry, therefore, is an important objective in the classroom. The benefits described above can occur only when children actually write. The task of getting learners to write poetry, however, is frequently not an easy one, because children often bring negative attitudes about poetry into the classroom.

Dealing with Negative Attitudes

It is not uncommon for students and adults to regard poetry as undesirable. While this negative attitude is not universal, it is prevalent in many classrooms. It may be even more common among boys because poetry is often seen as feminine in nature.

It is difficult to explain this widespread attitude. Perhaps part of the blame lies with the schools themselves, for poetry has usually been studied through detailed analysis that is irrelevant to the lives of the students. In addition, however, the nature of poetry has largely been misunderstood. The attitudes and misunderstandings have been passed on to younger children by those subjected to the analysis and by parents who remember their distaste from their own shool years. Even teachers who dislike and misunderstand poetry pass on their negative attitudes to children.

The common misunderstanding about poetry is that it must rhyme and have a rhythmic meter. While it is true that many poems have these qualities, they are not the most important characteristics. Yet, rhyme and rhythm seem to be the features that are the most frightening and difficult for the potential poet. There are, therefore, two strategies for dealing with negative attitudes toward poetry.

Reading Poetry to Children

Once children come to enjoy listening to poetry, they are likely to voluntarily attempt to write it. There is only one way to lead them to enjoy poetry and that is to expose them to enjoyable poems. This rather obvious statement has three implications.

First, time must be taken to read poetry to children. If the negative attitudes of a class are especially strong, it may be wise to read a number of interesting poems without announcing that they are poems. Especially if the poem does not contain stereotyped rhyme and rhythm, listeners may become intrigued with a piece of literature before ever realizing it is poetry. In any event, the introduction of poetry is probably easier if it is spread over several days or weeks. Taking a few minutes a day to share a new poem or reread one that is requested is a good investment of time.

The second implication is that the listeners' enjoyment must be the highest priority in the selection of poems to read. Aesthetic values, appreciation of the classics, and familiarity with the world's greatest poets could be considered when selecting poetry and eventually these qualities deserve some attention. While introducing children of any age to poetry, however, enjoyment is much more important. Without enjoyment from the beginning, appreciation will not be likely to develop and neither will the writing of poetry. Since age, socioeconomic background, geographic location, and many other factors influence the tastes of learners, it is not possible to develop a list of poems or poets that could be recommended for every classroom. However, among the favorite poets of children are the following:

Beatrice C. Brown
Lewis Carroll
John Ciardi
Elizabeth Coatsworth
Walter de la Mare
Eleanor Farjeon
Rachel Field
Robert Frost
Rose Fyleman
Langston Hughes
Eve Merriam
Carl Sandburg

There are a number of commercially available anthologies of children's poetry. Any of these offers the teacher a wide choice of poetry that is likely to stimulate interest.

A third implication of the approach that emphasizes exposure to enjoyable poetry is that children should not be expected to analyze poetry at this point. Detailed analysis of poetic devices, definitions, or even content seldom contributes to enjoyment. There is some question about the value of such analysis at any time, but during the time that negative attitudes are being overcome it is actually harmful. This is not to say that poetry should not be discussed at all during this time, but discussions should revolve around the reactions of the listeners.

Initiating Writing

Once individuals have come to enjoy listening to poetry, the teacher can begin the second major strategy for dealing with negative attitudes. This strategy consists of demonstrating to the children that they are capable of writing poetry. This is a form of confidence building and, therefore, should follow the guidelines described in the previous chapter. The initial step is to construct a situation in which every child can successfully write a poem. The best way to do this is to begin with a form of poetry that virtually guarantees success.

There are a number of types of poetry that are sufficiently structured to make the writing success rate very high. With one exception, these forms do not have rhyme or metered rhythm. As described earlier, rhyme and rhythm are often the most frightening aspects of poetry from the viewpoint of the beginner. Each of the forms is briefly described here and can be introduced in any order.

1. *Haiku.* Originating in Japan, haiku has recently become popular in American schools because it is beautiful and easy to write. Each haiku is made up of seventeen syllables and usually deals with some aspect of nature. The syllables are distributed among three lines with five syllables in the first line, seven in the second, and five in the third. Example:

   Leaves drift to the ground
   Twisting and turning as they fall.
   Autumn has arrived.

   Although children should not be held strictly to using the exact number of syllables, the structure of these numbers makes haiku easy for them to write. The format is introduced, several examples are given, and the writers can experiment with their own haiku.

2. *Cinquain.* Although cinquain uses a different type of structure—a certain number of words—it is just as easy to write as haiku. The format is as follows:

   First line: one word that serves as a title
   Second line: two words that describe the title
   Third line: three words that express an action
   Fourth line: four words that express a feeling
   Fifth line: a one word synonym for the title

Cinquain need not be limited to topics about nature. For example:

Pancakes
Sweet, delicious
Rising and frying
Make me love mornings
Breakfast

Cinquain can be introduced with the same technique as haiku.

3. *Tanka.* The tanka is very much like haiku except for its length. It contains thirty-one syllables distributed over five lines, in this pattern: five syllables, seven syllables, five syllables, seven syllables, seven syllables.

4. *Limericks.* Although more difficult to write than the three forms above, limericks are so appealing that they might be introduced shortly after the others, especially if the learners are older. Limericks rhyme and have a metered rhythm, but these can quite readily be learned through imitation. The way to teach this form, then, is to read a substantial number to the writers. Limericks have five lines, with the first, second, and fifth lines rhyming (actually, forming a triplet) and the third and fourth lines forming another rhyming pattern. Examples:

A puppy whose hair was so flowing
There really was no means of knowing
Which end was his head,
Once stopped me and said,
"Please, sir, am I coming or going?"[8]

A flea and a fly were caught in a flue
They cried out, together, "Oh what shall we do?"
Said the fly, "Let us flee!"
Said the flea, "Let us fly!"
So they flew through a flaw in the flu.

An example of a poetry-writing lesson might be helpful.

Mr. Cramer had approached poetry rather sneakily. Seeing the class reaction to poetry at the beginning of September, he left it alone for two weeks. Then one day, without warning, he recited a humorous poem that caused a great deal of laughter. He was requested to repeat it. He did, and he offered to share other funny statements (avoiding the word "poetry") from a book he had. When the students were thus intrigued, he was able to expand the topics and forms that he read to them over the following days and to begin using the word "poem."

After about three weeks of this type of expanding exposure, Mr. Cramer felt the class was ready to begin writing poetry. He brought several examples of carefully selected haiku to school. "Today, we're going to make you into poets," he began. After again expressing his confidence in their ability to write poetry, he told them about haiku and then read the examples. He asked them no questions and attempted no analysis, but he allowed them to ask and comment. Then, he gave them the directions about numbers of lines and syllables and repeated some of the sample poems. Next, the children wrote their own haiku, and volunteers shared them with the class. Mr. Cramer seemed delighted with each poem volunteered, and eventually that included nearly everyone.

Continuing the Writing

After children have some confidence in their ability to write poetry, they should be allowed and encouraged to use any form of poetry they have learned in any of their imaginative writing activities. When introducing haiku, cinquain, or some other form, the stimulus for writing is the new form itself. Once it is understood, however, each form can simply be added to the individual's repertoire of writing tools. When the teacher subsequently provides a stimulus for imaginative writing, as described earlier in this chapter, the writers can often have the option of responding in prose or any form of poetry that has been learned.

If the strategies to overcome negative attitudes toward poetry are successful, new forms can continue to be introduced. The forms that were suggested above may continue to be used long after they have served their initial purpose of building confidence, for each has its own style of beauty. But writers who become truly interested in poetry will want to learn more and more forms. Additional forms might include:

Sijo—a Korean form similar to haiku, sometimes with 3 lines of 14 to 16 syllables and sometimes with 6 short lines.

Senryn—a Japanese form using the same syllable structure as haiku, but dealing with human nature.

Couplet—a simple two-line, rhymed verse. Each line also has the same metered rhythm. If limericks have been learned, lines 3 and 4 are actually a couplet.

Triplet—in format exactly like a couplet except that it has a third line, this form usually tells a story and is frequently humorous.

Quatrain—perhaps the most commonly used form, with 4 lines of uniform length and a rhyming pattern. The pattern may be aabb, abab, or abcb.

Free verse—sometimes difficult to distinguish from prose, free verse has no rhyme or rhythm pattern and has no limitations on line length, format, or content.

Children who become intrigued with poetry will discover still other forms as they actively seek out interesting poems.

EXPOSITORY WRITING

Expository writing is somewhat the opposite of narrative. It has no plot, character development, or other characteristics of a story. Reports, critiques, summaries, letters, and descriptions are examples of expository writing. It typically has some practical purpose, whereas imaginative writing is usually written to entertain.

Expository writing is not often considered a part of creative writing. Using the definition of creative writing that is given at the beginning of this chapter, however, it needs to be included. Writers who express their own ideas, who think for themselves, are needed just as strongly for practical writing as they are for writing that is entertaining.

Writing Letters

It is quite apparent that letter writing is one form of writing demanded of nearly everyone. Almost every individual is called upon to write letters at one time or another, and some careers require a great deal of such writing.

The extent to which creativity is used in letter writing varies greatly. Usually a letter is more interesting and more effective when the writer puts down his or her own ideas rather than lifeless, stereotyped statements. Letter writing, in fact, offers about as many opportunities for creative writing as does a more imaginative form.

But how can children be led away from mundane writing and toward creativity? There are two types of strategies for doing this. The first is to use interesting and original letters as models and encourage children to follow them. This is especially true of group letters such as invitations, thank-you letters and announcements to parents or other classrooms. The second is to limit classroom letter writing to real, meaningful situations. Copying and correcting someone else's letter is a negative experience. Meaningful letter-writing situations might include:

Writing invitations to real events

Writing to pen pals in another school

Writing letters to the editor of a newspaper

Writing for free materials or information

Writing to a sick classmate

Writing to an author

The mechanics of letter writing can be found in any elementary-school language arts text. When they are taught in conjunction with real letter writing, they have a purpose and are more easily learned. In addition, the writing of meaningful letters encourages writers to approach the task with creativity.

Writing Critiques and Reviews

One of the more unpleasant tasks that students typically encounter in school is writing book reports. One of the reasons they are so often unpleasant is that creativity is not encouraged when they are written. When the sole purpose of such reports is to prove that the book was read and understood, it is no wonder that the products are uninteresting and unpleasant. When the task, instead, is to critique or review the book in the way professionals do, and when creativity is rewarded, the attitudes and purpose of the writers can take quite a different turn. Of course, overdoing book reports of any type can discourage free reading. But when reviewing and critiquing books is an interesting activity, this is much less likely to happen. Nor does the removal of book reporting as proof of reading involve much risk for the teacher, for students are more likely to read with honesty and understanding when the follow-up to the reading is interesting.

Of course, reviews and critiques need not be limited to books. In fact, writing about television shows is an appealing way to introduce this type of activity. Sports events, movies, plays, and other public performances also provide good material to review.

Perhaps the best way to encourage creativity in writing reviews and critiques is to first examine such works by professionals. The reviews in television magazines might be a good place to start. The one-line summaries of shows as well as the longer reviews of selected programs can be discussed by the class in terms of their validity and completeness. Older children can also profit from examining the book and movie reviews in the newspaper. Once interest is aroused, learners will want to try their hand at their own reviews. Only after confidence is well established should reviews and critiques be introduced as a way of reporting on books.

Writing Articles and Reports

Even when the objective of a writing activity is to report the facts or present a point of view, creative writing is needed. In fact, writing of this type may need the individual thinking of its authors more than other types. Putting facts together to form an article or report is a somewhat complex activity and is probably most appropriate in the middle grades.

There are a number of purposes for article and report writing. Although magazines often use the term "article" to refer to fiction as well as informational pieces, the article and the report are seen here as very similar writings. The general purpose of both is related to reporting information, and the various specific purposes of reporting can be met whether the product is called a report or an article. This category of writing includes reports on special-interest topics in science or social studies, library research reports, descriptions of places or events, news reports, written directions, and summaries.

Many teachers have seen the need to develop their students' independence in this area. Too often students have simply made minor changes in two encyclopedia entries and written them one after the other when asked to write a report. However, except for giving out poor grades on such products, few teachers have known how to deal with this lack of creativity.

Report and article writing must be learned. The first steps must be easy enough to assure success, so that confidence is established. The following steps suggest how this ability might be introduced:

1. Distribute copies of two descriptions to the class, both describing the same event but emphasizing different details.

2. Have the class discuss how the descriptions are the same and how they are different, and take suggestions about how ideas from both could be combined. Write this class report on the chalkboard or a chart.

3. On a subsequent day, distribute another pair of descriptions and again have the class discuss the similarities and differences. This time, however, have the individuals combine the two sources.

4. During lessons that follow, repeat the procedure with increasingly difficult tasks. Increase the length of the descriptions, add more differences between them, and add a third description.

5. Teach any skills in locating information in reference resources which the class or individuals may be missing.

6. Ask individuals to find their own resources and write reports that have some personal significance. This process can be successful, of course, only if individual expression of ideas is reinforced throughout the various steps.

Other Types of Writing

Not all writing fits into the categories of imaginative and practical. Biographies, autobiographies, and diaries, for example, have entertainment value, and yet they are reports of information. In addition, some of the practical products have imaginative components and vice versa. These types of writing are certainly as valuable as the ones that have been described, but they also frequently need the touch of creativity.

Biographical writing can be taught in much the same way as report and article writing. The steps outlined earlier can be used, or biography can be introduced after learners have practiced report and article writing. Instead of drawing from two descriptions of an *event,* of course, students practice using several sources about an individual's life. Biographical writing is an interesting variation on report writing because there are available resources about so many famous people.

Autobiographical writing is quite unique in that the main source of information is the writer's own mind. Teaching students how to draw from two or more sources, as with report or biographical writing, isn't necessary. In fact, autobiography can be introduced in the early grades. One interesting way to do this is to lead children to construct personal time lines. The life of a well-known person is first displayed on a time line, with major events represented by points on the line. The children then make their own lines and place important events on them (learning to walk and talk, vacations, starting school, and many more). They then turn the depicted events into words in the form of an autobiography.

Nearly any type of writing seems to demand some creativity. Only when the objective is limited to repeating someone else's ideas is there no room for creative writing. Original writing needs to be strongly encouraged in most written communication.

EVALUATING CREATIVE WRITING

The evaluation of an individual's ability to write creatively is usually part of an overall evaluation of his or her written products. It is quite logical to deal with all aspects of an individual's product at the same time, for that is how the author wrote them. At the same time, the teacher must be careful to avoid judgments about creativity that are based on the writer's mechanical abilities. There is a great temptation to be influenced by spelling, punctuation, and other mechanical elements, because it is very difficult to find concrete criteria for evaluating creativity in writing. In fact, it is often impossible to tell from the written product if the writer was using his or her own ideas. If creative writing is defined as that which is written when the author is thinking for himself or herself, the evaluation must be based on the child's ability to do so. The best source of information about that ability is the child.

In order to evaluate creative writing, therefore, the teacher needs to talk to the writer. This is best accomplished through an individual teacher-pupil conference. The conference can also be useful in evaluating other aspects of writing ability.

Individual conferences are not easy to arrange because they are very time consuming. However, the creativity of a child does not need to be evaluated every time she or he writes. The purpose is to assess development, not to assign a letter grade. If each learner can spend five or six minutes privately with the teacher every five or six weeks, the needed evaluation can be completed and the individual will see that the teacher is interested in his or her writing. Thus, time needs to be found for only a few conferences each time a writing activity is undertaken.

Besides showing an interest in and approval of the child's writing during the conference, the teacher needs to ask questions that lead to an understanding of his or her creativity. Certainly, the result will not be a creativity score or grade level. It will be a subjective understanding by the teacher of the type and amount of individual thinking that goes into written products. On the basis of this understanding, the teacher can more easily decide how much and what type of freedom, stimulus, modeling, praise, and guidance each child should have.

The following questions are examples of the type that might be asked in order to bring out the child's description of the independent thinking that went into his or her writing:

1. Suppose you were interviewed by a network television newsperson who asked you for a "behind the scenes" description of how you wrote this paper. What would you tell him or her?

2. What were some of the ideas you thought of but *didn't* use for this paper (like television outtakes)?

3. What part of this paper was the hardest to write? Why? The easiest? Why?

4. This is an interesting————(sentence, paragraph, idea, or whatever). How did you come up with it?

5. If you were allowed to share just one idea or one action from this paper with the class, which one would it be? How did you think of this idea or action?

SUMMARY

Creativity is an important ingredient in most types of writing. Creative writing does not develop by itself in school. In fact, the school must set up the right conditions, or creativity will be diminished instead of developed.

Among those right conditions is the freedom to write without fear of failure, to express ideas, and to choose one's own language. Such freedoms are necessary because writing must be the expression of the writer's own ideas if it is to be creative.

The writing that Mr. Compau assigned in the scene that begins this chapter violated much of this freedom. While the assignment gave them a great deal of choice about the topic (write anything about January), it gave them no stimulus for doing so and provided no ideas for a selected topic. Freedom to express ideas must be accompanied by some help in generating ideas. The freedom to select words and language was completely removed by the requirement to use the spelling words. There were implications that freedom from failure was also quite uncertain. Children could quite easily fail to think of a topic, to include every spelling word, or to fulfill other apparent demands.

In contrast, Ms. Snyder provided these freedoms quite imaginatively and stimulated the generation of ideas for writing. She furnished a meaningful experience, discussed it with the students in ways that reviewed their individual experiences, and was evidently willing to help wherever she was needed.

When learners are given the right conditions, they can use their creativity in various types of writing. Imaginative as well as practical writing becomes the field for their own ideas. Even poetry, a type of literature often regarded negatively, becomes part of the writer's repertoire. When young writers are free to do so, and are motivated and guided by their teacher, they develop into creative writers.

NOTES

1. Claudia Lewis, *A Big Bite of the World: Children's Creative Writing* (Englewood Cliffs, N.J.: Prentice-Hall, Inc., 1979), p. 67.

2. Walter T. Petty and Mary Bowen, *Slithery Snakes and Other Aids to Children's Writing* (New York: Meredith Publishing Co., 1967), p. 6.

3. Robert L. Hillerich, "Developing Written Expression: How to Raise—Not Raze—Writers," *Language Arts,* 56 (October 1979), 670.

4. E. Brooks Smith, Kenneth S. Goodman, and Robert Meredith, *Language and Thinking in School,* 2nd ed. (New York: Holt, Rinehart and Winston, 1976), p. 202.

5. Gary L. Gerbrandt, *An Idea Book for Acting Out and Writing Language* K–8 (Urbana, Ill.: National Council of Teachers of English, 1974), p. 42.

6. Joan P. Gipe, "Use of a Relevant Context Helps Kids Learn New Word Meanings," *Reading Teacher,* 33 (January 1980), 398–402.

7. Lewis, *Big Bite of the World,* p. 89–90.

8. Petty and Bowen, *Slithery Snakes,* p. 51.

CHAPTER EIGHT
TEACHING
WRITING MECHANICS

Scene A

"Class, open your books to page 47," said Mrs. Williams. "Today we're going to learn how to punctuate some abbreviations. Does anyone know what an abbreviation is?"

After several wrong guesses had been tried, Mrs. Williams called on Beth, who gave a definition very much like the one on page 47.

"Good, Beth. Now, who would like to read the directions for this page? Peter?"

After the directions had been read by Peter, another volunteer was called upon to read the list of eight abbreviations that served as examples.

"Are there any questions about how to do this page?" concluded Mrs. Williams. No hands went up, for all students were already bent over their papers and textbooks as the race to complete the assignment before lunchtime began.

Scene B

"How is your story coming?" asked Mr. Amoto as Andy approached the table.

"Everyone in my group thinks it's good," said Andy, "but there's this one place I can't figure out."

"Perhaps I can help. Where is it?"

"It's this place here," Andy replied, pointing. "I'm trying to say that this play belonged to everyone on the team, but I don't know what to do with that comma thing you put up in the air."

"You mean an apostrophe," Mr. Amoto offered. "Well, let's see."

After reading Andy's trouble spot, the teacher wrote several sentences using plural possessives on his note pad and led Andy to see their correct usage. The writer applied his learning to his own story.

A moment later Andy was eagerly continuing his proofreading, and Mr. Amoto was helping another student.

Learners who have gained some confidence in their ability to write, who believe that they have important things to say in writing, are ready to begin refining their abilities. Writing abilities include a variety of overlapping, intertwining skills and strategies, but we can generally divide them into two categories. The category of written expression includes the ability to write clearly, effectively, and appropriately. The category of writing mechanics contains the abilities or skills that are needed to write in an acceptable form. Since both are important for successful writing, they are treated separately in this text. Written expression is discussed in Chapter Ten, while writing mechanics are dealt with in this chapter and the next.

The term *writing mechanics* is used to describe an array of conventions or rules that are usually followed in formal writing as a courtesy to the reader or as a method of giving the message clarity. They include punctuation, capitalization, and several conventions of lesser importance. It is possible to include spelling and handwriting also in a discussion of writing mechanics, but in this text they are treated separately (Chapter Nine).

Emphasis on writing mechanics, as well as on written expression, is appropriately delayed until the potential writer has gained writing confidence. As this text has stressed in earlier chapters, writing instruction must be divided into two phases, and emphasis on written expression and mechanics must wait until the second of these. Creativity, positive attitudes, and acceptable mechanics themselves are more likely to result from a program that begins with an emphasis on success rather than one on correctness.

This is not to say that punctuation, capitalization, and other mechanics should be completely ignored during the time that confidence and creativity are being emphasized, whether to beginners or older students with limited abilities. Beginning writers can be exposed to many models of good mechanics, as they usually are in their beginning reading materials, and these forms of writing can be pointed out and discussed. Recognition can also be given to those children who discover how to use these forms on their own during their early attempts at writing. Older students who lack confidence and ability can be recognized for the mechanics they *do* know during the phase of their program that emphasizes confidence. But neither type of learner should be given the impression that form is as important as content. Normally, there is ample time to stress mechanics after confidence has been established.

When the time comes to increase gradually the emphasis on form, or mechanics, caution must continue. Confidence must be allowed to flourish even when a great deal of attention is being focused on punctuation, capitalization, and other mechanics. Learners should not be led to believe that any former writing they did was "baby stuff" or wrong. Their positive attitudes toward writing should be allowed to expand into the area of writing mechanics. This can best be accomplished by approaching mechanics through the concept of proofreading.

APPROACHING MECHANICS THROUGH PROOFREADING

Children who have confidence in their writing usually also take pride in their written products. Their self-concepts are such that they perceive themselves as writers. When they feel this way about themselves and their products, it is relatively easy to extend their pride into areas of correct form. When they believe that their writing is, in the eyes of others, worth reading, they will want their readers to understand what has been written. One way individuals can accomplish this, of course, is to get the teacher or someone else to polish their products for them, but with proper guidance they can learn to do this themselves.

Factors in Learning to Proofread

Learning how to polish or proofread written products involves several factors. One factor is understanding the *need* to have reasonably correct form in certain situations. Another is the understanding that writing often has more than one step, including at least a rough draft and a final copy. A third factor is the confidence that proofreading is not too difficult. Finally, writers need to acquire the skills or mechanical knowledge that it takes to make proofreading possible.

Creating a Need

The first of these, the need for proofreading, must seem genuine to the writers. If the primary purpose for producing correctness becomes that of pleasing the teacher, proofreading can actually be counterproductive. Students who proofread and rewrite because their teacher says they have to tend to write as little as possible so they will have less to rewrite. Sometimes they also become so concerned about mechanics during their original draft that quality of content and creativity suffer.

Genuine need is created when, first of all, the written products actually have readers who are interested. Writing letters to pen pals in another school, articles for a classroom newspaper, announcements or invitations for classroom events, or letters to authors and newspaper editors are examples that meet this criterion. Simply requiring students to exchange and read each others' papers will not usually suffice because such reading is not done by interested readers. Certainly, papers that are read only by the teacher do not create any genuine need for proofreading.

Secondly, need is created when writers become aware that uncorrected writing frequently leads to a lack of clarity. It is not enough to know that *some* people need punctuation and capitalization to be understood. Each writer must know that *his* or *her* writing lacks clarity without them. When teachers individually and privately point out such lack of clarity in a positive manner, some impact will be made. But children typically *expect* teachers to be concerned about mechanics. Therefore, the credibility of teachers' criticism, especially with older children, may not be good enough in this situation.

One way to overcome this difficulty is to set up proofreading groups for confident writers. Crowhurst has reported on the successful use of such groups in fifth grade.[1] Writers in these classes were eager to improve their first drafts. When an individual has written something that will eventually be read by someone else, the rough draft is given to the writer's partner or small group. The proofreading group does not critique the writing, for that could easily become very negative, but tells the writer specifically what message the writing is conveying. Of course, such groups would need training, guidance, and supervision, but the feedback from peers can have a powerful influence.

Children who are ready for proofreading can be taught to give useful feedback by practicing with simulated written products before dealing with those created by peers. The simulated products would have to be written and duplicated by the teacher. They should contain

One way to motivate proofreading is through the use of proofreading groups. (*Ken Karp*)

errors that make the message unclear, but the message should become clear once the errors are corrected. It would provide an easier lesson if all of the errors were of the same type, preferably of the type to be introduced first when the skills lessons begin in the following days.

For example, suppose the first writing skill to be taught is use of periods and question marks to end sentences. A paragraph like the following might be distributed to the class:

> Tom hated to go to the store for his mom walking down the hill to the store was easy, but carrying the bag of groceries up the hill was hard to get to the store he also had to walk past Brutal Bill's house getting beat up was always a risk he had to take

As a class, they discuss the meaning of the paragraph and what made the meaning unclear. After this activity is done as a class several times, small groups discuss other faulty paragraphs and report the results of the group discussions to the class. With teacher guidance, the groups should then be ready to tackle real written products supplied by peers.

Writers will also need feedback from someone more advanced than their peer group. The teacher must be available after the proofreading group is finished so that the individual can be given help and support as the revision is planned.

Multistep Writing

Another factor in learning to proofread is reaching the understanding that writing often involves more than one step. This understanding is difficult to give to student writers because it defies a natural tendency that we all have. We tend to regard the necessity for redoing something as a sign of weakness or as an indication of a poor performance. When a teacher asks learners to rewrite, then, it is natural for them to conclude their first writing was wrong or poor. Furthermore, teachers often add to this conception of rewriting by filling student papers with red marks and requiring children to "correct" the mistakes. As Schwartz has pointed out, when the writing procedure consists of the student writing, the teacher pointing out errors, and the student rewriting, the last step is an implied punishment that leaves the writer feeling defensive.[2]

If, on the other hand, learners see proofreading and rewriting as essential steps in producing written material that is to be shared, they are not likely to resist it. As artists continue to refine their work after the rough form is made, as a ball player continues to play after the first half ends, so the writer continues to write and refine after the first draft is finished. The teacher's role in this factor is to convince the learners that this is true.

One effective method for convincing students is to invite an author to the classroom who will share his or her own need to proofread and rewrite. The author need not be famous; a writer for a local newspaper, for example, is an excellent resource. When children learn that professional writers rewrite, they may accept this step more readily.

Another factor that encourages writing as a multistep process is the elimination of classroom practices that encourage writers to get it right the first time. These practices include requiring students to correct red marks, allowing only enough time for one draft, overstressing the importance of writing mechanics, and praising students for writing in good form on the first try. Gebhardt has reported that college writing teachers have regularly been able to help freshmen problem writers by freeing them from their fear of errors on the first draft.[3]

The example of the teacher is another effective practice. When student writers see their teacher proofreading and rewriting it has a positive effect. Finally, recognition and praise that are given to writers who improve their content and form from one copy to the next has a powerful impact on attitudes about rewriting.

Confidence in Proofreading

A third factor in learning to proofread is the confidence that it isn't too difficult. Learners need to feel that they are successful in their attempts to proofread as much as they need to feel success in creating the content of their papers. The most important strategy in developing this confidence is introducing proofreading gradually. In most cases, this means introducing one element of writing mechanics at a time. Learners are taught how to write the correct form of the element and how to proofread for it simultaneously. This usually involves several steps.

First, one or several lessons on the correct form of the element are given. If, without criticizing individuals, the teacher can relate the instruction to actual previous writings, it will be more effective. The lessons should include illustrations of the function of the element being taught, a display of good models, and practice in discriminating correct from incorrect form. It should include sufficient practice in

1.	2.	3.	4.	5.	6.	7.
Skill taught	Writing activity initiated	First draft written	Proofreading by groups	Rewriting	Conference	Spontaneous lesson (if needed)

FIGURE 8–1 Steps in teaching a skills element.

writing the element correctly, but only after the rationale, models, and discrimination practice have been provided.

Then, the teacher establishes the proofreading groups that were described above. The groups are instructed, while telling each other what messages the writings are communicating, to pay attention to the element of writing that has been focused upon.

After the proofreading groups have given their feedback and individuals begin to rework their writings, the teacher has a conference with each writer. Later, when this process has become well established, conferences can be limited to those children who express a need for them. When proofreading is first being introduced, however, a brief conference with each individual is important. During the conference the teacher checks to see if the feedback from the group was understood and directs attention to the element that was studied. The teacher does not usually tell the child what to correct or how to correct it, but offers guiding questions and encouragement. If the teacher discovers a needed but missing skill, a very brief spontaneous lesson is taught at this time.

When proofreading for the first element has been learned through practice, a second element is introduced. Proofreading groups and teacher conferences are then focused upon both elements that have been studied. In this manner, all of the writing mechanics are gradually introduced. Figure 8–1 is a graphic display of the process used with each writing cycle. It is also possible, of course, to introduce more than one skill in each writing cycle.

After several writing skills have been introduced, the task of proofreading groups becomes more difficult. Because it is difficult to remember a number of skills simultaneously while trying to focus on meaning, it may be wise for each student to have a checklist of all skills that have been introduced. The checklist can be developed, with teacher guidance, by each individual. Each time a new skill is introduced, learners can be helped to add a new item or question to their proofreading checklists. The lists can then be used as guidelines whenever the group gives reactions to written products.

The checklist might look like the one below after only one type of skills lesson has been taught.

```
        Proofreading Checklist
1.  Does the use of punctuation at the end of sentences
    make the meaning clear?
```

After three types of skills have been taught and the teacher has helped students add to their checklists, they might look like this:

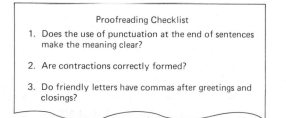

```
            Proofreading Checklist
1.  Does the use of punctuation at the end of sentences
    make the meaning clear?

2.  Are contractions correctly formed?

3.  Do friendly letters have commas after greetings and
    closings?
```

Obviously, this approach to teaching proofreading and mechanics together involves an extended amount of time. The idea that proofreading can be taught as a general skill and that individuals can then be expected to apply it to writing on their own is not very realistic. Proofreading needs to be related to each element of writing mechanics and taught in a meaningful context. As a result, learning to proofread is a process that not only lasts all school year, but continues as long as skills lessons continue.

In spite of the time involved, however, such an approach is necessary if children are to gain confidence, if they are to see that proofreading is not too difficult. If too much is expected of them while proofreading, they will be overwhelmed and frustrated. In that event, the mastery of writing mechanics will be delayed and possibly never accomplished.

Another important aspect of building proofreading confidence is giving recognition for success. Instead of recognizing and praising correct form on a writer's first draft, teachers need to reinforce growth in proofreading ability.

Learning Writing Mechanics

The remaining factor in learning to proofread is the acquisition of the writing mechanics that are used to produce good form. It is quite obvious in the paragraphs above that the mechanics are acquired in conjunction with proofreading, but the details remain to be explained.

Because the individual mechanics are the substance of correct writing, the following section of this chapter is devoted to discussing them.

METHODS OF TEACHING
WRITING MECHANICS

The approach to teaching mechanics that is most effective has already been outlined in the preceding section. Mechanical skills are introduced one at a time along with proofreading. As soon as a writing element is introduced, it is added to the list of items for which groups and individuals are expected to proofread. No element of writing mechanics is introduced without a known purpose. Before we examine the details of this approach, however, it is logical that we explore the process of selecting skills for instruction.

Selecting Mechanical Skills

There are two widely different views about selecting the sequence for teaching writing mechanics. One is that these skills should be taught as student writers need them. The other view is that they should be taught in some predetermined sequence. Both views have a reasonable basis.

Teaching as Needs Arise

The ideal time to introduce an element of writing is when a child discovers a need for it. As an example, suppose a writer's proofreading group has misunderstood a statement because it wasn't clear which of the words were a quote and which weren't. While the student is pondering methods for overcoming the difficulty, the teacher has a brief conference with him or her and discovers that the child needs to learn about quotation marks. This would be a far better time to teach such punctuation than would a time that fit a schedule but had no immediate purpose.

Teaching skills as they are needed is ideal because anyone learns best when the learning has a purpose. If children need certain writing skills because they want to improve the paper they are proofreading, the skills are much more likely to be understood and remembered. Such learning is the opposite of memorizing certain rules or procedures just long enough to please a teacher.

Teaching a Sequence

Any language arts textbook will, naturally, present the skills to be taught in some predetermined sequence. It is safe to assume that the writers and publishers of these materials designed the sequence carefully so that difficult skills follow those that are easier and so that the designated grade levels are appropriate. It is clear that most language arts instruction is based on textbooks, with some estimates indicating that as much as 95 percent of classroom instruction can be attributed to them.[4] The number of teachers who follow the prescribed sequence is unknown, but many who change the sequence only substitute one that is also predetermined. It is obvious, then, that many language skills are taught when the schedule or sequence dictates rather than when the learners need them.

The reason that skills, presumably including writing mechanics, are taught in this way has little to do with a recognized hierarchy of skills. There is little agreement, in fact, about which skills are more advanced than others. The sequence in which mechanics are presented varies tremendously from the textbook of one publisher to another.

Nor is the reliance on a predetermined sequence a result of teachers' resistance to the concept that learning is ideal when the learners see a need for it. Most teachers who follow a sequence would probably acknowledge that it would be better if they could teach mechanics as writing needs arise.

Writing mechanics are taught in sequence because it is a practical way to cover them. The ideal way to teach them is as they are needed, but little in the "real world" of school is ideal. When teachers follow the sequence in the textbook, they feel confident that all of the necessary skills are being covered. When instruction is limited to the mechanics for which the learners see a need, it is very easy to omit areas that might be important. Furthermore, the individualization required for teaching to needs appears to consume much more time and energy.

A Compromise

While it is not practical to suggest a program of writing mechanics that is limited to needs, a program that includes both needs teaching and a predetermined sequence might be very feasible. The steps described in the previous section for writing activities, proofreading groups, teacher conferences, and rewriting can be undertaken on a regular basis. When individuals or small groups experience a need, brief instruction can be given spontaneously, as shown in Figure 8–1. Between these writing sessions, each of which takes only a few class periods, the sequence of skills can be taught to the whole class or large groups as usual. There are a variety of ways this could be scheduled, but a logical one is to use three class periods every two or three weeks for a writing and proofreading activity.

When the teaching of mechanics is delayed until confidence is established and when several class periods are used each time a writing and proofreading session is undertaken, it is quite likely that there will not be time to teach every lesson in the textbook. Teachers would need to select only the important lessons from the textbook. This is a small concession compared to the gains to be made from teaching when a child wants to learn. The goal of the writing program is to produce children who can and will write, not to finish the book by the end of the year.

Teaching Punctuation

We have already seen that the most important part of any written product is its content. The most attention should go to the ideas being expressed. However, we have also seen that form has its importance. The various types of punctuation are among the most important elements of form.

The chief importance of punctuation lies in the fact that it helps to communicate meaning. Through the use of a number of agreed upon marks, a writer can show meaning that is only partially shown by the words. The meaning of the following sentences, for example, isn't clear:

No thanks to the coach the team won the game.

The meanings of the following sentences are quite clear:

No thanks to the coach, the team won the game.
No, thanks to the coach, the team won the game.

Not all punctuation makes such a dramatic difference. In fact, some punctuation adds nothing to meaning:

My friend Mary Wallace isn't here.
My friend, Mary Wallace, isn't here.

Generally, sentences in context depend less on punctuation to communicate meaning than do sentences in isolation, because the context carries a great deal of meaning.

Regardless of these facts, punctuation generally makes reading easier and makes the meaning of the message less likely to be misunderstood. It makes the written product easier to read because reading is a meaning-seeking process, and the more obvious the meaning the more easily the process is used. It makes the message less likely to be misunderstood because, as the first example above illustrated, the words themselves are frequently not enough.

In speech, meaning is aided by stress on certain syllables, by rising and falling voice tones, and by pauses of various durations. Facial expressions and other body language transmit meaning as well. To some extent, punctuation is the written replacement for these voice and movement qualities.

The punctuation that is usually introduced to children first is that which most closely matches the voice features that aid meaning. Periods and question marks at the ends of sentences, for example, are easy to equate with the fall and rise of voice tones at the ends of spoken sentences. Many uses of commas can be equated with substantial pauses in speech.

The match is far from a perfect one, however, and a person attempting to use punctuation solely on the basis of speech is likely to become confused. Normal speech, for example, makes frequent use of short pauses and it is difficult to determine from the duration of the pause in a spoken sentence whether a comma is needed in a written one.

There are also a number of punctuation elements which have no spoken equivalents at all. The underline for a book title, the quotation marks around an article or story title, and the period after an abbreviation are examples. Even quotation marks around quotations do not have a true spoken counterpart. Finally, there is some accepted punctuation, such as the comma or colon after the greeting of a letter, which serves no practical function and is quite arbitrary.

As a result, it is sometimes difficult to see the necessity of punctuation and frequently difficult to remember the many elements and their uses. Methods for dealing with these difficulties will be discussed shortly.

Determining What Punctuation to Teach

If at least part of the writing mechanics instruction in a classroom is given as proofreading needs arise, the content of this part of the instruction requires little selection. Students will be taught whatever mechanics they need to improve their papers. Whether or not the element of mechanics is at the appropriate grade level, is in the planned sequence of skills, or has been taught before, the writer is given what he or she needs to get on with the task.

As was pointed out above, however, it is not usually practical to expect that all writing mechanics can be learned as they are needed. There will be some punctuation for which student writers may never perceive a need. While care must be taken to avoid an overemphasis on any punctuation that is somewhat arbitrary, none of the forms that society demands can be totally overlooked. Therefore, some systematic method is necessary to teach children the punctuation they will need, to select from the textbook the lessons that are important.

The next question to be raised is almost certainly, "What is important?" This is not an easy question to answer because there is substantial disagreement about just what is necessary to produce acceptable writing. Evidently the authors of the textbook felt that all of their lessons were important or they wouldn't have included them. Of course, the decision about what is important should be influenced by the characteristics of the learners in the classroom, but a general guide might prove to be useful. Box 8–1 is such a guide. It shows the punctuation for which mastery is generally expected in the primary (grades 1–3) and middle (grades 4–6) years. The elements of punctuation are listed in a sequence that seems to increase in difficulty. However, there is no reason to believe that this is necessarily the best sequence to follow. The individual teacher is in the best position to know in what order to present the skills to a given group of learners.

In summary, this is the suggested method for combining the selection of punctuation content with the approach described earlier:

1. Punctuation instruction is delayed until a degree of confidence has been established.

2. When punctuation instruction is begun, the proofreading groups are established, and individuals are expected to proofread for each element that has been taught.

3. Individuals who need specific writing skills to improve their written products, after getting feedback from their proofreading groups, are given immediate individual or small-group instruction in that skill.

4. Between the regularly scheduled writing sessions, mechanics are taught from the textbook. Included in these mechanics are punctuation elements from Box 8–1. The least number of lessons necessary for students to master a skill are selected from the textbook.

BOX 8–1 *ELEMENTS OF PUNCTUATION*

Primary grades

Period after a sentence that tells something

Question mark after a question

Apostrophe in common contractions

Comma after the greeting of a friendly letter

Comma after the closing of a friendly letter

Period after initials and abbreviations

Comma between the day of the month and the year

Comma between the name of a city and a state

Apostrophe to show ownership with singular nouns

Period after a number or letter that shows an item in a list

Quotation marks before and after a direct quotation

Exclamation mark at the end of a strong statement

Middle grades

Apostrophe to show ownership with singular and plural nouns

Comma, question mark, or exclamation mark to separate a quotation from other parts of the sentence

Colon after the greeting of a business letter

Commas to separate words or phrases in a series

Comma before and after an appositive

Comma after an introductory clause

Comma after introductory words (yes, no, however, and the others)

Commas, periods, and quotation marks in footnotes

Methods of Teaching Punctuation

Two types of instruction have been described above, the spontaneous type when an individual or small group discovers a need while attempting to improve a first draft and the preplanned type that is used to deal with a sequence of skills. The spontaneous type is much shorter, because the child is eager to get on with polishing the story and because the teacher has no time to prepare a formal lesson. Yet, the two types of instruction are quite similar in nature.

Punctuation, like any skill, is best learned through discovery and in context. If learners can discover how an element of punctuation works by looking at models in which it is used correctly or by experimenting with it, they will understand it more readily than if they are simply told how it works. Certainly they will not learn to use an element of punctuation if they are asked to practice using it before they understand. If learners see the element in the context of real language, they will remember it more easily than if it is in isolated sentences. This is illustrated in a study by Calkins in which children who were taught punctuation through isolated lessons were able to use it less successfully than children who learned it while engaged in the context of actual writing.[5] This is why a teacher can usually be more successful in a very brief spontaneous lesson than in a longer preplanned one.

The spontaneous lesson uses discovery and context, but in an abbreviated manner. As the teacher has brief conferences with individuals who have received feedback from their proofreading groups, the needs are discovered. When the teacher sees that an understanding of commas in a series can resolve a question about the clarity of a writer's story, for example, models can quickly be supplied from which she or he can discover this element of punctuation. The model might be from a textbook, if examples of commas in a series can be located quickly. Sentences written by the teacher on a separate piece of paper are a more likely source of models. The model sentences should be similar enough to the sentences of the student writer that a generalization can be drawn, but not so similar as to solve the problem for the student.

It is not necessary that the learner be able to state any rule as a result of the lesson, but questions directed to the individual about the problem area ("Why was this unclear before?" "What has this punctuation done to the way someone now reads the sentence?") can often provide a quick check on understanding. This technique may seem to lack the use of context except for the isolated sentences provided by the teacher, but in reality it is the full length of the child's written product that provides meaningful context. A spontaneous lesson of the type just described can usually be completed in a minute or two. Many such lessons can be taught in a single class period.

The longer, preplanned lessons that are normally based on a language arts textbook must also make use of discovery learning and language in context. Some language arts teachers require a classroom of children to open their textbooks to a given page, explain how to do the practice exercise, and then assign the exercise as independent work. Such a practice can hardly be called a lesson. Not only is any instruction limited to the brief explanation of the exercise, but any opportunity for discovery and any use of context is extremely limited. It is true that the textbook usually gives a few example sentences that use the punctuation element. It is also true that some individuals may discover how the element works by completing the exercise. But the exercise is typically isolated from anything meaningful that might serve as context, and the children are typically preoccupied with completing the task rather than making discoveries.

The beginning step in a purposeful punctuation lesson is the display of a model that has a meaningful context. There are three aspects to this context. First, the learners must see why the punctuation is necessary, what function it serves. This is usually accomplished by giving them examples, preferably from their experiences, of the lack of clarity that results when the punctuation is missing. Second, the lesson must be related to something the students are doing or to some other part of their real-life situation. Whether in reading or writing, context is never limited to the words on the paper, but includes the knowledge and background of the reader or writer. Third, the written model must be of sufficient length to clarify the meaning of the language in which the punctuation appears.

An example of a lesson introduction might make the three aspects of context more clear. Ms. Ivory's class had been studying life in Japan during social studies. In the most recent writing activity, each individual had written to a different travel agency to request old travel posters, pamphlets, or other material about Japan. Reminding the class of the activity, Ms. Ivory displayed the following simulation of a letter:

> My class is learning about Japan. Please send me pamphlets about Japan that describe any river valley mountain resort hotel or any other tourist attraction. It will help me write a story article report or poem for my class book.

By asking for the number of places and uses listed, Ms. Ivory was able to lead the children to see the lack of clarity in the example and the function of commas in a series. The model was then supplied with commas in several positions (river valley, mountain, resort hotel; river, valley, mountain resort, hotel), and individuals volunteered the meaning in each case.

In this example, the model involved all three aspects of context. The function of the commas was demonstrated, the lesson was related to something meaningful the class had done, and the punctuation was shown in a paragraph that was long enough to give the commas a meaningful setting.

The second step in a punctuation lesson gives practice in discriminating correct usage of the element from incorrect usage. This is the step that most closely ties in with proofreading. It is done by displaying a passage that has, in the case of our example, commas correctly and incorrectly placed in a series and discussing each one. A passage is again recommended rather than isolated sentences, for the same reasons mentioned earlier. Through the displayed model in step one and through the discrimination practice, individuals are usually able to discover how to generalize use of the punctuation element to other situations.

Finally, practice is given in using the element independently. The practice exercises typically found in textbooks can serve this function, but it is far better if the students can practice on their own writing products. The ideal situation arises when the learner can use the element immediately in something she or he is writing, as is the case in spontaneous lessons.

Both spontaneous and preplanned lessons, then, can make use of context and discovery. Normally, the spontaneous lessons given during the teacher-pupil conferences that follow proofreading group meetings are more effective. However, the preplanned lessons that are based on a skills sequence can also be meaningful if they make use of these two factors.

Teaching Capitalization

Although capitalization is somewhat less functional than is punctuation, it plays an important role in giving a written product clarity. Capital letters are primarily signaling devices. They signal the reader that this is a special word or group of words or a special place. Among the special words and places signaled are proper nouns, initials, titles, and the beginnings of sentences.

Experienced readers can usually figure out what is said in a piece of writing that isn't capitalized. The following sentences, for example, are easy enough to read:

> the u.s. auto industry was explained by mr. carl jones.
>
> he quoted from *consumer reports* and other american magazines.
>
> "i feel like dr. jekel," he said.

The main difficulty with these sentences is that it takes longer than usual to read them. We are accustomed to the signals that capital letters provide, so reading without them is slower. While there are occasions when capitalization enhances meaning, then, its main function is one of courtesy to the reader. To some extent, punctuation is also a tool for showing social respect, as is the case with titles before people's names.

Determining What Capitalization to Teach

As with other writing mechanics, capitalization should be taught in spontaneous as well as preplanned lessons. Little decision making is needed to determine which elements of capitalization to teach in spontaneous lessons. As the teacher meets with an individual who is in the process of improving upon a first draft, the punctuation selected for instruction is that which is needed immediately.

Because preplanned lessons are normally based on some set or sequence of skills, however, decisions must be made about which elements of capitalization to teach. If the plan suggested in this text is followed, it may not be possible to simply teach every lesson in the textbook. Taking time to build confidence before skills lessons are begun and taking time throughout the program to schedule writing and proofreading activities limits the number of skills lessons possible. Therefore, a general guide might be a useful resource in helping teachers choose which capitalization elements to teach. Box 8–2 on page 186 is such a guide. It shows the capitalization for which mastery is generally expected in the primary and middle grades. The elements are listed in a logical order, one that seems to increase in difficulty, but there are other logical sequences as well.

The selection of capitalization elements to teach can be done in the same manner as the selection of punctuation. Preplanned lessons are taught to the class or large groups during class periods between the regularly scheduled writing sessions. With Box 8–2 as a guide, the smallest number of lessons necessary for students to master a skill are selected from the textbook.

Methods of Teaching Capitalization

The basic plan for teaching punctuation can also be used for teaching capitalization. Although spontaneous lessons based on needs discovered during individual conferences are more effective, it is practical to assume that skills lessons are necessary between writing sessions (see Figure 8–1). Both spontaneous and preplanned lessons are more meaningful and effective if they are based on context and discovery. As we saw in the discussion of punctuation, context has three aspects: an understanding of the element's function, a relationship between the element and real life, and a language setting of sufficient length.

Children are able to learn an element of capitalization in a complete context and discover how to apply it when three steps are followed properly. First, a model of sufficient length is displayed. Learners either draw conclusions from the model or experiment with it to learn the capitalization concept. The second step involves practice in discriminating between correct and incorrect usage of the capitalization element. Third, students practice applying what has been learned to a real writing situation.

BOX 8–2   *ELEMENTS OF CAPITALIZATION*

Primary grades

First word of a sentence
People's names
Names of other familiar things (pets, school, city, etc.)
The word "I"
The names of days, months, and holidays
First and important words in book and story titles
The titles Mr., Ms., Miss, Mrs., Dr.
First word of the greeting in a letter
First word in the closing of a letter
First word in a line of poetry or verse
Initials

Middle grades

All proper nouns and their abbreviations
Sacred names and pronouns referring to them
All titles used with names (President Smith; Pastor Jones)
First word of a quotation
Proper adjectives (French, Marxist, Christian)
First word of each line item in an outline

Following is an example of a capitalization lesson using these three steps. It is a preplanned type, perhaps based on a textbook lesson.

Mr. Lowes's third-grade class had decided to make a poetry book so that each child could give it to his or her parents as a gift for the December holidays. The poetry writing had already begun, but there was a week's time remaining before the children's products would be selected (making certain every individual had an entry) and published (mimeographed). During a language arts class, Mr. Lowes displayed a number of the class's favorite poems which he had copied in large letters onto chart paper. He also showed them a poem in which the individual lines did not begin with capital letters and asked the class which looked right. Several children were able to recognize the fact that the first word in each line is usually capitalized. He then divided the class into groups, distributed a book of poems to each group and asked them to find if this generalization is always true. After the class concluded that it probably is they speculated on *why* it is. Then, they practiced discriminating between correct and incorrect usage of the element. This practice was done independently with duplicated copies of poems from which some of the punctuation had been deleted. Finally, the learners were asked to look at the poems they had been writing to see if any additional capitalization was needed. When the poetry writing resumed two days later, proofreading groups and individual conferences focused on the beginning word in each line.

In this example, students drew conclusions from the model poetry that was presented. This is clearly a form of discovery learning. In addition, context was used in its broadest sense: the function of this element was subjected to speculation, a language sample of sufficient length to provide context was provided through the model poetry, and the relationship of the capitalization element to real situations was established when the children applied the lesson to their own poems. In other words, this lesson came about as close to the ideal as a lesson can without being based on spontaneous needs.

Other Writing Mechanics

In addition to punctuation and capitalization, there are a few other writing mechanics that require some attention. Correct word usage is important, including person, tense, and number agreement, but these are learned with oral language and applied to writing (see Chapter Four). Use of margins and indentations, abbreviations, quotations, and footnotes is unique to writing, however. The role of margins and indentations is simple enough to demonstrate and explain, but is not always easily remembered. Abbreviations are not easy to learn, because there are few generalizations that can be used to remember which letters to write for individual shortened words. The punctuation and capitalization of quotations have been discussed above, but the whole concept of when and how to use quotations requires separate attention. The usage and proper form of footnoting is rather complex and is usually not approached until late in the elementary-school years. As was pointed out earlier, spelling and handwriting might be considered writing mechanics, but they are in a separate chapter because of their unique nature.

Little more needs to be said about methods of teaching these less common writing mechanics. The use of margins and indentations, abbreviations, quotations, and footnotes can be taught in the same manner as that suggested for punctuation and capitalization. Both spontaneous and preplanned lessons are again recommended. Learning through discovery in context is the most effective way to master any area of writing mechanics.

EVALUATING WRITING MECHANICS

Methods for evaluating writing mechanics must be consistent with methods for developing them. In light of the positions taken in this chapter, it is appropriate to suggest that students' ability to write a first draft without great concern for mechanics, willingness to put sincere effort into proofreading, and maturity in rewriting should be evaluated. Mechanical knowledge is only one of the four factors described early in this chapter that are important in learning to proofread, so evaluation should not be limited to measuring isolated skills.

The best measure of writing mechanics is the study of the learners' written products. It is as student writers apply their skills to meaningful writing situations that their true abilities are demonstrated. As has already been pointed out, however, this does not mean that the teacher's evaluation should consist of marking all of the mechanical errors, assigning a letter grade, and returning the papers. Such a practice does more harm than good, because it can damage writing confidence if done often enough, and does far less to teach mechanical skills than the approach suggested in this text. If it is necessary to assign letter grades to students' writing mechanics, this can be done without touching a red pen to their written products.

One way to assign grades is to select three or four written products each marking period and determine the level of mechanical proficiency in those. Students may even do the selecting themselves if they have stored copies of their products in a file. This is much more sensible than grading and returning each paper. First, three or four papers a marking period is an adequate sample of the individual's writing competence, especially if they represent what the child has selected as "best." Second, such limited marking frees the teacher from a chore so time consuming that many teachers keep writing to a minimum in order to avoid it. Third, if every product is turned in for a grade, the message to the writer is that the purpose of writing is to satisfy the teacher. If writing has real purposes, the products will be mailed to the people for whom they were intended, printed in a publication, or actually used in some other way.

Evaluation, however, is different from grading. Grading may be based on evaluation, but the main purpose in evaluating mechanics or any area of learning is to find the individual's strengths and weaknesses. A logical follow-up to evaluation is a plan to build on strengths and decrease weaknesses.

The teacher who coordinates skills lessons, writing, and proofreading has several sources of information about the strengths and weaknesses of an individual's writing mechanics. There are the three or four papers that the teacher grades each marking period. These can be scrutinized carefully in addition to being graded. The individual conferences provide a brief but powerful source of information because the writer and the written product are seen together. Even the planned lessons and the practice done in them provide some clues about ability. When all of these sources are coordinated, an evaluation of the individual is possible.

Because writing mechanics is made of so many specific skills, however, it is not possible for any teacher to remember the strengths and weaknesses of every individual. The most practical solution for the majority of teachers is a checklist record-keeping system. Record keeping needs to be as simple as a checklist, so that teachers can put their time and energy into helping and teaching, not into bookkeeping. Yet, checklists need to be used cautiously. Mastery of a skill at one point in time doesn't guarantee understanding at a later time. Skills that aren't used are forgotten. A checklist with double columns, one for strengths and weaknesses and one for dates, would allow the teacher to see the recency of an entry on the list at a glance. Finally, a pencil should be used instead of a pen so that, as children change, the record

s = strong; w = weak Names:																								
Skill	s	w	s	w	s	w	s	w	s	w	s	w	s	w	s	w	s	w	s	w	s	w	s	w
Punctuation for sentence endings																								
Apostrophes																								
Commas in letter greetings and closings																								
Commas as separators																								
Periods after initials, abbreviations, and numerals																								
Quotations																								
Other commas																								

FIGURE 8–2   Record form for individual writing mechanics.

of their abilities can be changed. Figure 8–2 shows a recording device of the type just described. The spaces in such a record should be large enough that specific skill weaknesses can be written in.

SUMMARY

Emphasis on writing mechanics not only needs to be delayed until the writers are confident, but needs to be built on that confidence long after it has begun. The best way to accomplish this and still build a situation in which mechanics will be understood and used is through a proofreading approach. Learning to proofread involves several factors, including both knowledge and attitudes, and is usually best learned in conjunction with individual elements of writing mechanics. Two types of lessons are seen as necessary for teaching mechanics and proofreading, spontaneous and preplanned lessons. Spontaneous lessons, which are based on immediate needs, are the more effective type, but preplanned lessons based on textbooks are a practical necessity in most classrooms. The basis for either type of lesson and for the development of writing mechanics is the concept that writers who take pride in their products will want other people to read them with understanding.

The language arts class conducted by Mrs. Williams at the beginning of the chapter seemed to be based on little except a desire to cover a page in the textbook. If the learners saw any connection between this exercise and actual writing, they had to find it on their own. The page in the textbook was completely out of the context of their own lives, and there was little purpose in completing it except to satisfy the teacher's assignment. An exercise like this not only fails to build on the writer's confidence, but gives him or her no permanent learning about writing mechanics.

The conference held by Mr. Amoto, which is an example of a spontaneous lesson, is quite a contrast. Andy had a genuine need to learn about one element of writing mechanics, and Mr. Amoto was able to give it to him in the context of his own story and yet let Andy independently discover the principle in question. The boy was evidently eager to get on with his proofreading because there was some purpose for writing a story. Not only was the writer's confidence in writing encouraged, but he also learned a writing skill that may not need to be taught to him again if he has occasion to use it several times in the near future.

It is so sensible to tie writing mechanics to actual writing that it is amazing so few teachers do it. This chapter has attempted to show that skills teaching can be based on student writing, using context in a manner that allows children to discover correct uses of writing mechanics without abandoning language arts textbooks. Writing should not be delayed until mechanics are learned; writing and writing mechanics are natural partners.

NOTES

1. Marion Crowhurst, "The Writing Workshop: An Experiment in Peer Reponse to Writing," *Language Arts,* 56 (October 1979), 757–62.

2. Mimi Schwartz, "Rewriting or Recopying: What Are We Teaching?" *Language Arts,* 54 (October 1977), 756–59.

3. Richard Gebhardt, "The Timely Teetertotter: Balancing Discipline and Creativity in Writing Classes," *Language Arts,* 54 (September 1977), 673–78.

4. Donald H. Graves, "Research Update: Language Arts Textbooks," *Language Arts,* 54 (October 1977), 817.

5. Lucy McCormick Calkins, "Research Update: When Children Want to Punctuate," ed. Donald H. Graves, *Language Arts,* 57 (May 1980), 567–73.

CHAPTER NINE
SPELLING
AND HANDWRITING

Scene A

"OK. Put everything else away and get out your spelling books *and* your handwriting books. Get out both books because I'm going to tell you how to do your spelling and your handwriting now. When you're finished with your spelling, then, you can go right on to handwriting," Mr. Dennis explained to twenty-seven children.

After several minutes of delay, the teacher continued. "Today is Monday. Do you remember what we do in spelling on Monday?"

"The first column!" responded several voices in unison, referring to the first column of written activities in the text for that week's spelling lesson.

"That's right. *And* we spend at least five minutes studying the words by ourselves. Now, let's look at the first activity. The book says you should write all of the words that have an *–ie* in them. Are there any questions on this part?"

After Mr. Dennis explained the other activities in the spelling assignment, he went on to assign a page of handwriting practice. The children went to work and he went to his desk.

Scene B

"Today, we're going to study four words that have some things in common. I bet you'll see how they're alike quite quickly," Miss Goldstein explained to the nine children in the spelling group. "The first word is *table.* Here it is on the chalkboard. Mary used this word in her last story. Do you remember how you used it?"

"I said Sally hid under the table," Mary answered.

"Right. OK, the other words are *simple, bottle,* and *bubble.* Do you see how these words are all alike?"

All hands went up. "They all end with *l–e,*" Charles said when called upon.

After using all of the words in context, Miss Goldstein asked the learners for other words ending with *l–e.* Then she again drew attention to *table.* She covered the word. "Now try to picture the word in your mind. Then write it and I'll show you the word again."

Spelling and handwriting can be classified as writing mechanics. They are among the skills or abilities that are needed to write in an acceptable form. They could have, therefore, been included in the previous chapter. Because these two areas have unique characteristics, however, they require separate attention.

SPELLING

There are two reasons why correct spelling is important, and the first one is that it adds to clarity. When a reader encounters words that are spelled in the manner expected, he or she is less likely to misunderstand the writer's message. Writers should be concerned with spelling, then, so their messages are clear.

However, this is not a very urgent reason for spelling correctly. If the writer has spelled a word in a manner that gives the reader sufficient clues about pronunciation, the context will easily make the word recognizable. English was spoken and written for centuries without a standardized spelling system. Until Samuel Johnson developed the dictionary in 1775, most words had a variety of spellings. Of course, standardized spelling has many advantages in a literate and technologically advanced society, especially for the publishing industry. However, the degree to which exact spelling adds clarity to writing is limited.

The more important reason for correct spelling is that society places a great deal of emphasis upon it. Among educated adults, spelling that is anything less than exact is associated with ignorance and low intelligence. Such perfection is expected in few other activities of life. As unfair as it may be for society to place such high demands upon writers, the truth of this situation is quite clear. In the job market, the business world, and all scholarly activities, the good speller has an obvious advantage.

A realistic examination of these two reasons for good spelling provides us with an understanding of one of the chief problems in helping children develop spelling ability. Teachers are without a strong argument that correct spelling is essential for clarity, for children have little difficulty reading each other's misspelled messages. In addition, the social demand for exactness is essentially an adult one. There is not, therefore, automatic motivation among children to learn to spell correctly. Methods for dealing with motivation and other aspects of spelling instruction are included later in this chapter.

How Children Learn to Spell

It might be thought that learning to spell is simply a matter of memorizing the letter sequence of one word after another and practicing them until a vast collection of words is remembered. Recent linguistic research, however, has revealed that the process is much more complex than that. While memorization must be involved to some extent, children develop strategies for remembering the appearance of correctly spelled words and for spelling words about which they are uncertain. These strategies normally develop in several steps, which have been identified through linguistic research.

Steps in Learning to Spell

Chapter One points out that children do not learn language through imitation but discover how language works by formulating hypotheses and testing them. For example, a four-year-old might hypothesize that all words dealing with past things have an –ed ending. Only through testing, trial and error, does he or she learn when and when not to apply this generalization. Recent linguistic research, beginning with the work of Charles Read, seems to show that spelling is learned in much the same way.[1]

As children discover characteristics of spelling from which they can form hypotheses, they test them through use. Their development normally goes through three steps.

When young children first attempt to write, they use whatever they know of the relationship between sounds and letters. They tend to use letter *names* instead of letter sounds, perhaps because this is their earliest knowledge of letters. Thus, long vowels tend to be spelled with a single letter, short vowels are spelled with the long vowel that is closest in pronunciation, and consonants whose names are unlike their pronunciations are often confused. A "ch," for example, may be spelled with an "h" because the name of the letter ("ā ch") has the "ch" pronunciation in it. A child at this step in development might spell *cherry* as "h-a-r-e."

Gradually, early writers discover and test enough about their language that they move to the second step. At this point in their development children still base their spelling attempts on letter/sound relationships, but this relationship is understood much more thoroughly. Spelling errors made during this step tend to reflect the inconsistent nature of the letter/sound relationship in English at least as much as they do a lack of understanding. In other words, the writers tend to use a knowledge of phonics in spelling. Read and Beers and

Henderson, as well as other researchers, have found that this transitional period is characterized by such errors as overgeneralized long vowels ("ceme" for *came* because long *a* is pronounced "a–e") and "t" for –ed endings.[2]

Finally, as children become more familiar with the written form of their language, they move into the third step. They rely less and less on sound/symbol relationships to spell uncertain words and develop an awareness of structural patterns. For example, an individual who has already learned *geography* and *photography* is not likely to misspell the last part of *orthography*. Not only do they remember the appearance of many whole words, but also countless familiar letter clusters which they use in spelling less familiar words. Sometimes they even use sentence structure (syntax) and context meaning (semantics) to help them select a letter cluster when there are alternate choices. This learning is possible because, while the sound/symbol relationships in English are far from perfect, the patterns of letter clusters are quite consistent when syntax and semantics are considered. Children are not often consciously aware of these letter patterns, but learners who have reached this step have discovered them and use them without the help of stated rules. Those who have reached this step are usually quite able spellers.

The Role of Phonics

One of the larger controversies in the teaching of spelling is over the issue of phonics, the teaching of relationships between symbols (letters, or graphemes) and sounds (phonemes). Years of spelling research have not established whether the teaching of phonics helps learners develop spelling ability or not. The linguistic research described above, however, has shed some light on the value of phonics in spelling.

An understanding of which letter symbols typically represent which phonemes is useful to some degree in moving from step 1 to step 2 in spelling development. Children who still make some use of the letter *names* in deciding which letters to write while attempting an unfamiliar word will become more accurate if they replace this strategy with one that uses English letter/sound relationships. While phonics is probably a more useful tool in word recognition than in spelling, it is logical to expect that phonics instruction would help those who still use some step 1 spelling strategies.

Phonics, however, can't help learners move beyond the second step to the point where their spelling is based on familiar patterns of letter clusters, because this highest level of spelling ability isn't based on letter/sound relationships. It is fortunate that many spellers are able to achieve this highest level, for the letter/sound relationship is rather inconsistent. It has been shown that, if 166 different rules are used, about 90% of the selected one- and two-syllable words are spelled according to the rules.[3] However, 90% is not high enough and 166 rules are too many to be of practical help. Of course, few people would recommend teaching 166 rules. A more common recommendation would be to teach only the most functional phonics rules as an *aid* to the spelling of *some* words. The degree to which phonics can be an aid is still unclear, but it seems quite apparent, as noted earlier, that these skills are more useful for recognizing words than for spelling them. Only an intermediate level of spelling ability can be gained from application of phonics and even that level will be incomplete.

The Role of Visual Memory

The main strategy that good spellers evidently use is matching the appearance of a written word or letter cluster with their memory of its appearance. A word's spelling is tested by checking to see if it "looks right." An amazing feature of this visual matching ability is that its use is not limited to checking words after they are written, but guides the writer as the words are being formed. He or she usually knows in advance how the word *should* look. Another amazing aspect is that individuals who have this ability seem to be able to make the transitions from printed to typewritten to longhand words and still maintain full capacity for matching.

A great deal of mystery surrounds this matching ability, which could be called "visual memory," but it seems to demonstrate a key difference between individuals who are at step 2 and those who are at step 3 of spelling development. Except for children who still use letter names to spell words, it is doubtful that anyone completely ignores visual memory. The difference among individuals is probably the degree to which they use this matching strategy and to which they still rely on letter/sound relationships. Most words that any individual consistently spells with accuracy are probably based at least partially on visual memory. It is not known if some individuals have a greater natural ability to visualize words or if their development is simply more advanced.

An individual who has reached the third and final step in spelling development also uses this matching ability to spell words about which he or she is uncertain. In this case, letter clusters are matched instead of whole words. In the earlier example of *geography, photography,* and *orthography,* the writer's visual memory of the last six or seven letters would come into play.

The Role of Semantics and Syntax

There has been substantial evidence in recent years that able readers make extensive use of context in the process of reading. Context provides two types of clues: the meaning taken from the surrounding text (semantics) and the grammar or structure of that text (syntax). The linguistic research mentioned earlier has given us some reason to suspect that semantics and syntax are also used in spelling, especially when alternative spellings are contained in a person's visual memory. This would be most evident with homophones, words that are pronounced alike. For example, the spellings of *to, too,* and *two* and of *red* and *read* depend completely on context. It may be true that advanced spellers also use context to help them differentiate between such variant spellings of letter clusters as *–able* and *–ible, –ic* and *–ich,* and *–ent* and *–ant* rather than always placing whole words in their visual memory.

The Role of Self-Concept

Like the other areas of language, spelling is affected by the individual's self-concept. Children who have confidence that they are good spellers take more risks when they are writing, experiment more with spelling, and therefore frequently learn more letter clusters and words. Children who lack such confidence are likely to use only the vocabulary of which they are certain when they write or to spend a great deal of time asking for help with spelling or checking resources. Because the limited vocabulary is a more natural option for such writers, they experiment with and learn fewer words. Thus, confidence may not increase the odds for correctly spelling a given word at a given time, but in the long run it may have a large impact on the number of words and letter clusters an individual is able to place in her or his visual memory.

Implications for Learning to Spell

When the factors above are combined, it becomes apparent that the traditional weekly spelling lesson is not enough to provide many learners with spelling ability. The traditional weekly plan has three ingredients: practice in writing the weekly list of words, phonics activities, and spelling tests. In meaningful situations, practice in writing can be very beneficial because visual memory of spellings is developed through writing. However, when the writing is separated from any purposeful, meaningful context, as it often is during spelling lessons, children perform these tasks mindlessly instead of gaining visual memory. The phonics activities, we have seen, have a limited value. The tests, while useful for self-evaluation, don't aid in the actual learning of spelling. Thus, more than this is needed to help learners gain independence in spelling.

What is needed is a set of activities that match the factors described above. Children need to have a purpose for learning spelling and need to feel confident about their ability to do so. They need much exposure to written language so their visual memories can expand. Unless they are using *names* of letters as a spelling strategy, the earliest step in learning to spell, they need activities that de-emphasize letter/sound relationships. Activities that fulfill these needs are possible within the type of proofreading program suggested in Chapter Eight.

Method for Teaching Spelling

Spelling is learned more effectively through writing than through directed spelling lessons. Spelling is clearly a part of written language and cannot be learned in isolation any more than the other parts of language can. It is when writers experience a need for the spelling of a word that they are most likely to imprint it into their visual memory. Individual spelling needs can only be dealt with individually, so a part of the spelling program will need to involve individual teacher-pupil conferences.

On the other hand, it isn't practical to expect that the entire spelling program can be carried out through individual conferences. Those children who have weak spelling abilities need to spend more time with this area than such conferences could allow. An individualized program in which individuals construct their own spelling lists is one possible way to build in the additional time. However, the teacher's time constraints in a typical classroom situation often make such a program less than feasible. Although the traditional weekly spelling lesson has important flaws, an improved adaptation of that system may meet the needs of weak spellers in a more practical way. A form of directed lessons along with spontaneous teaching during individual conferences, then, appears to be the best combination for helping children learn to spell.

Spontaneous Lessons

Chapter Eight described a plan for combining proofreading with skills learning, and that plan can be expanded to include spontaneous spelling lessons. The plan calls for frequent writing activities with genuine communication purposes. Student writers produce a rough draft, submit it to their proofreading group, and use the group feedback to help them revise and polish their product. While the individual is revising, the teacher has a brief conference with him or her to check on understanding and give any needed spontaneous skills instruction. During that conference, individual spelling needs can also be handled.

The procedure is very similar to the one for teaching other spontaneous skills lessons. Context is used in that the word is needed in a meaningful piece of writing. Discovery techniques can also be included as learners see for themselves how their spellings agree and disagree with standard spellings. The procedure begins with an individual conference, during which one or more words are pointed out (by student or by teacher) with which help is needed. The student then writes the word, perhaps on scrap paper if it isn't already included in the written product. Then, the teacher writes the word and places this model underneath the student's. Attention is called not only to the discrepancies between the two spellings, but especially to the similarities. If the teacher sees or is aware of a pattern in the individual's misspellings, he or she could briefly demonstrate other words that follow the pattern. The student then writes the word and goes on with proofreading, while the teacher goes on to another individual. Individual conferences and spontaneous lessons such as this are held each time a writing activity is undertaken, which may be as often as every one or two weeks.

Directed Lessons

Some of the problems with traditional weekly spelling lessons were described earlier in this chapter. Such lessons are insufficient to help learners who have difficulties with spelling, and they are inappropriate for students who can already spell the words. This is especially true if teachers deal with this part of the curriculum by giving assignments from the practice pages of a spelling book rather than helping children spell. The practice activities vary from one publisher to another, but they are mainly designed to give students practice in writing the words, in using phonics, and in seeing common patterns of spelling. When these activities become mere assignments performed to satisfy a teacher, they are usually completed mindlessly by poor spellers, so that little visual memory is built. They are completed with no value at all by those who can already spell the words.

In its traditional form, then, the weekly spelling lesson is useless. Children with underdeveloped visual memories gain little from the

Monday through Thursday practice activities, learn to spell with varying degrees of success the night before the weekly test, and promptly
forget the words when the test is completed. Individuals who can
already spell the words gain nothing. In order to be of any value, such
a program must be modified. Only then can it be used along with
spontaneous instruction with any degree of success. Two basic modifications are necessary.

First, a system must be developed that recognizes the existing
abilities of proficient spellers. It is sheer foolishness to force children
who can already spell the words on the weekly spelling list to complete
the practice activities in the book. In fact, there is no need to study
known words at all. Manolakes found that the children in one school
district could, on the average, spell between 76 percent and 83 percent
of the words on the lists at their grade levels and between 58 percent
and 75 percent on the lists of a year above.[4] Some teachers attempt
to deal with this vast range of differences by adding words to the
regular lists for good spellers or by putting such students into the
spelling book a year above their grade level, but these practices do not
fully recognize the abilities of the better spellers. A more reasonable
practice is to release students from the requirement to practice words
they already know. One method for accomplishing this, one that is
already employed by many teachers, is to use the scheduled spelling
list but to excuse individuals from the study of any words that they
know on a pretest. The pretest is a test of the entire word list, given
at the beginning of the week-long spelling lesson and before students
study the words. Such a practice excuses all learners from meaningless
drill on known words and allows the better spellers to concentrate on
the few words they don't know.

The other modification that is necessary is to completely change
the method for helping learners who have underdeveloped visual
memories. Mindless activities must be replaced by group lessons that
focus on the appearance of the words. Among the possibilities for such
lessons are those that call attention to patterns of spelling. Thus, as
individual words are placed on the chalkboard, questions like the following might be asked:

How many other words can you think of that end this way?

When we add a (prefix, ending, and so on) to this word, what
happens?

How are these words alike?

In addition, learners of this type need help with their direct attempts to memorize words. Strategies such as the following are often recommended for individual study:

1. Look at the word.
2. Close your eyes and picture the word.
3. Cover the word and write it.
4. If an error is made in steps 2 or 3, start again at step 1.

Such a strategy is quite good, for the attention is focused upon the appearance of the word both in print and in the individual's own handwriting. However, it is usually more effective if the teacher directs the process instead of leaving it for independent study. In this way attention can also be focused on only a few words each day, an approach that seems to be more successful for children who have difficulty with spelling. On a given day, then, the teacher might select a few words from the spelling list and proceed with the following steps:

1. Put a word on the chalkboard, discuss its meaning, use it in context, and direct attention to any familiar pattern in it.
2. Cover the word and direct children to picture it in their minds.
3. With the word still covered, ask them to write it.
4. Repeat as necessary.

The problem spellers could then be tested at the end of the week to measure growth. Instead of a test that is dictated to the whole class, the teacher might use a less threatening method, that of having the words dictated by a partner.

Using this plan, at least two spelling groups would be in existence. Able spellers take a pretest, study incorrect words independently over several days, and take a retest with a partner. Less able spellers work with the teacher, using the approach described above, and also take a test with a partner.

Even with these modifications, the weekly spelling lesson is far from perfect. While some attention is paid to context in teacher-directed lessons, words are largely treated in isolation. For this reason, the spontaneous instruction connected with writing and proofreading, described earlier, must also be used.

Which Words to Teach

A final issue to which we should give some attention relates to which words to teach. During spontaneous instruction, of course, the spelling words selected are the words the individual needs to get on with the task. During directed lessons, however, the options are guided by two schools of thought.

One view is that words should be introduced on the basis of function. Since only 2,650 words make up 95 percent of the running words used by children and adults in their writing,[5] a word list of this size or somewhat larger is divided among the grade levels. The words that are taught first are those that are used most.

The other view is that words should be learned in groups that have similar patterns. In so-called "linguistic" spelling series, for example, groups of words ending in –tion or in –ture might be taught together. Or, words such as *bead, dream,* and *eat* might be taught with *bread, dead,* and *spread.* While this approach seems more logical in light of what we know about visual memory, there is little evidence to date that it produces any greater success than the functional approach. Perhaps this is because neither approach is very effective when words are isolated from writing in context.

In spite of the large amount of attention that has been given to the selection of spelling lists, then, this issue does not seem to be very important. Any recognized spelling series or word list would seem to serve as a basis for the directed part of the program. What is more urgent is that the importance of spelling be recognized and that spelling be related to context as it unfolds in the individual's writing.

HANDWRITING

One of the happiest changes in elementary education in recent years was the near end of nonsense in handwriting. For many decades children had been required to spend fifteen or twenty minutes a day drawing thousands of meaningless circles and slanted lines in the name of handwriting practice. Even when it was finally realized that such activities offered no positive results during authentic writing situations, daily handwriting practice throughout the elementary grades continued for another decade, this time through drawing thousands of isolated letters and words. Fortunately, most of this meaningless drill has ended, and educators have begun to allow handwriting to develop naturally in the context of other writing.

Children develop and refine their style of penmanship mainly through actual writing experiences. (*Ted Jursek*)

This change is a welcome one, but not because handwriting is *unimportant.* Not only is poor handwriting a hardship for the reader but it also makes the writer's task more difficult.[6] The move to a more natural method of learning letter forms is positive because such learning is more effective.

Actually, the only time children need instruction in the art of forming letters is when they sincerely don't know how certain letters are formed. There are two times when this type of help is especially needed. One is when children are first learning to write letters, usually in kindergarten or the first grade. The other is when they make a transition from the first form of writing, known as *manuscript,* to the *cursive* form that most adults use.

Manuscript and Cursive Writing

Although there are a few advocates of teaching beginning writers only the cursive form of writing, almost all beginners are taught manuscript. This form is often called *printing,* but it is much simpler than the print made by a printing press. It is made up of combinations of straight lines, circles, and parts of circles (see Figure 9–1).

Because manuscript is relatively simple and resembles the appearance of book print more than adult cursive writing does, it is generally recognized as a good way to introduce beginners to writing. The first time that a teacher needs to schedule handwriting practice and give direct instruction in letter formation, then, is when beginners are introduced to manuscript. Before long, most children see that their handwriting is not of the adult variety and they want to begin writing in cursive. Normally, this urge arises late in first grade or early in

ABCDEFGHI
JKLMNOPQR
STUVWXYZ
abcdefghijkl
mnopqrstuvw
xyz

FIGURE 9–1 Manuscript alphabet.

second. It is at this time that direct instruction is needed for the second time. Some teachers have insisted that by a certain time, for example third grade, all children must complete the transition from manuscript to cursive writing. While such a practice may not be very harmful to children, it is not necessary or helpful. Research has shown few advantages in speed, legibility, or efficiency for adults who regularly use cursive writing over adults who regularly use manuscript.

Role of the Teacher

We have seen that there are two times when teachers need to give preplanned direct instruction in handwriting. During the first of these, the teaching of manuscript to beginners, letter forms may be taught to the whole class, or at least to a large group. The letters may be

206

demonstrated and practiced in as much context as possible, one at a time, for short periods. Thus, children in the last months of kindergarten or the early part of first grade may actually need a fifteen minute handwriting period.

The second occasion for preplanned and directed lessons, when writers want to learn cursive writing, also comes early in most children's school career. Such teaching can probably best be done in small groups. When a few children begin to experiment with cursive writing on their own, they can be placed in a group and directly instructed in the formation of individual letters.

The procedures for teaching cursive letters will need to be varied to fit the specific situation. However, if the small group's interests don't suggest some other beginning, a good way to start is to show each individual how to write her or his name in cursive, because one's name is usually of interest. On subsequent days, a few letters at a time can be demonstrated to the group, gathered near the chalkboard. Sometimes there is value in letting individuals trace the letters that are on the chalkboard with chalk or their fingers. Most of the practice, however, should be on paper, where the letters will normally be used. The letters that are introduced should be selected carefully so that they can be used to spell several known words. For example, the first lesson might involve the letters *t, r, c,* and *a,* thereby allowing children to write *car, tar, cart, cat, tap, pat,* and so forth. These words should be used orally in sentences, and opportunities should be provided shortly thereafter for the words to be used in real writing situations. After a day or two of practice, more letters can be introduced.

Usually, when other children see what is happening, many of them will want to be included, for cursive writing has a "grown-up" status among most young children. One or more additional groups can be formed and similar procedures followed. After a group has been taught all of the letters, its members usually need very little additional instruction or supervised practice. The children who do not wish to learn cursive writing can be allowed to continue with manuscript.

While there are only two times in the school career of most children when handwriting instruction needs to be scheduled, the role of the teacher is not limited to those two brief periods. Once children have a rough idea of how letters are formed, they refine their letter formation and develop their own distinctive style of penmanship through actual writing experiences. This developmental process, which takes many years, needs the attention and guidance of a concerned teacher.

This attention and guidance has several parts. First, the teacher needs to be aware of individuals who still need help with specific letter formation and to give the help as needed. Second, the teacher needs to communicate the importance of legibility, and to some extent neatness, so that learners are continuously aware of it while proofreading. On the other hand, he or she needs to be flexible enough in setting legibility requirements that individuals can develop their own distinctive style without feeling guilty about any lack of conformity. The teacher needs to watch for writers who don't hold their pen or pencil comfortably or who sit in an awkward writing position, but once commonly accepted positions have been demonstrated, learners should again be allowed to develop their own techniques.

Left-Handed Writers

Individuals who write with their left hands have historically been treated badly. At one time they were regarded as evil or even demon-possessed. Although such attitudes disappeared long ago, a belief that left-handedness was bad persisted until recent years. Not many years ago, schools tried to force all children to write with their right hands. There is some evidence that such a forced shift in handedness is psychologically damaging to some children.

While left-handed writers should not be treated negatively, neither should they be ignored. Because our system of writing goes from left to right, these children have obstacles to overcome that right-handed writers do not. Their writing hand tends to hide their writing from their own view, making legible letter formation difficult. This factor, in turn, tends to cause them to place their wrists above the line of writing and bend their hand down into the famous "left-handed hook."

Children who have already developed the "hook" position and are already writing should not be forced to unlearn what they know and relearn another position. Beginning left-handers, however, can be taught to hold their pencil and paper in positions that are more comfortable and efficient than the "hook." Three adjustments from the typical right-handed writing position are especially important. Left-handed writers should be taught to do the following:

1. Hold their pencils farther from the writing tip—about one to one and one-half inches
2. Slant their paper to the right instead of the left
3. Slant their letters in the opposite direction from right-handed writers while writing in cursive

EVALUATING SPELLING
AND HANDWRITING

True evaluation of spelling and handwriting is based, not on the results of tests and practice activities, but on the purposeful writing that is done independently. If evaluation of spelling is limited to the number of correctly spelled words on weekly tests, the teacher learns little about helping children in situations where correct spelling is really needed. If evaluation of handwriting is based on practice during isolated drills, the whole concept of teacher guidance described above is violated. Measures of ability and of growth need to be applied to the written products that children complete.

Part of the evaluation should be based on the first drafts of independent writing and part on the final draft. As the teacher meets briefly with individuals who are proofreading (see Chapter Eight), he or she helps where needed with spelling, as described earlier in this chapter. The amount of help that is needed and the individual's level of spelling strategies can be noted and evaluated. The type of errors commonly made can lead the teacher to easily see at which of the three steps in spelling development the child is operating. Of course, the individual's spelling on the first draft should not be given a letter or numerical grade, for this would counteract the objectives of confidence building and creativity.

Handwriting, however, is probably evaluated most effectively if it is based on the final written product. The importance of legible and neat writing is evident only in products that have genuine purposes. Self-evaluation by students—comparison of written products completed at various parts of the school year—is also important for handwriting.

A method of record keeping is as important for spelling and handwriting as it is for other writing mechanics. The record keeping that was explained for evaluating punctuation and capitalization, however, can easily be expanded to include these two areas (see page 190). Separate lines for spelling and handwriting are simply added to the record sheet.

SUMMARY

The teaching of spelling and handwriting is similar in some ways to the teaching of writing mechanics described in the previous chapter. For practical reasons, all of these skills must receive some direct instruction, although handwriting requires a very limited amount. The similarity extends also into spontaneous lessons. As with the mechanics described in Chapter Eight, spelling and handwriting are usually improved more effectively during brief individual lessons that are spontaneous than they are during more lengthy, planned lessons. This is true because the individual instruction can be based on actual writing needs and can take full advantage of a meaningful context.

If, however, the planned textbook lessons are modified to better deal with a range of spelling abilities and with real handwriting needs, they can be used effectively along with spontaneous lessons. Able spellers should not be asked to study words they already know, and poor spellers should be helped to develop visual memories of words and letter clusters. Handwriting instruction should be given only when learners need help with letter formation. The system for proofreading that was described in Chapter Eight can be enlarged to give individual, spontaneous attention to these two areas.

Mr. Dennis, in the opening of this chapter, was quite ineffective in helping his class with spelling and handwriting. Assignments such as he gave lead to little else than "busy work." Filling in blanks and copying isolated words produces very little positive learning unless the learners see some purpose in it. It is very possible that neither the teacher nor the students had any objective in mind except to complete the tasks.

In Miss Goldstein's classroom, quite a different situation prevailed. Although it wasn't clear to what extent she also used spontaneous lessons, it was clear that this teacher realizes that some children need to be guided through the learning of spelling. A group of learners, probably those with less well-developed visual memory, were helped to use a familiar technique for studying words. Only a few were learned each day. Her approach was very much like the one described in this chapter.

When writing has a purpose, writing mechanics usually have one also. Spelling and handwriting are part of the communication process and are most easily learned in that context. When methods for dealing with spontaneous needs are combined with structured lessons, developing writers grow in spelling and handwriting ability along with the other aspects of writing.

NOTES

1. Charles Read, "Pre-school Children's Knowledge of English Phonology," *Harvard Educational Review,* 41 (1971), 1–34.

2. Ibid; J. Beers and E. Henderson, "A Study of Developing Orthographic Concepts among First Graders," *Research in the Teaching of English,* 11 (1977), 133–48.

3. Bruce Cronnell, "Annotated Spelling-to-Sound Correspondence Rules," 1971, cited in E. Brooks Smith, Kenneth S. Goodman, and Robert Meredith, *Language and Thinking in School,* 2nd ed. (New York: Holt, Rinehart and Winston, 1976), p. 246.

4. George Manolakes, "The Teaching of Spelling: A Pilot Study," *Elementary English,* 52 (February 1975), 242–47.

5. James A. Fitzgerald, *The Teaching of Spelling* (Milwaukee: Bruce, 1951).

6. Donald H. Graves, "Research Update: Handwriting Is for Writing," *Language Arts,* 55 (March 1978), 393–99.

CHAPTER TEN
TEACHING GRAMMAR

Scene A

"Who remembers what we call a word that names a person, place, or thing?" asked Miss Barnum.

"A noun!" responded several children in unison.

"OK, good. Now, do you remember what we call a word that tells an action?"

"A verb!" the same children responded. The other members of the class said nothing.

"OK, good. Let's say the meanings of these two words together. A noun names a person, place, or thing."

The class repeated the statement obediently.

"A verb tells an action." Again the class obeyed.

Miss Barnum continued. "Here's a sentence on the board. 'The dog ran.' What noun and what verb do you find in this sentence?"

After the class responded and after several other examples were demonstrated, Miss Barnum assigned a work sheet. The children were required to draw one line under every noun and two lines under every verb on the work sheet.

Scene B

"Yesterday Susan read us her story about her dog Sam," said Miss Clark. "She told us that she gave her dog a bath. She also told us that she gave her friend Sally a birthday present."

On the board she wrote, "Sally gave her dog a bath," and "She gave her friend a present."

"If you could rearrange the words in any way that made sense, how would these sentences change?" Miss Clark asked.

The class had rearranged sentences before and responded eagerly. "Sally gave her friend a bath. She gave her dog a present," said Kim. Laughter followed.

"Her dog gave Sally a bath. Her friend gave her a present," said Jeffrey.

"Does that make sense? Could her dog give Sally a bath?"

"Sure," answered Jeffrey. "He could shake water all over her."

"OK," answered Miss Clark. "Now let's go back to the original two sentences. Is there a way we can combine them?"

"Sally gave her dog a bath and her friend a present," Carlos said.

"Good. Is there a way we could combine the sentences so that the reader can tell which happened first?"

"After Sally gave her friend a present, she gave her dog a bath."

"Sally gave her dog a bath before she gave her friend a present."

The word *grammar* has come to mean different things to different people. To some, it has such a broad definition that it is almost a synonym of language arts in general. To others, it refers to everything on the mechanical side of writing and speaking and is seen as the opposite of creativity. To still others, it has a very specific meaning. Although there is little value in debating which is the "right" definition, the use of the word in a very specific sense is most useful to the purposes of this text. Before we discuss a definition of grammar, however, we will examine the purpose or goal of its study.

PURPOSE

For the student in school, the study of grammar is not an end in itself. Knowledge of grammar rules and concepts by itself is not a justifiable goal because it has no realistic purpose. Rather, its purpose is to aid the communication, to enable the individual to communicate more fully and with more understanding. The grammar that preschoolers learn on their own makes it possible for them to speak and listen as well as they do. In school, these two forms of communication are refined more fully, but grammar is studied mainly to improve reading and writing. It can contribute a great deal to the effectiveness and efficiency of reading and writing.

DEFINITION

In order to understand how grammatical knowledge can lead to effective and efficient reading and writing, we must know exactly what it is. In this text and in most current literature on language, *grammar* refers to the way that language is put together, to its *syntax*. Word order and the formation of phrases and clauses are part of syntax. The role or function of each word, phrase, or clause within a sentence is another part. These units of language fit together in a limited number of ways, even when a wide variety of words is used (see Box 10–1 on page 216). The patterns of syntax that are thus formed are comparatively easy to learn, but difficult to describe.

Because the syntax or grammar of English is difficult to describe, a number of branches or schools of grammar have evolved over the years. In Chapter Two, three areas of linguistics were described that are based on the three schools of grammar. Each looks at and therefore describes grammar in its own way.

BOX 10–1 *COMMON ENGLISH SENTENCE PATTERNS*

1. Subject-predicate, simple
    Examples: Dogs bark.
                The girls sang loudly.
                Does that quiet boy ever speak?
2. Subject-predicate, compound
    Examples: Dogs and cats fight.
                The men scoffed and criticized.
                Do these boys and girls ever play or laugh?
3. Subject-predicate-object
    Examples: Dogs chase cats.
                The children ate their hot dogs.
                Did your mother ever spank you?
4. Subject-predicate-direct object-indirect object
    Examples: The cat gave the dog a scare.
                Mrs. Smith read the class a story.
                Could you give me a little help?
5. Subject-linking verb predicate-noun complement
    Examples: The dog is a Beagle.
                That tall boy is a good athlete.
                Were you a teacher last year?
6. Subject-linking verb predicate-adjective complement
    Examples: The cat is white.
                Tom Smith's daughter is very beautiful.
                Were all of the people at the meeting angry?

Description of Grammar

Traditional

Developed in the 1700s and based on classic Latin, traditional grammar was the only form taught in school until recently. It classifies sentences according to their meaning and the writer's intention (*declarative, interrogative, imperative,* and *exclamatory*) and defines components of sentences. The definitions of components are based either on meaning (example: a noun names a person, place, or thing) or on function (example: a preposition relates its object to another part of the sentence). The difficulties of traditional grammar include the lack of close similarity between Latin and English and its relatively inflexible description of how English should be.

Descriptive Linguistic

Based upon recent linguistic research, descriptive linguistic grammar is a description of all the patterns into which English words can be arranged to convey meaning. Included in the description are systems for using inflectional (changing) word endings when the words are used in different ways (example: hurry, hurried, hurries). A clear distinction between this and traditional grammar is that it describes the way language is, whereas traditional sets up rules for how it should be. Descriptive linguistic grammar also recognizes differences between written and spoken language and differences in spoken language (dialects) among various groups of people within a language.

Generative or Transformational

Of even more recent origin, generative grammar or transformational grammar is a set of formulas that explain how all sentences are generated. It is based on the theory that basic ideas, called *kernel sentences,* are the foundation of the many forms that can be used to speak or write. Kernel sentences can often be transformed into several sentence structures. For example, the kernel sentence *The dog chased the cat* can also be stated as *The cat was chased by the dog.* The formulas also help us to see the vast differences in meaning between sentences that are similarly worded, such as *Mary was easy to please* and *Mary was eager to please.*

Limitations

These descriptions of grammar help us understand its nature. However, as Chapter Two points out, while the development of new systems of grammar has added many insights into language, and these insights have had an effect on teaching, the new grammar descriptions do not add a great deal to the content of language instruction. If anything, they have taken away from the body of content. The research that went into their development has helped us realize that speaking and writing abilities are not enhanced by learning *about* language through the memorization of rules or the analysis of sentences, but through practice in *using* language.

Evidence that the study of grammatical principles does not improve writing is not new. Since the early years of this century, research evidence has been accumulating which shows that identifying parts of speech, diagramming sentences, and learning rules has no influence on writing. In a 1963 summary of research about written composition, Braddock stated that the strong and unqualified conclusion to be drawn from research to that time was that formal grammar had a negligible effect on improving writing and might even be harmful because it took instructional time from more important things.[1] Of course, much of that research was done before modern grammars had entered the picture. But there is no evidence that studying the newer grammar descriptions has any more positive effects upon writing than did the study of traditional grammar.

It is not surprising that the study of grammatical principles is less than productive or that grammar is really learned through using language. Nearly every child who enters school for the first time already has an extensive knowledge of how to put words and other units of language together in ways that sound right and carry meaning. In Chapter One we saw that preschoolers learn how language works through trial and error. If it is simple enough for preschoolers to learn through usage, the structure of language must also be easy enough for older students to learn in the same manner.

The lessons of language that preschoolers learn are the essence of grammar. These young learners usually are unfamiliar with the words *syntax* and *grammar*. They can't explain one formula or rule about the structure of language or name any parts of speech. Yet, they know how language works. They can put units of language together nearly as well as the adults in their environment.

The emphasis for older students should also be on the functional. The abilities that students should gain from working with grammar are those that help them structure their language better when communicating, not those that allow them to recite rules and labels of language.

This is not to say that a society should avoid an understanding of its own language. The work of linguists and other language scholars is not only of interest to language users, but of great importance. Nor is it to say that the labels used to identify parts of speech (noun, verb, noun marker, and the others on page 25) should never be introduced to children. But certainly such material should never become a main component in the language arts program of an elementary school, and certainly it is not worth reteaching every year for six to ten years! Children have a much greater need for techniques that help them write and read.

When this text speaks of teaching grammar, then, it refers to teacher-guided activities that give learners the opportunity to experiment with and use language. The goal of such activities is to develop the individual's ability to use the structure of language effectively and efficiently. In terms of writing (and speaking), effective use of language is that which conveys the intended message clearly and produces the intended results. Efficient use of written language is that which gives a message appropriate depth using an appropriate *amount* of language. In terms of reading (and listening), effective and efficient use of language is that which allows the individual to understand the message in the easiest, fastest, and most appropriate manner. Children come to school with a vast amount of grammatical knowledge, obviously slanted toward the dialect of their environment. The school's job is to expand it and refine it.

Now that we have at least a vague picture of what grammar *is,* we must also look at what it isn't. The word *grammar* in this text is not a "cover-all" term that refers to all manner of language study. It does not deal with spelling, handwriting, punctuation, capitalization, or any of the other writing mechanics discussed in the previous two chapters. Nor does it deal with the tense, number, or person of verbs. Choosing the correct usage of *is, are, was,* and *were* or of *did* and *done* is a matter of word usage, not of grammar. Word usage is primarily a verbal form of language and is given sufficient attention in Chapter Four. *Grammar* is a specific term, as described earlier.

TECHNIQUES FOR TEACHING GRAMMAR

We have already seen that an understanding of grammar, that is, knowing how language works, is gained through experimenting with and using language and not through learning about it. Instead of assigning exercises in identifying kernel sentences or such parts of speech as nouns, verbs, and adjectives, teachers must guide the *use* of language in the classroom. Providing opportunities and purposes for experimenting with written forms of language must be the teacher's primary concern and technique.

A classroom that has many meaningful reading and writing activities already has much of what is needed to accomplish this, but a teacher can do more to help learners grow in their understanding of English syntax. Children should be challenged to explore and discover new and more expressive ways to construct English. They should also be challenged to read and understand progressively more complex forms of printed language.

There are two related types of activities that, together with purposeful reading and writing, seem to offer the most promise for building a knowledge of grammar. The first type uses activities that require learners to construct or manipulate (that is, rearrange) sentences. The other type uses sentence-combining and sentence-dividing activities.

Constructing and Manipulating Sentences

When students arrange or rearrange words or groups of words into sensible sentences or shorter units of language, they have the opportunity to explore and make discoveries about syntax. One logical way to develop concepts of grammar, therefore, is to set up activities that lead them to construct and manipulate sentences in this manner.

The purpose of such activities is not primarily to teach children to discriminate between good and incorrect sentences, although this is important and will be explored in the next chapter. The purpose is to lead them to discover the effect that word order and sentence structure have upon meaning. Learners don't arrange and rearrange parts of a sentence to find the *right* sentence, but to explore variations.

Here is an example of such an activity. Mrs. Campbell gathered her second-grade class into a circle and showed them several cards,

Children should be challenged to explore and discover new and more expressive ways to construct English. (Ken Karp)

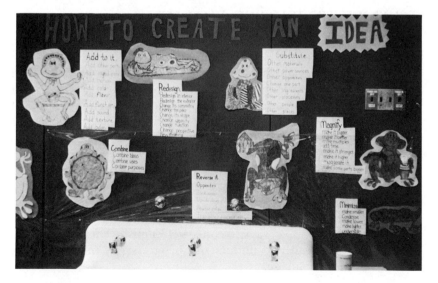

each having one or more words on it: *the ball, shaky, Mike, the fence, over, hit.* Next, she related the words to a class story from the previous day. She showed the children where each word was located in the story and read them the sentence from which each was taken. Then she placed the words on the floor and asked for a volunteer to arrange any of the cards into a statement that made sense. Jill selected three cards and arranged them to say, *Mike hit the ball.* Vern volunteered to add more to the sentence and produced, *Mike hit the ball over the shaky fence.* Mrs. Campbell asked where the ball was hit, what the sentence told about the fence (it was shaky), and what the sentence told about the boy who hit the ball (only his name). Then she removed the word *shaky* from its position in the sentence and placed it before the word *Mike.* She asked questions about the change in meaning that this made and, finally, asked for volunteers to rearrange the cards into any other statements that made sense.

In this example, the children responded to Mrs. Campbell because they were challenged and they learned through experimentation and discovery. The activity was made more meaningful by the fact that the language used was their own. All of these factors are important in teaching grammar.

Variations on this activity and other constructing and manipulating activities can be used, with some adjustment, at various grade levels. Some of these activities follow:

- Give ten to fifteen individual word cards to a group of children to manipulate. The cards contain several nouns or pronouns and several verbs written so that singular and plural forms of present and past tense appear on the same card, as shown in the diagram. When using cards with multiple words, children simply select the word that fits the sentence. One or two cards should also contain *the, a,* and *an.* Challenge the group to arrange the cards into as many different sensible forms as possible. Instead of using the words in the example, teachers will find an advantage in using the learners' own words or in relating the words to their interests.

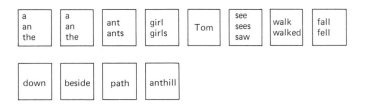

- Duplicate or copy a paragraph from a student's written product or some other source onto a chart with parts of several sentences missing. Small groups or the entire class fills in the missing language in as many sensible ways as possible. This activity is similar to a cloze activity, but whole chunks of language are omitted to be filled in by students.

- Omit single words from a paragraph and replace them with blanks to create a more pure form of cloze. In this case, challenge the students to supply for each blank a large number of individual words that make sense. It is important in this activity, as well as the one above, that learners should not attempt to search for *the right word* but for as many sensible words as possible. This objective is enhanced when the teacher lists on the chalkboard all of the suggested words for a given blank and repeatedly asks, "Can you think of any more?"

- Have two or more teams play an "Add a Word" game. Place a two- or three-word sentence on the chalkboard and let each team take a turn attempting to add a single word in such a way that the language doesn't loose its grammatical acceptability. Each team receives a point each time it can add a word to any part of the sentence in this way. The game continues until no additional words can be added or until a certain time limit is reached.

- Speed the trial-and-error process of discovering new sentence patterns by focusing attention upon certain types of sentences. If, for example, certain learners in a class seldom use "subject-predicate-direct object-indirect object" sentences (see Box 10–1), introduce this pattern by demonstrating sentences that contain it. Present a paragraph containing several such sentences to the students, and ask them what each of the sentences means. Then, ask them to word the sentences another way. This process should be repeated on a number of occasions. Allow time for some practice in rewording sentences so that they acquire the desired pattern.

Combining and Dividing Sentences

There is a second group of activities that develops concepts of grammar through experimentation and discovery. It deals with combining several sentences or other units of language into one, and with dividing longer sentences into two or more.

Sentence combining is a technique that has a substantial research base. Combs found several studies which indicate student writing can be improved through its use.[2] Following extensive practice in sentence combining, students write stories and essays that 1) consist of more mature sentences, 2) get better ratings by teachers and 3) show this superiority even eight weeks after the practice has stopped. Some of the research showed that growth in writing skills is encouraged by sentence-combining lessons and games as early as fourth grade.[3] We are not able to tell from these studies how well students could perform on a test of grammatical principles as a result of this technique, but we gain a more important insight, that of its applicability to writing.

In the report just described, Combs went on to suggest an additional benefit of sentence combining. In conducting his own research study, he found that reading comprehension test scores of seventh graders who had been trained in sentence combining improved significantly more than those of seventh graders who had not been so trained. There is an indication, then, that this technique provides some necessary grammatical or syntactical background not only for writing, but also for reading.

While some would consider the technique to be too simple to be of value, such combining operations evidently challenge and stretch the understanding of syntax. Two sentences with separate simple subjects and different predicates can be combined by simply inserting conjunctions such as *and, or,* or *but* (Examples: *Tom pitched the ball. Bill swung the bat. Tom pitched the ball and Bill swung the bat.*) However, most sentence combining is more complex than this. It is usually necessary, therefore, to develop student independence in this technique gradually.

This independence can be partially achieved by providing planned lessons. To keep the lessons from becoming meaningless school tasks, sentences are selected that reflect classroom events or that are based on students' writings. Two or three sentences are placed in a group, and the teacher guides the learners through the process of combining them. O'Hare has suggested the use of a signal system to help beginners learn sentence combining. The signals, consisting of words written in predetermined ways, give the student clues about how to join the sentences into one.[4] One such system might include suggested conjunctions or other joining words placed in parentheses and words that can be easily omitted printed in all capitals. Other words may also be omitted by the student, but the meaning must be unchanged. The following set of sentences, for example, might be used in the lesson:

Coach Jones could see SOMETHING.

(that)

Andre didn't know SOMETHING.

He needed to know how to swing his bat.

With the teacher's guidance, the students produce the sentence *Coach Jones could see that Andre didn't know how to swing his bat.* After students have been guided through several of these, they can do them independently. More and more complex sentence patterns are used, and then the signal system is gradually withdrawn.

Sentence combining can also be practiced through the use of games. Perron has suggested modifications of such games as beanbag, concentration, and tennis to provide practice in this technique.[5] In each case, individuals must combine two or more sentences to continue with the steps in the game.

Combs has detailed the steps of a sentence-combining dominoes game (see Figure 10–1).[6] Cards are constructed like dominoes with a

FIGURE 10–1 Sentence-combining dominoes.

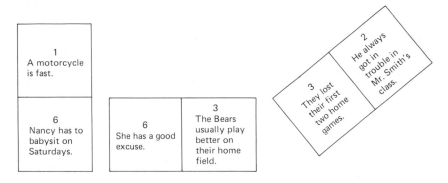

Construct dominoes cards with the following features:

1. Each card has on each end a numeral between 1 and 6 and an accompanying sentence.
2. Any sentence accompanying a given numeral can be combined with any other sentence of that numeral.
3. Construct the following numeral combinations.

    6/6 6/5 6/4 6/3 6/2 6/1
           5/5 5/4 5/3 5/2 5/1
                4/4 4/3 4/2 4/1
                      3/3 3/2 3/1
                             2/2 2/1
                                     1/1

numeral on each end. Each end also contains a sentence constructed so that the sentence on any number 3 card can be combined with that on any other number 3. The same is true of the other numbers which appear on the cards. The game is played with dominoes rules, except that a player must correctly combine the sentence on the domino he or she is playing with the sentence on the domino against which it is being played. In the example in Figure 10–1, the player who is placing her number 3 domino against the number 3 that is already in place must say a sentence such as this: "The bears, who usually play better on their home field, lost their first two home games." If she says this, or another sensible combination, she will earn six points, the total of the two dominoes that are joined.

The cause of the success of sentence-combining activities has not yet been determined. Perhaps a number of factors are in operation when students analyze how two or more language units can be rearranged into one. It is clear, however, that it is the individual's use of syntax or grammar that is brought into play and expanded in this analysis.

Sentence dividing is the opposite of sentence combining. Students begin with a compound or complex sentence and reword it so that it becomes two or more sensible sentences. There is no research base for this technique, but it is logical to assume that the same type of syntactical growth occurs through its use as through combining. It may, therefore, be used along with the other techniques described above.

Parts of Speech

Little has been said so far about the traditional practice of teaching parts of speech. Schools, it seems, have always taught children to discriminate among, and label, nouns, verbs, adjectives, adverbs, and prepositions. While many schools have made the transition to the more accurate "linguistic" labels for parts of speech (see Chapter Two), the practice continues. In fact, many students fill in practice sheets, diagram sentences, and label words in a similar way year after year. Little has been said about it in this text because there is little to say. We have already seen that research shows no evidence that such study improves writing, reading, or any other form of communication. The value of learning labels for types of words is limited to the convenience it offers in talking about our language. This limited value hardly warrants large blocks of instructional time year after year in school.

Labels for parts of speech can be learned, to the extent that they are needed, in an informal manner. If teachers use the word *noun* often and consistently in speaking of words that follow noun markers, children will come to understand that label in the same way they do *cocker spaniel, willow,* or *Buick.* Lefevre has suggested adding color coding to activities of the type described earlier in this chapter.[7] When manipulating and constructing sentences, children use word cards of various colors. One color is used for nouns, another for verbs, and so on. This gives learners much exposure to parts of speech without stressing labels and without any useless memorization of definitions. Parts of speech learned in such an informal manner can contribute to the real purpose of grammatical study, as described in this chapter, and yet give children enough vocabulary about word labels that they can talk to others about their language.

EVALUATING GRAMMAR

The child's use of grammar can be evaluated at two levels. At one level, the individual's ability to perform the tasks that are described in this chapter can be evaluated. Information about this ability can be very useful, but more is needed. The second level of evaluation is in the child's application of this ability to real communication situations in writing and reading.

Grammar Tasks

As children participate in activities of constructing, manipulating, combining, and dividing sentences, the teacher can determine the performance level of each individual. This might be done informally as they work in groups or as a class. The amount of an individual's participation in manipulating the word cards in the examples given in the previous section, for instance, can be noted. The ease with which sentences can be combined or divided and the number of responses to sentence tasks can be observed. Some teachers may find it beneficial to record individual progress for each of these grammatical tasks on a checklist or other form of record. If so, the checklist suggested for record keeping in Chapter Eight can be expanded to include the several lines necessary for this addition.

A more formal evaluation of grammatical tasks can also be conducted. Sentence construction, rearranging, combining and dividing lend themselves well to paper-and-pencil forms that can be used as tests. While the multiresponse activities suggested earlier are probably more beneficial for instructional purposes, grammatical tasks can be structured for *evaluation* purposes so that only one answer is correct.

Writing and Reading

Because grammar instruction is not an end in itself, evaluation of it isn't complete without examining its application. The areas in the school curriculum to which grammar are most directly applied are writing and reading. Evaluating the individual's ability to apply what he or she has learned about grammar, however, is not as easy as evaluating grammatical tasks. The learner's ability to apply an understanding of grammar to reading can be determined to some extent through miscue analysis. This technique is discussed in Chapter Twelve.

The ability to apply an understanding of grammar to writing can be examined from several angles, again including an informal measure. To some extent, it can be assumed that children who use good written expression have a good working knowledge of how language works, for this is an important component of written expression. Conversely, one possible cause of poor written expression is lack of this knowledge. When written expression is evaluated, as Chapter Eleven describes, some implications can be drawn about grammar.

A second and more direct evaluation technique is an examination of the sentence patterns used in the student's writing. Going by the common English sentence patterns (see Box 10–1), the teacher can determine with what variety the child writes. While there are few guidelines about the ideal type and quantity of sentence patterns in good writing, the individual's use of variety in sentences can be used to make inferences about his or her understanding of sentence patterns. Patterns that aren't used may not be understood. The process of labeling every sentence on a child's paper is, of course, very time consuming. Such an evaluation may be possible for each individual on only a few randomly chosen papers throughout a school year.

A final evaluation of the ability to apply grammar to writing is related to quantity. Hillerich has described a technique that involves counting the number of words per "T-unit" in a child's writing.[8] A T-unit is any independent clause with all of its subordinate clauses and modifiers. The technique is based on the assumption that longer T-units tend to be more complex. As mechanical as this technique is, research by Hunt and by Loban has demonstrated that this is a good measure of the writer's language sophistication.[9] Perhaps some combination of the techniques suggested in this section can give the best picture of the student's grammatical knowledge.

SUMMARY

Young children learn a great deal about grammar with no instruction. By trial-and-error experimentation, they discover so much that they can speak and listen to language that is very adultlike before they ever enter school. Learning through experimentation is also very effective once children enter school. The understanding of grammar that learners need to become good writers and readers can be taught through activities that lead them to experiment with language. Research consistently shows little value in techniques that require students to label parts of speech or memorize rules.

The introductory section of this chapter depicts a scene from the classroom of a teacher who seems to understand learning through experimentation. Miss Clark set up an activity in which the learners experimented with sentence rearranging and then sentence combining. Instead of guessing at or searching for the one right answer, students tried to find all of the sensible responses they could. Before sharing sensible answers with the class, they had to mentally experiment with various word orders and sentence structures. Such activities expand understanding of how our language is put together.

The other scene depicts a teacher who apparently believes that the study of grammar for its own sake is worthwhile. The children were expected to remember labels for words and to become familiar with label definitions, both of which were based on a Latin grammar rather than English. The practice exercise that was assigned had little to do with any communication in which they were engaged. Such techniques are highly unlikely to have any effect on the writing or other communication abilities of the participants.

Grammar, or syntax, is a very important element of a language. It is completely impossible to use a language even minimally without understanding how it is put together, how word order and sentence structure control meaning. But that understanding is not acquired by learning *about* the language. It is learned by experimenting with it and using language in real communication.

NOTES

1. Richard Braddock, and others, *Research in Written Composition* (Champaign, Ill.: National Council of Teachers of English, 1963), pp. 37–38.
2. Warren E. Combs, "Sentence-Combining Practice Aids Reading Comprehension," *Journal of Reading,* 21 (October 1977), 18–24.

3. Jack D. Perron, "Beginning Writing: It's All in the Mind," *Language Arts,* 53 (September 1976), 652–57.

4. Frank O'Hare, *Sentencecraft* (Boston: Ginn and Company, 1975).

5. Perron, "Beginning Writing."

6. Combs, "Sentence-Combining."

7. Carl Lefevre, *Linguistics, English, and the Language Arts* (Boston: Allyn & Bacon, Inc., 1970).

8. Robert L. Hillerich, "Developing Written Expression: How to Raise— Not Raze—Writers," *Language Arts,* 56 (October 1979), 776.

9. Kellogg W. Hunt, *Grammatical Structures Written at Three Grade Levels* (Champaign, Ill.: National Council of Teachers of English, 1965); Walter D. Loban, *Language Development: Kindergarten through Grade Twelve* (Urbana, Ill.: National Council of Teachers of English, 1976).

CHAPTER ELEVEN
WRITING EXPRESSION

Scene A

"Well, class, I've handed back all of your compositions now. Some of you did a beautiful job and some of you have a lot of red marks on your papers," said Miss Ziph. "I want to talk to some of you who need help. You're first, William. Please bring your paper up to my desk. The rest of you begin rewriting your papers."

As two of his classmates smirked at him, Willie trudged up to the teacher's desk carrying his paper.

"You had some good ideas in your composition, William," Miss Ziph began. "You were supposed to write about freedom and you seemed to know what it is. But you made a lot of mistakes on sentences and paragraphs. Do you know what a sentence is?"

Willie tried to search his memory for the right words in spite of the anxiety he was feeling, but he couldn't remember.

"It's a group of words having a subject and a predicate that makes sense by itself," she offered. "Can you say that?"

Willie repeated the words obediently.

"Now," the teacher went on, "does this group of words make sense?"

"I-I guess not," mumbled Willie staring at the red marks.

After going through a number of sentence errors and mending each one in the manner Miss Ziph suggested, and after going through a similar process with his paragraphing errors, Willie was sent to his seat. He was still confused, however. He couldn't figure out what it was his teacher wanted.

Scene B

"Hi, Charlie," said Mr. Wang. "How's your letter coming?"

"Well, I think it's convincing," he answered. "My proofreading group thinks the editor might like it so much he'll print it in the newspaper. I'm still working on this one part, though. I'm having trouble coming up with the right words to say how run-down the ball field is in the park. I don't want it to sound like I'm just complaining."

"Let me look at it," said Mr. Wang. After a pause, he said, "I think you've chosen your words well, Charlie. Perhaps the problem is in your organization. Remember what we said about organizing a paragraph around a topic sentence?"

"I think so. Write a topic sentence; then write others to support it."

"OK, good; you remember. What's your main point in this part?"

"That the city should fix up the ball field. Oh, I know! I'll say that in one sentence and tell why in the others. Thanks, Mr. Wang!"

"Check to see if every sentence in the first paragraph is correct," he said as he smiled and walked to another desk.

When learners have gained enough confidence in their writing abilities that they can seriously begin to deal with writing mechanics, it is also time to begin working on written expression. Two types of mistakes must be avoided. One is emphasizing written expression too early, before confidence has been established. The other is emphasizing mechanics or creativity so strongly that expression is inadequately treated.

Written expression is a set of abilities and an awareness that leads the writer to write effectively. The abilities cover a wide range, but they are all geared toward the purpose of the written product. The awareness is that of knowing what the purpose is and who the product is written for. Like other aspects of writing, expression is gained over an extended period of time, is learned partially without instruction, and can be aided through appropriate teaching.

Expression is a very important part of writing. The most mechanically correct and creative paper, if it is not written effectively, is largely a waste of the writer's time. If it does not accomplish the purpose for which it was written, it has little value. In fact, attention to writing mechanics is justified mainly as a complement to written expression. Mechanics help make the writing clear, so that its purpose is not thwarted.

Of course, the purposes of writing vary. Every item we write has a somewhat unique purpose, but purposes fall into categories. Some things that we write, such as a grocery list for ourselves, are easy to write in a way that accomplishes their purposes. Other things that we write, such as a letter to the parents of a student, are difficult and frequently don't accomplish their purpose completely in spite of our efforts. As stated above, written expression involves not only an awareness of the written product's purpose, but a set of abilities required to write effectively for that purpose.

It is not as easy to identify the specific abilities used for expression as it is, for example, those for mechanics. Perhaps they differ from one individual to the next just as writing style does, and from one piece of writing to the next. However, a number of abilities are quite clearly needed most of the time and can be taught, or at least enhanced, in school. These are the ability to use grammar and write sentences, the ability to use vocabulary effectively, and the ability to organize writing around a purpose. An awareness of audience is just as necessary, although it can't be regarded as an ability or a skill.

GRAMMAR AND SENTENCES

If writing is to be effective, it must be executed in a manner that is understood by the reader. This can happen only if the writing uses a

Writing practice with feedback leads to effective written expression. (*Ken Karp*)

form that is familiar to the reader, which in nearly every case means a form that uses familiar language patterns. Because English syntax or grammar is rather uniformly consistent, the writer must know how to put language together in a manner that is grammatically appropriate. The degree to which the grammar used must follow rules of "standard" English depends on the purpose of the writing. A formal letter or report to educated people usually needs to be complete and "proper," but a note to a family member only needs to be understood.

Similarly, the degree to which a writer must use complete sentences depends on the purpose of the writing. A list, a schedule, or a reminder may be more effectively written with incomplete sentences. Certainly, there is a sharp limit to the types of writing that can be done effectively without understanding how to construct acceptable sentences.

Although they overlap, knowledge of grammar and knowledge of sentence structure are not the same. Preschoolers have a good working knowledge of grammar, and they apply it to their speaking and listening continuously. Yet, the majority of their speech is not in sentences. Even adults who know grammar very well speak mainly in other units of language-phrases, single words, and strings of language that are not confined to subject and predicate structures. Yet, such oral utterances are based on grammatical understandings, on knowledge of how language works.

Sentence construction is largely confined to communication that is written. It too is based on grammatical understandings, but requires an additional understanding as well. Both spoken and written language depend upon knowledge of how words and phrases modify each other, how one type of word (for example a noun marker like *a, the, this,* or *another*) signals that another type of word is about to follow (for example, a noun), and how word order affects meaning. But written language also depends upon an understanding of the "two partedness" (subject and predicate) of sentences.

Teaching Grammar

Although every child comes to school with a vast working knowledge of grammar, many children need to further develop this knowledge. Growth in grammatical understandings must be accomplished through guided *use* of language, not through study of its nature. Techniques for developing grammar were explained in detail in Chapter Ten.

Teaching Sentence Construction

Learning to write effective sentences involves at least three levels. At the simplest level, the child must learn what is and what isn't a sentence. To be effective, the learner must next learn how to write a variety of sentence patterns. Finally, the ability to select the most appropriate sentence pattern for a given occasion must be learned.

None of these levels is learned by memorizing rules. The child's ability to recite the words, "A sentence is a complete thought" or "A sentence has a subject and a predicate" may have nothing to do with sentence-writing ability. In the same way that they learn grammar, individuals learn to construct sentences by receiving guided practice in constructing them. Children who have many opportunities to put predicates and subjects together and to write and receive feedback on sentences are far more likely to develop the ability to write sentences than those who learn *about* sentences.

Putting together subjects and predicates is a good practice activity for a whole class. One effective way to do this is to let children manipulate subject and predicate strips or cards. An example may make this clear.

Miss Ellis distributed a strip of paper containing either a sentence subject or a sentence predicate to each second-grade child and kept one of each for herself. Calling the class to a part of the classroom where they could work on the floor, she laid out her two strips, "the dog" and "chased the cat."

"Does this sound like a sentence?" she asked. After an affirmative answer, she asked, "Does it *look* like a sentence?" The children knew that it didn't and paper punctuation and capitalization symbols were used to make the appearance right.

Miss Ellis then pulled the two strips apart and asked if anyone had a strip that could be added to the first one, "the dog," to make a sentence or a statement that sounded right. Connie placed "ate the sandwich" after Miss Ellis's subject card. After the class agreed that it was a sentence and after the capitalization and punctuation were taken care of, other volunteers placed sensible predicates on the floor. Then the same procedure was used to complete Miss Ellis's predicate strip. Finally, all of the subject strips were placed in one column and all of the predicates in another and the class manipulated them until thirteen sensible sentences had been constructed.

As an independent activity, children were allowed to write other sentences on paper strips, cut them in the right place, and put the two pieces in the proper columns on the floor. Thus, the learners had the opportunity to make discoveries about sentences, first by manipulating sentence parts in a structured situation and then by writing their own.

Similar types of activities can be used to practice the construction of other sentence patterns (see Box 10–1 in Chapter Ten for a list of common sentence patterns). With more complex patterns, such as the "subject-predicate-direct object-indirect object" pattern, it may be beneficial to use three strips of paper for each sentence (see Figure 11–1). In this way, learners can practice the second level of sentence writing development described earlier, writing a variety of patterns.

Even the third level of development, learning to select the most appropriate pattern for a given occasion, can best be learned through practice. Certainly, there are no rules that can be taught to help writers decide when to use certain types of sentence patterns. Manipulating subject and predicate strips, however, isn't helpful at this level. Such decision-making ability comes from practice writing in meaningful situations. An individual system for integrating context and purpose must be developed by each writer. The proofreading groups and teacher conferences described in Chapter Eight can be the most valuable resources to the developing writers who are experimenting with sentence patterns.

VOCABULARY

One of the most outstanding characteristics of effective writers is their ability to select words. By contrast, a common complaint of those who struggle with writing is that "the words just won't come." It would

FIGURE 11–1 Sample of scrambled sentence strips for a subject-predicate-direct object-indirect object sentence pattern.

seem, therefore, that teaching learners large quantities of words would help them a great deal with their writing. This is not necessarily the case, however.

Using Words in Writing

It is obvious that a person has to know some words, both in pronunciation and meaning, to be able to write. With the exception of some severely handicapped individuals, however, every schoolchild knows many hundreds, and most know thousands of words. They understand the words when they listen, they use them when they speak, and they know what they mean. If there is some minimal number of words that one must understand to be an effective writer, nearly everyone over the age of six has mastered it.

It is not the size of the writer's stock of words that makes her or him effective, it is the ability to select the right word at the right time. Of course, the individual who has a larger vocabulary has more choices, more selection capability. There is some advantage to knowing more words, especially if one of the purposes of writing is to impress someone. But this is of far less importance than the ability to *select* words.

Written expression is often used as an excuse for teaching large amounts of vocabulary and often for teaching it in negative ways. This happens because it is assumed that a large vocabulary is a very important factor in effective writing. It is also often assumed that such techniques as drills which promote memorization of isolated words and definitions, assignments to look up and copy dictionary definitions, and weekly vocabulary tests are effective in expanding vocabularies.

This latter assumption has a basis in research. Consistently, "direct instruction" in vocabulary has produced better vocabulary test scores than "incidental" learning, a term usually used to describe a program that encourages large amounts of independent reading. Vaughan, Crawley, and Mountain reviewed some of the reading research on this question, research conducted over a period of thirty years, and repeatedly found this result. There is very little agreement, however, about what is meant by direct instruction.[1] When success is measured in terms of students' ability to define words on vocabulary tests, many methods of vocabulary instruction have met with success. Some authorities have simply concluded that some instruction is better than none. As a result, even the bad techniques listed in the previous paragraph are widely used to increase test scores.

The problem with instruction that is geared toward better vocabulary scores is that effective writing depends on one's ability to *select* the right words, not on an ability to define them. It is better to use a small vocabulary effectively than to use a large one ineffectively. Furthermore, the techniques that are mentioned above tend to produce only short-term effects unless the learners have a true desire to learn the words. Far too frequently, the words and definitions are quickly forgotten once the test or practice activity has ended.

Improving Vocabulary

There are, however, three types of activities that teachers can use to improve writers' abilities to use words effectively. The first is wide exposure to language, the second is practice in meaningful writing, and the third is development of word flexibility.

Exposure to Language

Although the research discussed above gives strong evidence that direct instruction does more to improve vocabulary test scores than independent reading does, we have seen that this growth may be largely limited to test results. Broad exposure to literature, that is, to large quantities of reading in various fields, builds vocabulary also. It isn't as helpful for test scores, but reading gives learners countless models of words being used in meaningful ways. The same is true of exposure to language in other forms. By reading, listening to stories read to them, listening to meaningful speech, and conversing with peers, children learn how to use words in the same manner as they learned before they entered school.

Writing Practice

When left on their own to write, children tend to use words with which they are familiar in ways that are familiar as well. Sometimes new word uses are discovered this way, but writing without feedback doesn't usually result in much change. When proofreading groups and teacher conferences are used, however, vocabulary can grow along with writing mechanics, grammar, and spelling abilities. The techniques that are discussed in earlier chapters, then, are also useful in helping learners develop the ability to select words effectively.

Developing Word Flexibility

Writers can learn to make better use of the words they know if they can develop flexibility with them. Activities can be designed that give them practice in looking at words in several ways. Flexibility seems to rely on a full understanding of three concepts:

1. Many words have more than one meaning, and the appropriate meaning is determined by context.
2. Usually there is more than one word that can be selected to express an idea (synonyms).
3. Words can be selected on the basis of categories to which they belong.

Activities designed to develop flexibility will necessarily use specific words. The objective of the activity, however, is not that the learners remember the words or their definitions, although in some instances that will happen also, but that they expand the effectiveness of the words they know. Some examples follow.

*   *Identifying similar meanings.* Students are given a list of sentences, each containing the same word. Some of the sentences use the word in a manner that makes the meanings similar. Students find which sentences they are. For example:

Rob swung his *bat* at the ball.
The *bat* flew out of the cave into the dark night.
Mom put my *bat* and glove into the closet.
It's hard to hit with a broken *bat.*
It's your turn to *bat.*

* *Matching meanings.* Students are shown two columns of sentences. Every sentence contains the same word, but within each column it has a different meaning in each sentence. Students match a sentence from the first column with a sentence from the second column—both with words that have the same meaning. For example:

We had to *run* all the way home.	Will a stream *run* uphill?
Don't let the water *run* from the faucet.	Nylon material will easily get a *run.*
Dick got his second *run* of the game.	I'll *run* in the next race.
There was a *run* in her stocking.	The pitcher let in another *run.*

* *Challenge chart.* Students are challenged to find as many synonyms for a word in context as possible. After the teacher shows them a sentence (example: "The car *went* down the street"), they list words that could be used in place of the underlined word. As synonyms are given, the teacher records the words for all to see.
* *Ranking synonyms.* Johnson and Pearson have devised an activity which leads children to investigate the differences in shades of meaning among synonyms. A list of five or six synonyms is placed on the chalkboard and the class makes group decisions, by voting if necessary, about which of the words has the most intensity, strength, or approval. They then rank the remaining words in the same manner. Sometimes a helpful class discussion precedes these decisions.[2] Examples of such lists of synonyms are:

Loathe	Small	Like
Despise	Little	Tolerate
Dislike	Tiny	Love
Hate	Undersized	Adore
Abhor	Microscopic	Admire

- *Creating categories.* After students have been shown what to do, they create categories and then find words to fill their own categories. To demonstrate and explain the activity, the teacher might select two or three interesting categories and put them on the chalkboard. For example:

Sports	
Basketball	Field hockey
Baseball	Soccer
Football	Swimming
Hockey	Polo

Words that show anger	
Rage	Resentful
Irritated	Infuriated
Furious	Wrath
Mad	Peeved

Students then individually create categories and fill them with words. Discussions of how categories overlap might follow.

- *Categories game.* Groups of three or four students are formed and each individual competes against the other members of his or her group. Each player makes a small grid and places letters that have been agreed upon above the columns of the grid. Categories are determined and written beside the rows. For example:

	f	m	a
Vehicles			
Animals			
Liquids			

When the signal is given, each player tries to fill each box with a word that begins with the letter at the top of the column and belongs to the category indicated to the left of the row. Individuals attempt to use a word that they believe is different from the words used by others in the group. A point system is used to reward the use of unique words. After three to five minutes, time is called and the players in each group compare answers to determine scores. For every box each person receives the following scores:

For having a word different from that of anyone else, 10 points

For sharing a word with one other player, 5 points

For sharing a word with 2 or more other players, 1 point

For a blank, 0 points

For an incorrect word, minus 10 points

None of these activities is likely to greatly increase the number of words that learners can define, but that is not their purpose. These activities are designed to develop in children a sense of word flexibility. This is a third way that developing writers can improve their effective use of vocabulary.

ORGANIZING WRITING AROUND A PURPOSE

All of written expression makes sense only in the context of the purpose for the writing. Sentence structure, choice of words, and to some extent even writing mechanics are effective primarily to the extent that they fulfill that purpose. A distinct difference between writing which is expressive and that which is not is that the former consistently and continuously works toward an objective.

Of course, sentence structure, vocabulary, and mechanics are not enough to make a written product effective. All of these have to work together. They have to flow in a logical, smooth progression if the purpose is to be fulfilled. In other words, the writing has to be well organized. But the best organization for a given piece of writing also depends upon its purpose.

Establishing a Purpose

The first, and a crucial, step in any writing, then, is establishing a purpose. It is not usually difficult to determine the purpose of one's writing. When we write, we almost always know why. A difficulty in school writing is that frequently the real reason for writing is "the teacher says we have to," a purpose that most students would be reluctant to verbalize in class. If satisfying the teacher or getting a good grade is the real purpose for writing, it may be difficult for the student to identify another purpose when questioned by the teacher. The ideal solution to this problem, of course, is to use writing activities that have meaningful purposes, as discussed in earlier chapters.

Because school is not an ideal place, however, it is impossible to always create writing situations that are meaningful to every child. It is necessary, therefore, to guide many children in setting a purpose for writing. Setting purposes is not a "skill" in the usual sense of that word. We can't teach a child how to set them, give him or her practice in doing so, and hope that from then on he or she will always know how. It is, instead, an expectation. When learners have been led to identify the purpose of writing (beyond satisfying the teacher) often and consistently, they gradually develop the expectation that writing must have a purpose and they must be aware of what it is.

Each writing activity that is undertaken in a classroom, then, should include some attention to purpose setting before the first words are written down. If the whole class has the same purpose (as, for example, inviting parents to attend something at school), it can be briefly discussed with everyone. If each person has a somewhat different purpose (as when preparing for a language arts fair), individual attention will be needed. The teacher can circulate among the writers as they are beginning in a manner similar to that used later during proofreading conferences (see Chapter Eight). The brief amount of time that it takes to ask the class or individuals to simply identify their purposes is a good investment in later written expression.

Organizing the Writing

Once a writer has her or his purpose clearly in mind, it is possible to organize what he or she wants to say. As stated earlier, the best organization for a given piece of writing is the one that best fulfills its specific purposes. It is impossible, as a result, to set down rules or even guidelines for organizing one's writing. It is possible, however, to make students aware of, and give them practice in, three types of organizational strategy: sequencing, elaborating, and summarizing.

Sequencing

Putting thoughts in logical order is an important part of organization. What is and isn't logical not only varies from one situation to the next, but from one person to the next. The logic that is used, of course, must be the writer's, but the teacher can make writers aware of the importance of good sequencing and give them practice in thinking it through. The ability to put things in logical order is difficult for young children, but work can begin even in the early grades.

The easiest place to begin sequencing is in relating incidents in the order in which they happened. If there are not too many details, even young children can remember and record what happened first, second, and so on. Sequencing should not stop with chronological order, however. Learners should gradually be introduced to the importance of finding the best order for major ideas and specific sentences in all types of writing.

This ability can be approached at two levels, working through the sequence of another author's writing as a group or class and developing an awareness of sequence in the students' own individual writing. Like the other aspects of organization, direct instruction is impossible, but the teacher has an important role in guiding practice. The teacher can set up activities that vary with age.

- Children who have not yet learned many writing abilities can be helped with the first level, sequencing another author's writing, by deciding upon the logical order for pictures or simple line drawings. For example:

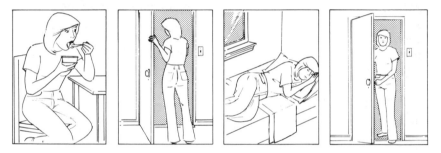

  Learners might arrange the cards on which the drawings appear in a number of sequences that make sense. Individuals who arrange the cards in a given way (perhaps by placing them in a chalk ledge) tell brief stories to accompany their selected sequences. The individual frames from comic strips can be cut apart and used in the same manner by individuals and small groups.
- Older learners who still need help with sequencing can practice ordering the sentences of a paragraph that has been cut apart. To avoid the implication that there is only one right order in which the sentences can be placed, this is better done by the whole class or in group discussion. Obviously, if the paragraph deals with a topic of interest to the learners, the practice will be better motivated.

Such activities, however, serve mainly to make potential writers aware of the *importance* of sequencing. The extent to which sequencing ability can be transfered directly from such activities to their own written products is unknown. Yet, this is where organization really counts. Once awareness has been achieved, the teacher can help writers apply sequencing to their writing through frequent reminders and feedback. The reminders can be given at the beginning of writing activities or at any other time, and the feedback from the teacher can be given during conferences. When learners find that order receives this much attention in the writing program, they begin to anticipate including it when they are polishing their writing and meeting in proofreading groups.

Elaborating and Summarizing

Saying the right amount at the right time is another aspect of good organization. Telling too much or too little about a given idea within a written work can bore the reader, give insufficient information, or misplace the emphasis. Similarly, the entire piece of writing can be inappropriately lengthy or short for its purpose. As with sequencing, there are few guidelines that can be learned and applied to all writing, for the purpose again determines organization.

One rule of thumb, however, that can easily be learned and adapted to most situations is that length greatly influences emphasis. Generally, ideas that deserve greater emphasis within a written work should be given more space. Another rule of thumb that is helpful in some situations is the journalists' list of "who, what, where, when, and why." In many types of writing answers to these questions serve as a minimum.

In order to adjust length, students of writing need to learn how to elaborate and summarize ideas. Children who have made normal progress in school should be ready for this aspect of writing by the time they are in third or fourth grade. Elaborating involves adding more details, background, or support information to an idea, not just adding words or repetitions. Summarizing usually means finding a way to say an idea in fewer words by reporting only the most important details, background, or arguments.

The overall approach to helping learners improve their elaborating and summarizing is like that of sequencing. Students practice with the writing of other authors so that they become aware of the importance of these two techniques, and then they are guided to use them in their own writing. One important difference is that passages of greater length are usually needed to practice elaborating and summarizing, for the role of length in establishing emphasis can rarely be demonstrated in the space of a simple paragraph. Here is a logical sequence for building these techniques:

1. Give middle-grade learners clearly stated passages and let them list the author's points or ideas. Then let them judge the emphasis placed on each point by looking at the space devoted to it.
2. Hand out passages of various lengths, for each passage guide students to find the main idea or ideas, and let the class rework the writing into a brief summary.
3. Read or tell a series of events, a set of arguments, or some other presentation. Show a brief written summary of the presentation. Have the class elaborate on the summary.
4. Through reminders and individual conferences, guide students to apply appropriate summarizing and elaborating techniques when meeting in proofreading groups and when polishing their own writing.

Paragraphing

Stallard describes the typical student approach to paragraphing in the following manner: "When the urge hits them they indent and go on until the urge strikes again."[3] He points out that this gross misunderstanding of the nature and content of a paragraph is a result of insistence by schools that children use paragraphs without first teaching them other aspects of composition. Perhaps his assertion that most students write this way is somewhat overstated, but paragraphing is clearly difficult for many children, and the reasons he gives for this seem plausible.

Paragraphing is easy to learn only after the other components of written expression, as described above, are understood. A purpose and a sense of organization are especially needed before paragraphs can be written effectively. If writing does not follow a sequence geared toward an objective, if it does not flow from one point to the next, dividing it into paragraphs doesn't make a lot of sense.

Only two paragraphing concepts, both of which are related to the content of the writing, need to be mastered by the student who already knows how to deal with purpose and organization. The first is that the central idea of paragraphing is that each paragraph has a central idea. In order to construct paragraphs, learners must be led to see that their writing is most effective when they explain one idea at a time. The other significant concept that must be learned is that a paragraph has a topic sentence upon which all the other sentences are built. When these two concepts are understood, knowing where to end a paragraph and remembering to indent are relatively easy.

In most cases, the content material that should be used to introduce the two major concepts is, again, that of another author. The student should be led to examine a passage containing several paragraphs, to identify the overall topic or purpose of the passage, and to decide what the topic of each paragraph is. This can probably best be done as a class activity rather than as an independent assignment, so that discussion and group interaction can add to the learning situation. After all, there is usually room for some opinion when trying to decide upon the specific topic someone else had in mind when writing. The objective of this passage examination is *not* to identify the *right* paragraph descriptions, but to build awareness that each paragraph has a topic.

As the paragraph topics are identified, they can be listed on the chalkboard in outline form. This not only builds the desired concept, but gives students a realistic view of outlining. There is a controversy among language arts experts about whether or not students should be asked to outline their ideas before they begin a writing product of any length. One view is that such a practice is very useful in the development of a sense or organization. The other view is that such a practice throttles creativity and individual style because good writers usually develop their content as they write. A realistic solution to the controversy is to teach outlining as a self-checking technique that individuals can use *after they write,* to see if their material is organized.

After analyzing and outlining other authors' material on several occasions, students are usually ready to begin working on their own paragraphs. If they have been confused about the nature of paragraphs until this time, or if this is their first exposure, a very simple beginning should be used. In spite of the advantage in most situations of using larger context, it is probably best to take one paragraph at a time at first. Recalling what was learned about paragraph topics earlier, each individual writes a sentence describing or stating something and then writes several sentences elaborating on the first one. One good approach for introducing this type of technique is to ask, "What is your favorite———?" (example: television show, sport, singing group). In the first sentence, the writers identify their favorite and in the other sentences tell why. Other types of paragraphs are then introduced.

When the two concepts of paragraphing have been learned through such activities, learners should be encouraged to follow through in their regular writing program. As with the other parts of written expression, this encouragement can come through proofreading groups and individual teacher conferences.

AWARENESS OF AUDIENCE

Gearing writing toward the specific audience for which it is intended is one of the most important aspects of written expression. We have seen that the organization, choice of vocabulary, and other components of expression make sense mainly in the light of the *purpose* of the writing. Usually, the purpose is slanted toward a certain person or toward specific groups of people. For example, if a businessman writes a letter to a congressional representative who supports a bill that threatens his business and another letter to a potential customer, the two letters must contain different lines of reasoning, different organization, and different types of vocabulary. Yet, the purpose of each is to convince someone. A teacher writing an evaluation of a student and a report to parents would experience some of the same differences, because effective writing is geared toward its audience.

Rosen has identified four main categories of audience: self as audience, teacher as audience, another known audience, and an unknown audience.[4] Nearly all students learn to write with an awareness of their teacher as audience, sometimes paying so much attention to what the teacher wants that creativity is limited. However, other types of audience awareness are often neglected.

Gearing one's writing to a certain audience involves somewhat advanced abilities. Kroll has suggested that the ability to put oneself in the shoes of the listener or reader is beyond the potential of the typical primary-grade child. While young children can easily identify whom they are writing to or for, they are unable to adjust their writing accordingly.[5] Piaget has explained this inability in terms of young children's egocentrism, their underlying assumption that if they understand what they mean their audiences must also.[6] Developing the ability to write for an audience, therefore, is another challenge with which the writing program must deal.

Developing Audience Awareness

There are a number of strategies that can be used, and a number of practices that can be avoided, by the teacher to bring out awareness of audience. It is evident that awareness needs to be brought out, for many students become adults without ever developing the ability to gear their writing to an audience. Perhaps an unpleasant, but not so uncommon, description of what can go wrong in a classroom writing program will clarify this point.

In many classrooms, children in primary grades are given countless writing tasks. Some are simply filling in blanks, while others are larger and may sometimes be related to more interesting topics. All of these writing tasks are similar in that the unspoken purpose is to please the teacher, a purpose that is easy for most six- to nine-year-olds to adopt. The blanks are filled in so they can be marked as correct by the teacher, the assigned sentences and similar tasks are done for the same reason, and "creative writing" is done to win positive symbols or comments. As the children mature and their egocentrism declines, they reach a point where they could deal with seeing the reader's viewpoint, with writing for an audience. However, they have been silently and unknowingly trained for several years to believe the teacher is the only audience that counts. Instead of learning to deal with other audiences, they become more aware than before that writing for the teacher is important. Thus, some learners become very good at writing for the teacher.

The teacher's praise gives some of them the confidence to become good writers even for other audiences. For the children whose poor writing mechanics or other problems prevent them from learning the necessary techniques to please the teacher, however, there is no happy ending. Usually, the rejection prevents them from ever becoming confident as writers, and they certainly never develop a sense of audience. Possibly, some of the students who learn to write for the teacher never develop very effective techniques in writing for other audiences as well. None of the students in such an unhappy situation develop as much awareness as they might.

Practices to Avoid

The practices that teachers should avoid, then, are those that approximate the situation first described. Even in primary grades, writing to win teacher approval should be de-emphasized. Feedback that is limited to an overall grade or evaluation or that is mainly concerned with writing mechanics should be avoided. Finally, the practice that most needs to be avoided is *ignoring* audience awareness.

Techniques to Use

On the other hand, there are techniques that can be used to foster such writing abilities. In the primary grades, when little can be expected in the actual audience slant of the writing, the emphasis will be limited to recognizing for whom the writing is intended. Even this

is important, however, for young children who are constantly re-
minded of who their audience will be are less likely to think of the
teacher as the only audience. Reminders from the teacher before and
during writing activities help. Evaluative comments during individual
conferences that speak to how well the intended reader will receive the
written product help even more. Of course, all of these suggestions
presuppose that there really *is* an audience, that much of the writing
that occurs in school is meaningful and has a genuine purpose.

Middle-grade learners can be guided to begin the type of writing
that is actually geared toward an audience in choice of content, selection of organization and vocabulary, and use of sentence construction
and paragraphing. As with the other areas of written expression, there
are no specific skills that can be taught or rules that can be laid down
that will fit all occasions. Instead, developing writers need to experiment with slanting their writing to accomplish a specific purpose with
a specific audience, receive feedback on their attempts, and practice
frequently.

Specific Activities

There are some specific activities that can be used to provide
these three ingredients. They all involve giving writers a reason for
writing differently for different audiences. For each of the following
suggestions, the teacher should first make certain the writers understand the purpose, lead a discussion on the nature of the audience, and
point out some possible general strategies in writing for that audience.

- Students write letters of invitation to at least two classrooms,
  inviting them to an event in their own classroom. Students write
  a letter to children of at least their own age and one to young
  children, gearing the letters to the appropriate age level.
- Students write a news article from two points of view. One way
  to do this is to supply the class with copies of a briefly summarized ball game between two fictitious or real teams (see Box
  11–1). Half the class rewrites the story as if they were sportswrit-
  ers from the losing team's hometown and the other half from the
  winning side's. Samples of both points of view are then shared
  with the class. This activity is also useful when each individual
  writes both points of view, and it certainly need not be limited to
  sports reporting.
- Students write directions to a simple game or other physical
  activity. The directions are then given to other students who have

WHOSE SIDE ARE YOU ON?

In a close game, the Bakersville Birds defeated the Lewistown Lizards last night 7 to 6. The first 2 innings were scoreless. In the 3rd inning, the Bird's Bert Jones and Len Smith each singled. After a walk by John Johnson, Bill Benson doubled and drove in 2 Bird runs. The 4th inning was scoreless. In the 5th, Lizard Bob Bone doubled and his team mate Mark Maze walked. After the next 2 batters struck out, Kent Clark hit a home run, giving the Lizards a 3 to 2 lead. In a series of walks and singles, the Birds scored once more in the 6th. In each of the next 2 innings the Birds scored twice while holding the Lizards scoreless. A home run by Marty Clobber with 2 men on in the 9th gave the Lizards 3 more runs, but the game ended at 7 to 6.

never played the game or performed the activity. The writer observes the attempts to follow the directions, noting what problems arise, but does not make further explanatory comments. The writer then rewrites the directions and tries them out with other students until they are followed satisfactorily.

Combining Purpose with Audience

In the world outside of school, the purpose of a piece of writing and its intended audience are usually so closely intertwined they can't be separated. A letter is written *to* a friend *for the purpose* of informing her of personal news and of convincing her that the friendship is still strong. A requisition is written *to* a superior *for the purpose* of convincing him of the need for new equipment. A letter is written *to* an editor *for the purpose* of evaluating some event.

After learners have used some practice activities dealing with audience awareness, therefore, they need to apply their emerging abilities to real writing situations. They must develop the expectation that before any writing is begun, the purpose as it relates to a given audience must be determined. In establishing this audience purpose, it is useful to know four general types of objectives that are available to writers (and speakers).

The four objectives are informing, convincing, entertaining, and expressing emotions. Informing includes such specific tasks as describing, giving directions, evaluating, and questioning. Certain types or parts of letters, reports, applications, and news articles are examples of writing to inform. Writing to convince can be found in such products as sales literature, personal letters, and letters to editors or government officials. Writing to entertain or express emotions is usually limited to personal or private communication. Details about building abilities to inform, convince, and so on are found in Chapter Four, "Developing Verbal Expression," and can easily be adapted to the area of writing.

EVALUATING WRITTEN EXPRESSION

There are standardized tests that claim to measure aspects of written expression. However, these tests do little to measure expression as it is discussed in this chapter. While such abilities as identifying good and poor sentences, choosing the best word or expression, and sentence arranging are sometimes included, they are out of context. They don't tap the writer's ability to determine a purpose for a given audience and organize a piece of writing around it. The information that the teacher can gain from such measures of general abilities in paragraphing, sentencing, and other areas is useful, but standardized tests don't measure the real essence of written expression. Much more is needed.

The real evaluation of progress in written expression must come from the students' meaningful written products. As the teacher holds brief individual conferences with children and as the final written products are surveyed, evaluations must be made in terms of the various elements of expression that are discussed in this chapter. Each written product of each individual must be evaluated separately, because the purpose and audience of that specific product must be considered before the evaluation can be completed.

Of course, a teacher can't possibly remember and compare the progress of every individual child over a very long period of time. As with many of the other areas of language arts, some type of recording system must be used to keep a history of progress. A checklist is probably the most practical tool, especially with children in the middle grades, from whom most of the expression growth is expected. Because this aspect of writing will be evaluated during the same individual conferences with writing mechanics and grammar, it would make most sense to add the components of written expression to the checklist already recommended for these other areas (see Figure 8–2). The items to be included in such a checklist are the ones discussed in this chapter:

Sentence construction

Vocabulary

Setting and following a purpose

Organization

Paragraph writing

Awareness of audience

By the time the checklist in Figure 8–2 has additions for spelling, handwriting, grammar, and written expression, it could become quite lengthy. However, not every area of writing needs to be recorded for every child every time he or she writes. Rather, the evaluation and record keeping need to be an ongoing process in which the teacher notes the greatest strengths and needs whenever the circumstances call for it and time allows. Enough information needs to be recorded to give a picture of progress, but evaluation procedures should not be so time consuming that they interfere with teaching or learning.

SUMMARY

Written expression is an aspect of writing that is often neglected by schools. Yet, it is at least as important as the other aspects. A written product with near-perfect punctuation, capitalization, spelling, and other elements that doesn't accomplish its purpose is of little value.

Written expression is a set of abilities and an awareness that enable a person to write effectively, to accomplish the purpose of the writing. The awareness involved is that of knowing the purpose and the audience for whom the writing is intended. The abilities required vary greatly, but usually include those of using grammar, selecting sentence patterns, choosing vocabulary, organizing, and paragraphing in ways that best fulfill the purpose.

The best method for helping children develop such awareness and abilities is to give them many guided writing experiences. This chapter also includes specific activities that help student writers see the importance of various components of expression and develop some general strategies. However, there are no rules or specific skills in selecting sentence patterns, vocabulary, and organization that can be taught. Written expression is learned as students are guided through frequent and meaningful writing activities.

The two teachers illustrated in the episodes in the chapter opening were much different in their apparent understanding of these facts. Miss Ziph evidently believed that rule learning was the key to correct sentences and paragraphs. She also provided a writing experience that had doubtful purpose or meaning to the writers. The student involved had no intended audience except the teacher and the purpose seemed to be to please her. Mr. Wang, the other teacher, seemed to have a much better understanding of written expression. The writing activity was meaningful, the purpose and audience were clear to the student, and the learning of abilities was largely through discovery and experience. Of course, the two teachers also had a vastly different approach to relating to children and, therefore, to building confidence as well.

This and the previous five chapters have all dealt with the school's writing program. This is appropriate because writing is certainly an important part of the language arts. If there is a theme to be found in all of these chapters it is that writing is learned mainly through writing. This concept leaves the teacher with an enormous task, that of providing students with meaningful writing tasks and using these tasks to help learners discover how to write. This is a greater challenge than simply teaching prescribed skills from a text book.

NOTES

1. Sally Vaughan, Sharon Crawley, and Lee Mountain, "A Multiple-Modality Approach to Word Study: Vocabulary Scavenger Hunts," *Reading Teacher*, 32 (January 1979), 434–37.

2. Dale D. Johnson and P. David Pearson, *Teaching Reading Vocabulary* (New York: Holt, Rinehart and Winston, 1978), p. 41.

3. Charles K. Stallard, "Writing Readiness: A Developmental View," *Language Arts*, 54 (October 1977), 777.

4. Harold Rosen, "Written Language and the Sense of Audience," *Educational Research*, 15 (1973), 177–87.

5. Barry M. Kroll, "Developing a Sense of Audience," *Language Arts*, 55 (October 1978), 828–31.

6. Jean Piaget, *The Language and Thought of the Child*, trans. Marjorie Gabain (New York: New American Library, 1955), p. 119.

CHAPTER TWELVE
READING AND LANGUAGE

It has long been acknowledged that reading and the other language arts are closely related. The fact that reading is one of the four major forms of communication is seldom disputed. In practice, however, reading instruction is usually totally isolated from language arts instruction. In the vast majority of classrooms, a language arts period is scheduled separately from reading; language arts and reading are regarded as two separate subject areas, each with its own textbook; and the two subjects are not coordinated in any manner.

Even in the classrooms where a conscious effort is made to combine reading and the other language arts, the relationship is usually limited to the concept of one area helping the other. Reading is used to help writing by providing a basis or springboard for the writing. Reading is used as a means of developing listening comprehension. Listening to children's literature is a technique used to help build reading motivation or interest. To be sure, all of these coordinated uses of communication forms are excellent. Teachers who use reading as a device to help writing and other areas should be commended for their insight and often for their courage. However, such activities do not necessarily reflect a total understanding of the relationship between reading and the other language arts.

In recent years, a great deal of theory construction and research has centered around the relationship of language and reading. Some of the research deals specifically with the relationship between writing and reading.[1] But the more general overall relationship of reading and language has received even more attention. Three general points of view seem to have emerged, and reading experts tend to lean toward one camp or another. In order to better understand how reading and language are related and how this relationship affects the classroom, we must first look at the three viewpoints.

THREE VIEWS OF READING AND LANGUAGE

The three theories that have emerged in the area of reading are not actually *limited* to the relationship of reading and other forms of language. They are models or theories that attempt to explain the entire reading process, the mental procedures followed when a reader interacts with a page. The central issue in the three views, however, is how the reader uses language to read. The popular names for the three are *bottom-up, top-down,* and *interactive.*

Reading is one of the major forms of communication. (*Ken Karp*)

Bottom-Up

The several bottom-up theories share a common belief that reading is a process of recognizing words and their individual meanings and then piecing these together to derive sentence and paragraph meaning. The popular name comes from the fact that word recognition is regarded as a low level or "bottom" process and understanding the meaning is a high level or "top" process. Word recognition may include use of phonics or other "sounding out" techniques and may include recognition of whole words or "sight words." Thus, bottom-up theories hold that the reader starts at the bottom, with word recognition, and ends at the top, with meaning.

Such a viewpoint gives very little recognition to the role of language in the process of reading. All that is needed, according to this view, is that readers understand the language of the text well enough to piece together the individual word meanings. The process involves something similar to listening to yourself to find out what you're saying. As the reader identifies word after word, silently or orally, he listens to himself to find familiar language, and this is how sentence meaning is derived. However, the role of language context in helping readers to identify words, or even to skip over words and seek meaning directly, is not dealt with in this view.

Top-Down

Top-down theories adhere to the belief that the process of reading, at least for good readers, begins with meaning rather than with words. Readers already have a pretty good idea about what a group of words will say before they look at them, if the words appear in a large context. From their understanding of the author's message in previous groups of words, sentences, and paragraphs, readers are able to predict approximately what the author will say in the next group of words before focusing upon them. Only enough information needs to be gained from the words themselves to be able to confirm or alter the prediction. Thus, top-down theories hold that proficient reading starts at the top, with meaning, and goes down to word recognition to the extent that it is necessary.

Such a viewpoint gives a person's knowledge of language a great deal of credit in making reading function properly. It is the reader's understanding of language on a much larger scale than that of individual words that makes predicting possible. The reader is unaware that he or she is using context or that individual words receive limited attention, for meaning of the passage as a whole is kept at the front of attention. Two properties of language are seen as contributing clues to the reader so he or she can make predictions—semantic and syntactic. Semantics, the underlying meaning of the author's message, contributes clues because the reader is able to take advantage of the redundancy that is so common in language and to follow the author's sequence or line of logic. Syntax, or grammar, provides clues because the reader is familiar with the sentence patterns and informal rules of language that are used again and again and is therefore able to predict the form or structure of the next group of words. Smith compares this process of predicting and confirming to the procedures used by scientists to generate and test hypotheses.[2]

Interactive

Interactive theories lie somewhere between the other two. The reading process, as seen from this viewpoint, continuously uses both word recognition and higher-level meaning clues. Stanovich has developed an explanation of reading from this view which he calls the *Interactive-Compensatory Model.*[3] According to this view, readers use word recognition and meaning clues simultaneously. Meaning is the objective, but the process involves both sources of clues, and the degree to which each is used depends on the individual and the situation. If a person is weak in either word recognition or the use of semantics and syntax, either source of information can partially compensate for the other.

This compensation is seen as an explanation for individual differences in learning to read.

Interactive theories view the reader's use of language in much the same way as top-down theories do. The reader uses the same two properties of language, semantics and syntax, to get meaning from the author's message. The reader is again unaware of how context and individual words are being processed. The difference between these two theories is in the *amount* of dependency the reader has upon language knowledge. In top-down theories, reading depends very heavily upon the meaning and structure clues found in the language of the surrounding context and uses the individual words only to check predictions. In interactive theories, reading depends somewhat less on language, because word recognition and clues from context interact with each other.

Evaluation of the Three Views

As is common with most systems of classifying ideas, the differences among the three viewpoints just described aren't as clear as their supporters might contend or as Figure 12–1 might imply. This is especially true of the top-down and interactive theories. Even Kenneth S. Goodman, whose theory about reading as a psycholinguistic guessing game is cited by many as the original top-down theory, denies that his position is really top-down.[4]

FIGURE 12–1 Three theories about language and reading.

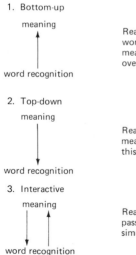

1. Bottom-up

   meaning

   word recognition

   Reader begins by recognizing words and then pieces word meanings together to construct overall meaning.

2. Top-down

   meaning

   word recognition

   Reader understands overall meaning of passage and uses this to predict specific words.

3. Interactive

   meaning

   word recognition

   Reader uses meaning of the passage and word recognition simultaneously.

However, the research evidence that reading is *not* a bottom-up process is mounting and becoming more and more convincing.[5] The idea that good readers identify the pronunciation and meaning of each word and then piece these together to understand the author's message is no longer acceptable. Some of the problems with a belief that reading demands exact word recognition can be illustrated.

First, notice how long it takes you to answer the question in the box.

How quickly can you
find the error in
in this sentence?

If you are like most experienced readers, you had to read the sentence several times before you noticed the repeated word. This small illustration may remind you of proofreading that you have done. Most of us sometimes fail to notice obvious errors, especially in our own writing, even if we have carefully proofread the written product. It may even be embarrassing to have someone else show us how obvious the undiscovered error was. When we proofread our own writing we know what the text was supposed to say and don't notice what is really there. Both of these experiences illustrate the fact that often we read what we *expect* to see on the page rather than using a process that recognizes each individual word.

A second illustration deals with reading when parts of the words are missing. The following sentence is probably difficult to read because so much has been left out.

the- sec- - - ba- - - - - cau- - - - l-n- dr- - - a- - thr- - - - h-m-.

If, however, you know that the sentence came from a description of a baseball game, the sentence is easy to read. Of course, it still would be difficult to someone who knew little about baseball. Because most of our reading is in areas with which we are already familiar, however, we can usually read without looking at each letter or even each word. In this illustration, only twenty letters were left in the sentence and twenty-six were taken out. Simply knowing that the sentence was about a baseball game gave us enough clues to read the sentence. When a sentence or group of words appears in a complete passage, the number of semantic and syntactic clues available from context is even greater.

This seems to clearly indicate that good readers don't *need* to look at every word.

A final illustration that reading doesn't depend on word recognition will require that you time yourself as you read. Better yet, if someone else times you, accuracy in timing may improve. Below are two groups of words. Read the first one with as much speed and accuracy as possible while being timed. Note the number of seconds and then do exactly the same thing with the second group of words.

> his the Mrs. tried eyes the silently his would focused all print the hoping to run of on to him frightened seemed but read Jones one together child in he notice blue on today him sat his wouldn't keep page to into call large teacher chair

> The frightened child sat silently in his chair, hoping his teacher wouldn't notice him. He tried to keep his eyes focused on the page, but all of the print seemed to run together into one large blur. Would Mrs. Jones call on him to read today?

Both groups of words are exactly the same except for word order and punctuation. Unless you totally gave up on the first group of words and simply skimmed through it, you probably read the second group much more quickly. Your time on the second reading probably approximates your normal reading rate. If you had to look at every word, as you did with the first reading, you would usually read more slowly. This illustration seems to show that good readers normally don't take the time required to read each word.

The most logical explanation of the evidence brought out in these illustrations and shown by recent research is that good readers use something more than lower-level word recognition to process the printed page. The "something more" is a combination of background experience and understanding of language.

Experience allows the reader to use semantic, or meaning, clues more easily because the familiar is always easier to understand than the unfamiliar. Just as the sentence with the deleted parts was much easier to read once it was associated with a familiar sports activity, anything is easier to read when it can be associated with familiar experiences.

Knowledge of language aids in the use of semantic clues also, for the person very familiar with his language realizes how repetitious or redundant it tends to be. Knowing what meaning to anticipate or to predict in the upcoming group of words is partly a result of language knowledge. Evidently, however, an understanding of language is even more useful in using syntactic, or grammatical, clues. If English is repetitious in its systems for representing meaning, it is more so in its use of sentence patterns. A reader is usually able to use her or his understanding of common sentence patterns and grammar to predict what *kinds* of words are in the upcoming phrase or word group. It may not yet be clear how important the distinction between top-down and interactive theories is or which one is more accurate, but the importance of language and experience is becoming very clear.

The evidence is growing, then, that bottom-up theories of reading don't explain very much of the reading process. Yet, school reading programs that are committed to bottom-up approaches are abundant. Word recognition, in fact, is being given more attention now than ever before. Many schools are even subscribing to so-called *systems* approaches to reading, wherein the reading program is divided into thousands of small teachable pieces with little regard for the role of language. There is a great need for teachers and schools to become aware that reading is an interaction between a page and a reader who brings large quantities of experience and language to the situation.

IMPLICATIONS FOR THE CLASSROOM

An understanding of how reading and the other language arts are related should lead to some changes in the school's instructional program. This usually doesn't mean throwing away the existing reading program or the purchase of any new instructional materials. The attention to language that is needed can be added to nearly any reading approach that isn't limited to word recognition. However, there is a need in many programs to make a shift in emphasis and to modify several practices that are frequently used in the teaching of word recognition and comprehension. Because the teaching of reading could never be adequately described in a single chapter, this text doesn't deal with specific techniques for doing so. It is important here, however, to explore the implications of the reading/language relationship upon word recognition and comprehension instruction.

Word Recognition

The three major theories of reading are concerned mainly with how individuals read after they are proficient in the process. An understanding of proficient reading is absolutely essential if a reading and language arts program is to have realistic goals. However, the theories do not deal at all with *learning* to read. Yet, learning is the area with which teachers are most concerned. One of the greatest concerns is over word recognition. If proficient reading seems to use clues from language more than clues from individual words, is there a place for word recognition in school?

By most definitions, word recognition consists of four somewhat separate groups of skills: phonics, structural analysis, word patterning, and sight-word recognition. Phonics skills are used to associate sounds with individual letters or groups of letters in order to, piece by piece, determine the pronunciation of a word. Structural analysis skills are used to take words apart into such units as syllables, prefixes, and suffixes in order to determine the pronunciations of these larger units within words. Word patterning skills are used to determine the pronunciations of words that are members of patterns, such as *Dan, fan, man,* and *tan.* Sight words are recognized as word wholes without any need to "sound out" components of the words.

While there is some controversy over the amount and the type or types of word recognition skills that should be taught, few reading authorities deny their importance. Even from a top-down point of view, clues from individual words are used to the extent that they confirm or alter the reader's predictions. From an interactive point of view, word recognition may sometimes be as important as the use of semantic and syntactic clues.

The main function of word recognition skills, however, is to get children started in reading. Because the theories described above do not deal with methods for beginning reading instruction, it is impossible to determine from them what role word skills should play. There is, however, a general consensus among teachers and reading authorities that learning to read begins with recognizing words. There is also research evidence that children learn to read individual words before they learn other aspects of the reading process. Delores Durkin, for example, found that preschoolers who taught themselves to read did so mainly through reading, writing, and asking questions about specific words.[6] Evidently, word recognition is the device that triggers later reading ability.

Once the initial stage of learning to read is past, on the other hand, the importance of word recognition begins to decline. The use of context, that is, semantic and syntactic clues, gains more and more importance. The degree to which the use of these clues replaces word recognition is uncertain. According to interactive theory the two ideally become somewhat equal, and according to top-down theory the use of context clues becomes the primary force in reading. It is clear, though, that word recognition is mainly a set of skills to get young readers started. The goals of a reading program must deal with the use of context clues at least as much as with word recognition.

These theories provide a number of implications for the classroom. Each of the implications below is based on the assumption that word recognition must be taught with the limitations in mind that were just discussed.

1. Phonics, structural analysis, word-pattern skills, and sight words should be taught as part of a beginning reading program.

2. In order to keep a continuous focus on the fact that the purpose of reading is to understand meaning, the word recognition skills in the first item should be presented in a meaningful context. This can be done in a number of ways. Once in a while, a teacher can take advantage of a situation where children need to learn a skill in order to read something they *want* to read. Usually, however, the context will consist of applying the skill to a written passage at least one paragraph in length. For example, after children have been taught a common pronunciation of a letter, they should be given a paragraph to read in which they must apply their new knowledge, even if the teacher must help them read the other parts of the paragraph. No phonics or other skill lesson should end without some direct and obvious tie being made between word recognition and the process of getting meaning. Children should never be misled into viewing word skills as an end in themselves.

3. Learners should be encouraged to make sense of what they are reading rather than to pronounce each word exactly. Remembering that good readers don't even look at each word, teachers must stop giving the impression that reading is word perfection. When a child is stuck on a word, the teacher should ask, "What would make sense here?" or "What would make sense here that starts with the letter *b*?" The typical demand in such situations to sound out the word is usually unfair and, when repeated continuously, discourages use of context. Oral reading in front of an audience, especially when it is unrehearsed, also needs to be severely limited for the same reason.

4. When students have achieved a reasonable degree of fluency in reading and give evidence that they are using language context, word recognition instruction should stop. Exactly when such fluency occurs is not clear and probably varies, but a reasonable

guess is that learners who can read third-grade material with understanding need little more word skill instruction.

5. Children who develop some reading ability but continue to focus on each word individually ("word by word" readers) need help with using context rather than with more phonics or other word skills.

Comprehension

The three theories discussed in the first part of this chapter deal primarily with the way good readers use language to get meaning from print. Getting meaning is usually referred to as *comprehension.* As with word recognition, however, the theories never deal with methods of teaching comprehension.

By far, the most common way to deal with comprehension in the schools' reading programs is to use the format provided in the teacher's guide of most elementary-school reading texts. Sometimes called a *directed reading activity,* this format calls for an elaborate introduction of a story or other reading passage and substantial guidance from the teacher as learners read a few pages at a time. The guidance consists mainly of question asking, with the questions coming largely from the teacher's guide.

Neither a top-down nor an interactive view of reading speaks against the use of guided reading. But if language and reading are closely related, and if reading makes heavy use of context clues, some changes are necessary in the way that such guided reading is used. The following implications seem reasonable.

1. Because readers' expectations about a passage have a large influence on their ability and motivation to make predictions from context, it is important that they have a meaningful purpose for reading. All too often, students read because they "have to" or because they need to please the teacher. Such a purpose greatly reduces comprehension. Teacher's guides usually identify a purpose, but *telling* readers why they should read is ineffective unless they adopt the purpose as their own. One way to give classroom reading a better purpose than that of pleasing the teacher is to supplement textbook reading with purposeful reading such as letters from pen pals, directions for games or interesting activities, or scripts from television shows. Another way to give meaningful purposes is to allow time for, and to encourage, a great deal of independent, self-selected reading. When guided lessons

from reading texts are used, students can be given a voice in selecting which story they will read next, even if this means that not all of the reading text will be "covered" in a year. Having a choice in what one reads allows a person to identify with the choice and to establish one's own purpose.

2. Learners' overall comprehension abilities will probably improve as their overall language abilities improve. Both semantic and syntactic context clues are useful to the reader only to the extent the language is understood. In Chapter Ten the point is made that knowledge of grammar is useful in both writing and reading. This is true because grammar, or syntax, provides one of the main types of context clues described earlier in this chapter. Therefore, the practices and techniques which are described for developing knowledge of grammar in Chapter Ten should be used also to improve reading comprehension. In addition, the teaching techniques suggested for speaking, listening, and writing that are given throughout this text will help readers. Experience with language itself, which these techniques provide, gives readers the background necessary to take advantage of semantic clues.

3. The emphasis of teachers' questions must be on the message of the author rather than on specific facts within the text. Several types of research have shown that the majority of questions asked during classroom guided reading seek "literal" answers, those that are explicitly stated in the passage and require only sheer memorization by the child. Such questions are necessary some of the time, but an overemphasis on them over a period of time is likely to develop habits of reading for details that please the teacher rather than developing the expectation that reading should make sense.

Reading as a Whole

As the implications listed in both the word recognition and comprehension sections above indicate, there is more to reading than using a collection of skills. Children cannot be taught a series of isolated word recognition skills and some so-called comprehension skills with the expectation that this is all they need to learn to read. The fact that many children learn to read in spite of such an approach is evidence of their ability to make sense out of nonsense, not evidence that reading ability is a set of skills.

Word recognition skills and comprehension strategies need to be included in a school reading program, but they should never replace or even outweigh the attention that must be given to reading as a wholistic act. We have already seen that the importance of individual word recognition skills fades as reading ability grows. The focus of the reading program, then, must be on meaning.

The teaching techniques that have been described above contribute to a focus on meaning, to a concentration on reading as a wholistic act. When word recognition is tied to context, when readers are encouraged to use context along with word skills, and when reading is made meaningful through purpose setting and appropriate questioning, children are likely to develop a realistic picture of reading. In addition, the teacher must avoid any other general approaches that emphasize bits and pieces of the reading process at the expense of the quest for meaning. It is the learner who must see that reading makes sense.

EVALUATING READING AND LANGUAGE

The topic of evaluating or measuring reading is so large that a number of textbooks have been written about it. Certainly a discussion of all of the approaches to reading diagnosis is beyond the scope of this chapter. The purpose here is to explore the relationship between reading and the other parts of language. Therefore, the discussion of evaluation techniques will be limited to this relationship as well.

At the present time, the most effective technique for evaluating the child's ability to use language in reading seems to be *miscue analysis.* This is a technique that looks at the errors or "miscues" that an individual makes while reading orally. It is built around the assumption that readers use the same strategies whether they read exactly what's on the page or whether they add, delete, or substitute words. By examining the words that don't follow the text precisely, it is possible to gain clues about the kinds of strategies the reader is using. In other words, it is possible to learn how much the reader uses word recognition and how much he or she uses semantic and syntactic clues from context while reading.

Goodman and Burke have developed a detailed description and guide for using miscue analysis. When the examiner can afford to spend several hours with each individual, this complete analysis gives a clear picture of the word and context strategies the reader uses. It also includes norming scales to be used in comparing a child to other readers.[7]

In most situations, however, there simply isn't time to do such a thorough analysis. Few teachers can afford to spend several hours per child. Much of the information that is needed to evaluate the child's use of language while reading, however, can be obtained with a much less detailed and less formal version of miscue analysis. The next few paragraphs describe one such simplified version.

First, give the reader a passage to read aloud. As the individual reads, mark any words that are omitted, added, or substituted on a second copy of the passage. If the reader corrects any of these miscues, note this also. The reading should continue until approximately 20 or 25 miscues have been accumulated. Then several steps are taken to analyze each miscue. This is probably more easily done if an analysis sheet is constructed similar to the one in Figure 12–2. Using the form, follow these steps:

1. Copy each miscue onto a separate line of the form.

2. Decide upon the similarity between the word in print and the miscue. If the miscue either looks very similar or is pronounced much like the printed word, check the "high" subcolumn under graphic similarity. If the miscue is unlike the printed word, check the "low" subcolumn. Use the middle subcolumn if the miscue seems to fall between the two. In judging the similarity, pay special attention to the initial letter of the word because readers usually focus on this letter more than on the others. Only substitutions can be judged for similarity; omissions and additions can't be compared with anything.

3. Decide upon the semantic acceptability of the miscue. If the substitution, omission, or addition does not change the meaning of the sentence or phrase, check the "high" subcolumn. If the meaning is changed or disrupted greatly, check the "low" subcolumn. The middle subcolumn is used for two situations: (a) the meaning is changed somewhat, and (b) when the meaning of the immediate context, usually that of the phrase in which the word is located, is unchanged but the meaning of the whole sentence or larger context is disrupted.

4. Decide upon the syntactic acceptability of the miscue. If the miscue leaves the phrase and sentence grammatically sound, check the "high" subcolumn. If the grammar of the sentence is extensively changed (as when a different part of speech is used), check

	Graphic Similarity			Semantic Acceptability			Syntactic Acceptability			Cor-rected	Comment
Miscue	Hi	Mid	Low	Hi	Mid	Low	Hi	Mid	Low		

FIGURE 12–2 Sample miscue analysis form.

the "low" subcolumn. The middle one is again used when the grammatical change is moderate (as when an ending changes tense or singular/plural).

5. If the individual has self-corrected the miscue, rate it as described above, in spite of the fact that corrections are a sign of good reading strategies. Then check the "corrected" column for that line.

6. Although this simplified miscue analysis does not produce scores that can be compared to a table of norms, the examiner can obtain a picture of the reader's relative strengths in using word,

semantic, and syntactic clues by adding the columns. The most important information is found in the totals of the "high" sub-columns. If the total in the high graphic similarity column is substantially higher than those of semantic and syntactic accept-ability, the reader probably depends too much on word recogni-tion. If the three "high" columns are about equal, or if the semantic and syntactic categories are higher than the graphic one, the reader probably makes good use of language context clues. Because omissions and additions are not scored in the graphic column, better accuracy can be obtained by calculating the percentage of highly similar or acceptable miscues from the total of those scorable in a given category. If, for example, all 25 miscues can be rated for semantic and syntactic acceptability, but only 17 can be scored for graphic similarity because the other 8 were additions or omissions, it isn't fair to simply add up the "high" subcolumns.

7.   Determine the type of miscue that is more often corrected by analyzing the "corrected" column. Usually, a high percentage of self-correctioned words with high graphic similarity is another indication of good use of language context.

It is evident that, like many of the evaluation techniques recom-mended in this text, a simplified miscue analysis is rather subjective. Accuracy and consistency depend largely on the person making the decisions about ratings. The teacher can use such evaluation tech-niques only to gain *clues* about learners, not to gain concrete facts. Of course, the same can be said of more formal and standardized tests, which usually have less accuracy and consistency than many users believe. Evaluation is, in the end, a series of decisions that must be made by a knowledgable teacher.

SUMMARY

Reading and the other language arts are closely related. There is growing evidence that good readers use clues from the language con-text when they read at least as much as they use the words themselves. There is more to reading than simply identifying words and piecing them together. It is a wholistic process involving an interaction be-tween the printed page and the reader, a reader who uses a vast amount of experience and language background.

The implications of this language/reading relationship are significant. Word recognition instruction needs to be given in such a way that the learner never loses sight of its purpose—to aid in getting meaning from the page. Comprehension instruction must steer the reader toward the overall sense of the passage rather than toward memorization of details. The other areas of language arts discussed in this text must be given adequate attention, for they too contribute to the language knowledge that is needed for reading with understanding. Reading and language can't really be separated, for one is a part of the other.

NOTES

1. Marilyn J. Wilson, "A Review of Recent Research on the Integration of Reading and Writing," *Reading Teacher,* 34 (May 1981), 896–901.

2. Frank Smith, *Comprehension and Learning* (New York: Holt, Rinehart and Winston, 1975), p. 12.

3. Keith E. Stanovich, "Toward an Interactive-Compensatory Model of Individual Differences in the Development of Reading Fluency," *Reading Research Quarterly,* XVI (1980), 33–66.

4. Kenneth S. Goodman, "The Know-More and the Know-Nothing Movements in Reading," *Language Arts,* 56 (September 1979), 657–63.

5. Stanovich, "Toward an Interactive-Compensatory Model," p. 35.

6. Dolores Durkin, *Children Who Read Early* (New York: Teachers College Press, 1966).

7. Yetta M. Goodman and Carolyn L. Burke, *Reading Miscue Inventory Manual; Procedure for Diagnosis and Evaluation* (New York: Macmillan, Inc., 1972).

CHAPTER THIRTEEN
CHILDREN'S LITERATURE

Books and other literature written especially for children have two important functions in school. They play an integral part in the development of all language arts and are useful in other subject areas. They can also influence nearly every other aspect of children's lives. Because children's literature can be very useful in helping learners grow in their listening, speaking, writing, and reading, it deserves special attention in this text. But such literature also has value in and of itself because it helps children associate reading with pleasure and helps them grow as individuals. It is impossible to discuss one use of literature without the other.

The definition of children's literature varies among authorities and teachers. On one hand, the term can be limited in meaning to children's fiction and poetry. On the other hand, it can refer to all printed material designed for children, including textbooks. In this chapter, it is used to describe all magazines, books, and similar materials written especially for children, except those designed to be used as textbooks or text materials. The types of available literature are discussed later in this chapter.

THE VALUE OF LITERATURE

In most schools today, there is an overemphasis on teaching skills. In the areas of language arts, there seems to be a widespread belief that the teaching of listening and speaking skills and especially writing and word recognition skills provides the surest way of building able communicators. One result of this unfortunate belief, as other chapters in this text have demonstrated, is the neglect of creativity, confidence, and reading for meaning. Another result is a de-emphasis on the importance and value of children's literature.

If teachers are to give literature its proper place in school, they must be acquainted with its various forms and with many individual titles and pieces. This acquaintance can be developed by enrolling in a course in children's literature or by self-study. In a simple chapter within a language arts text, the exposure necessary to build familiarity with children's materials is impossible. Therefore, no attempt is made to do so. There are many complete texts available for that purpose. What this chapter *does* attempt to do is establish the twofold purpose of literature in school and describe some effective techniques for accomplishing that purpose.

Literature for Its Own Sake

Even if literature didn't provide an excellent tool for building language arts and aiding other subject areas, it would be very important. Literature for children has a value of its own, a value that should give it a high priority in a school program. Among the reasons for its importance are the pleasure it can give the reader, the general life understandings it can produce, and the improved self-concepts it can stimulate.

Giving Pleasure

While some "back to basics" proponents seem to feel that pleasure and school should never mix, the pleasure of reading is one of the most important discoveries a child can make in school. The individual who learns to love books as a child is much more likely to become an avid reader as an adult. The adult reader has an option for leisure time activity that isn't available to the person who dislikes reading. It's an option that leaves the timing, topic, pace, and location entirely open to the individual's taste. Furthermore, the well-read adult is frequently a better citizen and a better person as a result of his or her exposure to print. It is doubtful that many children who hate reading grow up to be avid readers.

The way to teach the joy of reading and the value of literature, of course, is not through formal lessons. Few of our attitudes are learned by having someone *tell* us what we should believe or feel. The way to foster an enjoyment of literature is to make it enjoyable. There are several qualities about the act of independent reading that can make it pleasurable, and many of these can be facilitated by the school.

First, literature can be a release from the routines and even the difficulties of life. Everyone needs to escape from the realities of life part of the time, and reading is a safe, wholesome way to do so. While there is no evidence that regular readers are less likely to turn to drugs and other abuses to accomplish temporary escape, the prospect of that possibility is logical. In books, the young reader can find release in adventure, comedy, excitement, fantasy, and identification with heroes.

Second, literature can give pleasure by simply filling leisure time. Children can find in books an alternative form of leisure just as adults can. In an era when television typically consumes large amounts of students' time, an alternative is especially desirable. Literature can be more enjoyable than television, because the individual is not dependent upon the programming of others to satisfy her or his interests.

A third reason that literature can produce pleasure is that much of it deals with *feelings* rather than facts. Huck says, "Most of what children learn in school is concerned with *knowing;* literature is concerned with *feeling.* We cannot afford to educate the head without the heart."[1] Identification with the feelings of characters in stories not only brings the joy, victory, and relief of the book into the experience of the reader, but aids in the development of emotions as well.

Increasing Life Understandings

While direct experience may be the most effective way to learn, it is seldom the most efficient. We probably learn more through secondhand or *vicarious* experiences. By listening to and watching others, we can be exposed to much more than if we depended entirely on direct experiences. Literature can open a vast field of vicarious experiences that increase life understandings and provide insight into human behavior. By reading, the individual is able to see the world not only through his or her own eyes, but also through the eyes of others. When children are motivated by the pleasure reading can give and when they are permitted to make their own reading selections, literature can help them make sense of their world.

Books play an integral part in the development of language arts and influence nearly every other aspect of children's lives. (*Ken Karp*)

Much of what has been written for children has the potential to ease personal problems and build self-concepts. Frequently known as *bibliotherapy,* the emotional help available from books has been recognized for many years. Such emotional help, however, must be self-directed; the teacher cannot direct or prescribe bibliotherapy. Neither teacher nor anyone else can ever decide for an individual what book "would be good for him." While potentially helpful books can be made available to the individual, the child must discover the potential for herself or himself.

Greer has described how this process works. The reader identifies with or emotionally matches events, states, objects, or, usually, characters in a story.[2] The reader not only recognizes the problems, emotions, and other feelings of the story character, but actually shares in them. In effect, she or he temporarily *becomes* the character. According to several authorities on bibliotherapy, this identification process can have at least two positive effects. By giving vent to pent-up emotions, the child experiences psychological relief.[3] The reader realizes vicariously that troubling problems and feelings are also common to others, and this produces self-awareness and sensitivity to other people.[4]

Of course, there is no guarantee that bibliotherapy will work. The very individuals who most need the emotional help that books can give are often the ones who resist reading and literature the most strongly. The most the teacher can do is make the books available and provide the environment and motivation described later in this chapter. Even if a child picks up a book that seems to deal with the same type of problem he or she is having, there is no guarantee that identification will take place and that emotional help will result. Furthermore, children with emotional problems frequently need other help, sometimes professional, in addition to that provided by bibliotherapy.

The opportunities for children to find emotional relief through literature are greater today than they have ever been before. Writers and publishers have produced books and articles that deal with nearly every type of problem children have experienced. There are stories about children whose parents have been divorced, whose mother or father have died, who can't get along with siblings, who can't afford the things their friends can, who are shy, and who don't succeed in school. There are stories that deal with loneliness, fear, anger, resentment, and guilt. These books are not usually negative. On the contrary, they allow the reader to identify with characters who work through such problems in realistic ways. Thus, the opportunities available today for emotional release through literature are truly manifold.

Literature as a Tool

In addition to the value that literature has for its own sake, it can be a very useful tool in teaching the various subject areas of school. Informational books about social studies and science topics can provide alternatives to textbooks in those subject areas. Biographies of famous people can be drawn upon to demonstrate how a famous scientist made use of the scientific method, how the values of those in leadership positions affect millions of people, or how people thought and behaved in a given historic era. In addition, even fiction can be used to motivate or initiate the study of a topic.

Probably the subject area that can benefit the most from literature is language arts. One of the most important aspects of teaching listening is developing the attitude among learners that school is filled with content worth listening to. When the teacher reads a variety of literature to the class frequently and effectively, this attitude is advanced enormously. Books and other children's material can provide the stimulus for much of the peer discussions that promote growth in speaking abilities. Because reading involves a process of making predictions based partially on understanding the syntax of printed language, as Chapter Twelve describes, the familiarity with printed language patterns that results from exposure to literature can aid in the development of reading ability.

The writing program is especially geared to benefit from children's literature. It can lead to many writing activities that are truly meaningful. Children can write letters to authors after they have read their books, articles, or editorials. They can write their own myths, poems, science fiction, or whatever after they have become familiar with types of literature through reading or listening. Story endings, alternative versions of an event, or descriptions from a new point of view can be written, if the writers see the purpose for doing so, after literature has been shared with them. In some classrooms, children's literature forms the backbone of the writing program.

TYPES OF LITERATURE

There are a number of ways that children's literature can be categorized. There probably is no single "right" way or best way to place individual pieces of literature into categories, for the purpose of such categorization is limited. Certainly children shouldn't be expected to memorize a list of categories or even to practice correctly placing literature into categories. An understanding of the types of literature is something of value mainly to the teacher.

The whole purpose in discussing the various types is to provide the teacher with a means of exposing children to a wide variety of literature. Odland makes this point strongly, "The major efforts of the teacher during the entire elementary-school literature curriculum are directed toward providing children with an opportunity to hear and to read different types of literature."[5] It is quite essential that a teacher be acquainted with the various types of literature if children are to be exposed to each of them in school.

One way to categorize literature is by the response or "stance" expected from the reader or listener when encountering it. Rosenblatt has devised such a system with only two categories, *efferent* and *aesthetic*.[6] Efferent reading, that which usually results from factual reading, requires the attention of the reader to be focused on things to carry away or remember when it is finished. Aesthetic reading, which is usually used with poetry and fiction, focuses attention in a different direction. Sound, rhythm, associations, and sense are all perceived together. While the distinction between these two types of reading has important classroom implications for introducing various pieces of literature, a two-part system of categorization hardly provides the teacher with a tool that meets the purpose stated above.

Another way to categorize literature is by topic. Categories might include mystery, adventure, horses, racing, detectives, and myths. While such categories are sensible for organizing a classroom library, they again aren't very useful in giving learners wide exposure to literature. The categories fail to distinguish between fiction and nonfiction and vary greatly in width and scope.

One reasonable category system, one that fits the stated purpose, is outlined here. A teacher selecting books from each of these categories over a year's time will be exposing his or her pupils to a wide variety of literature.

Fiction	Nonfiction	Poetry
Realistic	Biographical	Mother Goose
Science fiction	Informational	Free verse
Fantasy	Modern	Structured
Modern	Historical	Lyrical
Folktales		Limerick
Fairy tales		Haiku
Myths		Cinquain
Legends and fables		Sonnet

USING LITERATURE
IN THE CLASSROOM

As stated early in this chapter, children's literature is frequently de-emphasized in today's school. The enormous value of literature, both for its own sake and as a tool, is overlooked in far too many classrooms. One possible cause of this neglect is a current emphasis on "basics" and their accompanying multitude of skills.

This de-emphasis is reflected in a list of five general types of school literature programs that Odland has identified.[7] They and their variations represent current practices in elementary schools.

1. Literature is taught as a separate subject, frequently only to up-per-grade high achievers and usually in place of the "reading" class. Sometimes it involves assigning a book and accompanying discussions to a group of students.

2. Learners have access to the school library. Either through sched-uled class visits or through an informal "open library" system, the entire literature program consists of making the library avail-able.

3. Except for teachers or other adults reading to their classes during spare time, there is no program.

4. Literature is used strictly as a tool or as an independent activity. Sometimes book reports are assigned.

5. A planned program with literature for enjoyment as the main objective is carried out as a regular part of the school program. Children are read to and are encouraged through various tech-niques to read independently in addition to guided activities.

Odland points out that numbers two through four above are the predominant systems for dealing with literature in the elementary school. Thus, it is clear that in many classrooms literature does not receive the time and attention that is necessary for it to achieve the potential value described earlier.

How, then, should literature be used in the classroom? The fifth type of program in Odland's list comes closest to the ideal approach. A planned program with enjoyment of literature as the main purpose can best provide the benefits of children's literature.

The nature and content of such a program will necessarily be quite different from the literature classes most of us remember from high school and college. In order to build enjoyment of books and other literature, the program should contain these items:

1. Reading aloud to the class on a regular basis
2. Adult modeling of reading as enjoyable and useful
3. Use of literature as a tool in various subject areas, especially language arts

These three components are individually discussed next. In addition, two controversies about the use of children's literature are discussed.

Reading to Children

Reading regularly to children of any age has a number of benefits. Young children first learn what the language of books is like from being read to. This speeds their development of reading strategies that make use of context, as Chapter Twelve explains. Vocabulary is learned from listening to literature as much as it is from reading it. Tastes related to a variety of types of literature can be learned when the reading is drawn from a wide sample of materials.

But reading to children can also contribute to the enjoyment of literature. It is a form of selling the idea that books are fun. Just as the commercial makers of many products spend a great deal of advertising energy just to get customers to sample their products, teachers should channel some of their energy into getting children to sample literature. No sales pitch is more effective than reading to the children. Sometimes the reading can stop at an exciting place so that the listeners will pick up the book to see how it ends. However, this isn't always necessary, for children frequently enjoy rereading what they have already heard. Good books "sell themselves" in this way.

With so many benefits coming from reading to the class, there is little reason for minimizing the amount that it is used. One of the reasons the literature program must be planned is so that such reading is done on a regular basis. Reading to children every day is not too often. If time constraints are severe, as they are in most classrooms, ten minutes can be taken daily from the reading or language arts periods. It is difficult to argue that some other type of language study could have a greater impact in ten minutes' time than this. Nor is there any reason to stop reading to students when they move into upper-elementary grades. In fact, these learners frequently need a stimulus to enjoy literature more than children in primary grades do.

Reading literature aloud must be done well. Unless the teacher has an unusual ability to read spontaneously, the reading should be practiced before it is presented. Too much is at stake for the technique to be used in an ineffective manner. Reading aloud by students should be practiced and done well for the same reason. This certainly precludes any use of "round robin reading," the practice where children take turns reading unrehearsed from a text. Any reading should have a purpose, and literature should always be enjoyable.

Adult Modeling

Most of the attitudes that children develop are learned from imitating or modeling important people in their lives. Attitudes toward literature are no exception.[8] Thus, the examples that teachers, especially elementary teachers, set in the classroom have a large effect upon the learners' enjoyment of literature. There are a number of things that teachers can do to model reading as useful and enjoyable.

Reading, as a general tool, can be pictured as something useful when the teacher uses it in the classroom for specific purposes. Using resource books to find needed information or answer questions, using stories and poems to illustrate situations and demonstrate ideas, and reading excerpts from newspapers and magazines are examples of ways that reading as a useful tool can be modeled frequently. Using literature in other subject areas may help also. When children see that their teacher regards reading as something useful, they are more likely to adopt this attitude themselves.

Literature for enjoyment can be modeled in a similar manner. When students see that their teacher loves to read books, poems, and other types of literature, it has a positive effect upon their attitudes. Some of this modeling takes place when the teacher reads literature to the class with obvious enthusiasm. There are, however, other ways of modeling as well.

One of the most effective ways to model reading enjoyment is through a relatively recent technique, usually known as *sustained silent reading*. This is another part of the literature program that needs to be planned, in that time needs to be set aside for it. The technique consists simply of a scheduled time when everyone in the classroom reads self-selected material for sheer enjoyment. "Everyone" includes the teacher and any other adult who happens to be in the room.

In fact, it is the teacher's demonstrated enjoyment of reading that is the key to the success of the technique. McCracken and McCracken found, in their survey of teachers who had difficulty with sustained silent reading, that a main cause of unsuccessful attempts was the teachers' failure to participate in the reading.[9] If students are actually expected to spend their time reading, and if the objective is to stimulate reading enjoyment, the teacher must put aside the temptation to grade papers or engage in any other activity and must read along with the students.

The technique is usually initiated by challenging the learners to sustain themselves with the same books for a short time, often five or ten minutes. The teacher then ignores the class and silently reads a book that is honestly enjoyable, not a textbook or a child's book. If any student behavior less than an emergency needs attention, it can be dealt with after the brief period is ended. In fact, it is best if the teacher doesn't even look up during the five or ten minutes. Such a suggestion sounds quite risky to many teachers who fear chaos will erupt in the room, but few teachers who have tried it have found any problems after the first few days, as long as they actually read along with the class. When the time is up, the teacher shares one happening from, or one reaction to, his or her book and any volunteers are invited to do the same without any threat of criticism. On the following days the procedure is repeated and the time is gradually expanded to fifteen or twenty minutes a day. On some days the period ends with a volunteer sharing time, as mentioned above, and sometimes provision is made for those who would like to continue reading longer. The emphasis, in any event, is always on enjoyment.

Using Literature in Other Areas

Earlier in this chapter the use of literature as a tool was described. Materials for children should not be used in subject areas to the *exclusion* of their use for enjoyment. In fact, the use of such materials in language arts and other areas will not be very effective unless the students have first learned to value or enjoy literature. But once this attitude is established, the benefits that are described earlier can result.

Some of the benefits of using literature come quite automatically from the activities that promote reading enjoyment. When the teacher reads to the class frequently and effectively, the attitude that there are things in school worth listening to is promoted, and language understanding is gained that aids in reading and writing. When children read more because their teacher serves as a model for reading enjoyment, they gain the practice that improves their reading abilities and the vicarious experiences that help them in writing.

Other benefits result from planned and careful use of literature in various subject areas. Materials must be chosen carefully to fit into a science or social studies topic, and the manner in which they are used must be planned. They can be read and discussed with the entire class, multiple copies can be read and discussed by a small group, or they can be used as a resource by groups working on a project. Discussions, whether whole-class or group, don't become successful automatically just by making the literature available, but must be carefully planned. Writing activities that are based on such materials must also be planned so that the learners see a purpose in moving from what they have heard or read to expressing their own ideas in writing. A literature program, then, must be given schedule time and must be planned if it is to reach its full potential.

Analyzing Literature

One of the controversies that surrounds the use of children's literature deals with the question, "Should elementary school children be led to analyze the literature they read?" Should groups or whole classes of children be required to read the same literary work and then be guided through a study of its techniques? We may have unpleasant memories from high-school and college literature classes that required us to memorize definitions of literary terms and devices and then scrutinize famous works to identify them.

Fearing that such analysis of literature will turn children against literature and its enjoyment, some critics have taken a stand against any analysis in the elementary school. Children are better off without a thorough understanding of certain literature selections, they argue, than they are without a joy of reading. Literature should be shared and enjoyed, but not analyzed.

Another viewpoint, however, is that literature can be analyzed without destroying its enjoyment or appreciation. Some authorities claim, in fact, that an appropriate type of analysis will actually enhance the enjoyment and appreciation of literature. Of those who hold this view, few agree on what is an appropriate type or amount of analysis.

Strickland has suggested a form of literature study that calls attention to literary techniques only subtly. As the teacher reads aloud to children, pauses, repetitions, and sometimes discussions are used to emphasize certain words or expressions. When discussions are used, they are usually limited to descriptions of the mental pictures created by the author.[10]

Another approach to literature study for elementary-school students is the comparison of stories which have similar plots. Folktales lend themselves well to this kind of comparison because they have a good deal of consistency to them. Western suggests that learners read and compare several versions of the same folktale so that they gain a deeper understanding of folktale structure and an appreciation for these tales and literature in general. Kimmelman suggests comparing several folktales within and among certain categories. After identifying three common patterns of plot structures into which most folktales fall, she argues that children can be led to see the similarities within each category. From this, they can learn to make predictions about other folktales and can learn about literary devices without directly studying them. Both of these authors recommend informal and indirect teaching techniques that take nothing away from literature for enjoyment.[11]

If enjoyment continues to be the main goal of using literature in school, then it would appear that informal analysis of literature has merit. This can be done with no formal instruction in literary devices, with no boring or painful scrutiny of literary works, and with no negative attitude development. After learners have heard or read a story, their interest and understanding is extended in a manner that bears some resemblance to the conversation friends might have about a book they have read.

Using Literature for Reading Instruction

Another controversy surrounding the use of children's literature in school deals with its use to teach reading. Many authorities fear such use for the same reason they warn against analyzing literature—that enjoyment will be destroyed. Because most reading instruction today is highly skill-oriented, the stories to be read are broken into digestible segments, words are pulled from the stories for the purpose of teaching word recognition skills, and comprehension instruction emphasizes finding facts or remembering details. Certainly, good literature can be ruined when it is subjected to such treatment. On the other hand, other authorities argue that good literature can provide more motivation, purpose, and variety to a reading program than the type of material written specifically for reading texts. Literature typically represents excellent writing, continuity of longer stories, and more interest appeal.

The answer to this controversy seems to be similar to the one related to literature analysis. If reading instruction is largely limited to skills teaching and if children are seldom given the opportunity to interact with the entire reading selection, literature is best kept out of the program. If, however, the focus of the reading program is on making sense, and comprehension is treated in the manner suggested in the previous chapter, literature can be a welcome addition to the program. Paperback books in multiple copies can be used part of the time to replace sections of the reading texts. Some teachers even find it possible to use an individualized program where each child selects books to read and then schedules private conferences with the teacher. A teacher must follow the reading program that is established for a school, but there are many opportunities to expose children to literature in nearly every situation.

SUMMARY

Children's literature can be a very useful tool in the teaching of language arts as well in other subject areas. It also has its own value: It helps learners enjoy reading and contributes to their growth as individuals.

Therefore, literature should be used extensively in school. A planned program is usually the best way to guarantee its use. The program should include reading to children, adult modeling of reading enjoyment and usefulness, and use of literature in various school subject areas. If enjoyment of literature is the primary purpose, the analysis of such materials on an informal basis and their use as reading instructional material can also be valuable. Children's literature should be an important part of the classroom.

NOTES

1. Charlotte S. Huck, "No Wider than the Heart Is Wide," in *Using Literature and Poetry Affectively,* ed. Jon E. Shapiro (Newark, Del.: International Reading Association, 1979), p. 28.
2. Margaret Greer, "Affective Growth through Reading," *Reading Teacher,* 25 (January 1972), 336–41.
3. Richard L. Darling, "Mental Hygiene and Books," *Wilson Library Bulletin,* 32 (December 1957), 293–96.
4. Patricia Gianciolo, "Feeling Books Develop Social and Personal Sensitivities," *Elementary English,* 52 (January 1975), 37–42.
5. Norine Odland, "Planning a Literature Program for the Elementary School," *Language Arts,* 56 (April 1979), 364.

6. Louise M. Rosenblatt, "What Facts Does This Poem Teach You?" *Language Arts,* 57 (April 1980), 386–94.

7. Odland, "Planning a Literature Program."

8. Jon E. Shapiro, "Developing an Awareness of Attitudes," in *Using Literature and Poetry Affectively,* ed. Jon E. Shapiro (Newark, Del.: International Reading Association, 1979), p. 5.

9. Robert A. McCracken and Marlene J. McCracken, "Modeling Is the Key to Sustained Silent Reading," *Reading Teacher,* 31 (January 1978), 406–408.

10. Dorothy S. Strickland, "Promoting Language and Concept Development," ed. Jon E. Shapiro (Newark, Del.: International Reading Association, 1979), pp. 40–41.

11. Linda E. Western, "A Comparative Study of Literature through Folk Tale Variants," *Language Arts,* 57 (April 1980), 395–402; Lois Kimmelman, "Literary Ways toward Enjoyable Thinking," *Language Arts,* 58 (April 1981), 441–47.

CHAPTER FOURTEEN
ORGANIZING THE LANGUAGE ARTS PROGRAM

Throughout this text, the role of the *teacher* in the language arts program has been stressed. The teacher doesn't simply follow a textbook or even a curriculum guide established by the school, school district, or state. Certainly such resources are important, but they are to be *used,* not followed. The key to a successful language arts program is the teacher.

The day-by-day role that the teacher must fulfill, however, isn't always clear. This text, instead of reducing the task, makes dozens of suggestions about context to include and techniques to use above and beyond those which are typical of the language arts textbook. A real problem for the teacher, then, is one of scheduling. How can all of this content and all of these techniques be included?

Even before scheduling decisions can be made, however, the nature of the program must be determined. This involves decisions about the characteristics of the learners and the relative importance of each of the component parts of language arts. In addition to a range of differences, do any of the learners have special needs? Should oral language or writing, skills or confidence, be emphasized? Perhaps it shouldn't be surprising that many teachers blindly follow the textbook or guide, for attention to so many details can be overwhelming.

The purpose of this chapter, then, is to show that it is possible to organize and teach language arts in a manner that shows concern for the child's overall communication abilities. The many decisions that must be made and the details to which such a teacher must attend need not be overwhelming. The teacher must, however, have an organizational plan.

WHAT EVERY LANGUAGE ARTS PROGRAM NEEDS

At a superficial level, it seems obvious that what a language arts program needs is attention to speaking, listening, spelling, grammar, writing, and the other language arts. But we have seen that there is more to a program than component parts. The total child as a communicator must be dealt with for two reasons. First, a child and his or her language can't be separated, for interaction with others and thinking itself relies heavily on language. Second, within any individual person, the several forms of language (speaking, listening, writing, reading) are interrelated and affect one another. Therefore, what every language arts program needs is a set of strategies for dealing with the total child as a communicator rather than just a set of objectives related to skills.

In this text, several overall strategies of this type have been proposed. They are reviewed below for the purpose of providing a framework upon which a program can be established. A teacher has to have a framework or set of strategies, because the specific details of language arts instruction can be planned only after the basic nature of the program is determined.

Meaningful Context

Language is only learned when there is a purpose for it. The first type of strategy that every language arts program needs is one that places language learning in a meaningful context. The school can't provide a setting for language that is as natural as the home in which most children first learned to talk, but there is much it can do to provide real communication situations upon which language instruction can be built. Writing letters to real people, writing stories and reports that are shared with interested audiences, and writing poetry for a classroom publication are examples of meaningful contexts that are based on real communication. The more such situations the teacher can create, the more effective will be language arts instruction.

Coordinating Lessons with Context

Some language arts authorities have suggested that if programs were devoted entirely to meaningful language situations, no direct instruction would be necessary. Most teachers, however, find such a suggestion less than practical. Fearing that some important content may be left out of the learners' development, most practitioners have used direct instruction in the form of classroom lessons to instill language growth. A balance between these two positions seems best. The teacher can set up meaningful situations as described in the previous section, work with individuals while they are writing, and teach important skills to the class, all within one program. Several suggested schedules are included later in this chapter to show how the classroom time can be arranged to make such a combination possible.

The only way that the direct lessons can benefit from the context of meaningful communication is if they are coordinated in some way. It is ideal if the writing skills lessons on Monday and Tuesday, for example, can be applied directly to the writing activity that begins on Wednesday. It is far from ideal when the lessons in skills are isolated from any meaningful speaking or writing activities. Children who mindlessly fill in blanks day after day learn little language. The ideal is seldom possible, but the teacher can usually point out how a given skill relates to one or more of the recent or future language activities. Furthermore, if the overall program is meaningful, confident students will want to improve their communication abilities and will view the lessons as a means of doing so.

Adjusting the Emphasis

The third type of strategy for language arts, especially for writing, is a gradually shifting emphasis. Students need a solid base in oral language (speaking and listening) in order to become effective readers and writers. Oral language should receive attention throughout a communications program, but it is especially important in the beginning. When oral communication is established, the greatest attention needs to be focused upon building confidence and creativity. Learners need confidence as writers if they are to take the risks necessary to try out new skills and ideas. They need the freedom to be creative if they are to develop expressive writing. When these areas have a strong foothold, individuals will have the abilities and motivation to improve the mechanics of writing and written expression.

Although oral language, confidence building, creative writing, writing mechanics, and written expression should all receive attention throughout the years of elementary school, the emphasis should gradually change from oral language to confidence and creativity, and then to mechanics and expression. In an ideal situation, this change in emphasis would occur slowly as the children advance through their years of school. Realistically, however, many teachers of higher grade levels must develop confidence and creativity before beginning on mechanics and expression.

Meeting Individual Needs

Finally, every language arts program needs a strategy to deal with individual differences. Meeting individual needs in language arts is not extremely difficult, for much individualization can occur within group or whole-class settings. Although the whole class may share an experience and then discuss it, each individual responds in his or her own way. The teacher responds to and evaluates each child's oral language individually. Although the class may have the same stimulus and purpose in completing a writing activity, each individual responds at his or her own level.

Other individualization is also important. During writing activities, individual attention should be provided first by proofreading groups and then by the teacher. Reading, handwriting, and spelling

The key to a successful language arts program is the teacher. (*Ken Karp*)

can each make use, at appropriate times, of ability groups. Finally, in all aspects of language learning, self-concepts must be considered and dealt with.

Usually, therefore, the suggestions made in this text for dealing with the whole child as a communicator will take care of needs for individualization. Some learners, however, have such needs that additional adjustments must be made to the program to accommodate them. Mainstreamed, gifted, and bilingual children usually require some adjustments. They will each be discussed in turn.

TEACHING MAINSTREAMED CHILDREN

In 1975 Public Law 94–192, the Education for All Handicapped Children Act, was passed, and all educational systems in the United States were affected. The law states that all mentally retarded, hard-of-hearing, deaf, speech impaired, visually or health impaired children and children with specific learning disabilities are guaranteed an education in a placement that gives them the least restrictive alternative. This means that many children who were once placed in institutions or special education classes now spend some or all of their school hours in regular classrooms along with nonhandicapped children. Not all handicapped learners are placed in regular classrooms, but each child is placed in a setting that is as close to a "normal" environment as her or his handicap allows. Decisions are required to be made on the basis of multiple tests, consultations with parents, and observations by school personnel. The several alternatives that are typically available for placement are shown in Figure 14–1.

The full- or part-time placement of handicapped children into regular classrooms has been called "mainstreaming" because such placement puts them into the *mainstream* of education. Debate about the value of mainstreaming, as it is currently being implemented in American schools, could easily fill a separate textbook. The point here is that today's language arts teacher is typically faced with at least a few children who have special problems and special needs. No longer are all children who bear a certain special-education label being kept out of the regular classroom.

What can a teacher do to help children with special handicaps, especially in the area of language arts? The answer, of course, depends on the nature of the handicap and of the child. There are differences among the groups mentioned above and among the subgroups, of which there is an even larger number, but there are also differences between any two children even within a subgroup. The teacher's first task is to make the mainstreamed child feel welcome and the second

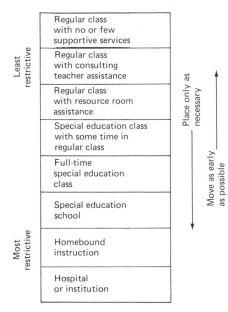

FIGURE 14–1   Placement alternatives for handicapped children.

is to gain as much information about each individual as possible. Files, previous teachers, parents, and special education consultants should all be used as information resources. Only then can adjustments in the language arts program be planned.

Because every mainstreamed child is different, this text can't provide teaching formulas for each of them. However, a number of general suggestions can be made that may help in adjusting the program.

1. Handicapped children acquire language in the same manner as do other children, by using it in meaningful ways. The blind and visually impaired can't learn from print, the deaf and hard of hearing can't base their written language on oral forms, and nonverbal children with severe physical handicaps must resort to special techniques perhaps as slow and awkward as a head stick that points to a language board. However, all these children, and those with all other types of handicaps, learn language by being exposed to and using it. Breaking language into many bits and pieces and isolating them from real communication is no more appropriate for these children than for any others. Edelsky and Rosegrant, in fact, warn that such treatment of language may put mainstreamed children into a *more* restrictive environment, the exact opposite of mainstreaming's intent, because their language training is so unlike the real world.[1]

2. The greatest gift a teacher can give a mainstreamed student is the freedom to respond at his or her own level without ridicule or shame. As explained above, the language arts program allows teachers to do a great deal of individualization while teaching groups or even the whole class. The presence of mainstreamed children doesn't change this fact, for the individualization is to be found in the individual responses of the students and in the teacher's reaction to those responses. When children whose language is noticeably different are in the classroom, the adjustment that must be made is not in the *form* of individualization, but in the teacher and peer reactions. If the teacher shows annoyance with or ridicules the struggling learner, there will be few positive accomplishments. But if the teacher serves as a positive model in accepting the child, students are likely to follow.

3. Positive self-concepts are often even more important for mainstreamed learners than for others. The handicaps that these individuals have had to live with frequently have made them see themselves as less adequate people. Morehead and Morehead

have pointed out that communication difficulties and the emotional and social life of the child can have a reciprocal and devastating effect.[2] Other handicaps can have a similar effect. Success, therefore, is a vital component of the program for mainstreamed children. Much of the success can be provided in the ways already described in this text, but sometimes other special adaptations can be made:

a.   Use pictures or concrete manipulatives where appropriate.

b.   Use a "buddy system," where a more able student is seated next to a mainstreamed child and gives help as needed.

c.   When a task is beyond the writing ability of a child, a tape recorder can sometimes be used to receive responses.

d.   Whenever possible, use a differentiated assignment system so that various individuals have different tasks to perform. In this way, mainstreamed students who need shorter and simpler assignments can be given them without making these students feel set apart.

e.   Where school policy allows it, use a report card system that doesn't let low grades destroy the mainstreamed child's confidence. One way of doing this is to grade by comparing performance with ability and then indicating at the bottom of this child's report card that he or she received special consideration through an individualized program.

4.   For students with attention and concentration problems, special provisions should be made for seating and group arrangements. They need to be seated in places where they will not be easily distracted. For example, the most heavily traveled routes in a classroom usually lead to the pencil sharpener, the door, and the closet. Students with attention and concentration problems should not be seated near these "freeways" of the classroom.

5.   Learners who have physical handicaps, on the other hand, should be seated so that they have easy access to the materials and resources they need as well as to the teacher.

6.   Use activities that don't publicly call attention to the mainstreamed child's weaknesses. Various types of group activities can be used to involve individuals in their areas of strength. Choral reading, learning games, and dramatics are examples of such activities.

7. Set and maintain realistic standards for all handicapped children. Many mainstreamed children have normal intelligence and should have standards that match it. Standards and expectations that are either too high or too low can have a negative effect on learning.

TEACHING GIFTED CHILDREN

In recent years, some attention has been called to another exceptional segment of the school population, the academically talented and gifted. In many schools, a part-time program, in some states mandated by law, exists to deal with the special needs of these exceptional learners. One common type of program removes them from their regular classrooms for a few hours a week to work with fellow gifted students in challenging and interesting activities.

By and large, however, the needs of gifted students are still not being adequately met by the schools. Too frequently, such children do the same work and sit through the same lessons as other learners, even when the challenge and level of difficulty is far too low for them. One of the reasons for this is a lack of financial support for programs for the gifted. Another is the lack of time that teachers contend with as they struggle to help learners who are having difficulties in school. Still another reason is an attitude among educators and others that, because these students are already performing at or above grade level, they don't need additional help. The language needs of gifted children are especially ignored because they tend to have large vocabularies, read well, and write imaginatively.

There are two serious dangers in ignoring gifted learners. One is that they easily become bored with school and either exhibit behavior problems or develop clever strategies for performing as little as possible during learning tasks. The other danger, partly as a result of the first, is that they never come close to reaching their potential in school, and possibly in life. Yet, there is evidence that a large majority of our present-day leaders in business, industry, government, and many other areas were gifted students when they were in school. To offer less challenge and development to the potential leaders of our society is to risk reducing the quality of leadership in future years.

Highly developed communications abilities are very important for students with above-normal potential. The language arts program, then, must deal with the needs of gifted students. Before we explore techniques for adjusting the language program to meet these needs, two strategies that we must *not* use have to be clarified.

1. Do not ignore the gifted child. For all the reasons given above, he or she needs attention.

2. Do not simply give him or her more work to do, especially if that work is not challenging or interesting. Sometimes gifted students rebel against boredom by completing tasks in less than perfect ways. A perceptive teacher must be able to discern such behavior from lack of ability. Mountains of meaningless homework or drill activities do nothing to meet the needs of the gifted.

Fortunately, some of the needs of the academically talented and gifted can also be dealt with through the type of language arts program advocated in this text. The individualization that is needed is fulfilled partly through responses that the learners give to learning and practice activities and the reactions of the teacher to those responses. Just as teachers' expectations can be adjusted to the levels of mainstreamed students, they can be adjusted to the levels of the gifted. The teacher does not have to *assign* longer written products or more difficult tasks, but can communicate in many informal ways an expectation that such individuals are capable of more. This is especially possible during the individual conferences that are held whenever written products are being polished.

In addition, much of the need for challenge and diversity can be met within the framework of language arts by encouraging, but not forcing, the development of optional interest areas. When the use of real communication situations makes the program meaningful, gifted and other students often voluntarily undertake projects or areas of study above and beyond those required. At other times, a simple suggestion from the teacher or an offer of "extra credit" can spark such undertakings. Among the many language-related activities that can be suggested for the gifted are:

- *Word study.* With only a little guidance, the study of connotations, synonyms, figurative language, and etymology (word histories) can become independent activities. The teacher's role is to suggest and explain the study, provide ample resource materials, and be available at times to answer questions. Dale and O'Rourke have suggested that learners can study etymology by analyzing the meaning of vocabulary in nursery rhymes as evidenced by the context of the words.[3]

- *Crossword puzzles.* The availability of crossword puzzles at many levels of difficulty makes them a natural for these students, if they are not overused. Even more appropriately, the *construction* of these puzzles can be undertaken independently. Certainly, they can be made to fit the interests of the writers and their development is indeed challenging. Other types of word puzzles are also appropriate.

- *Creative reading.* While prediction is a necessary part of any mature reading, gifted learners can be encouraged to extend and elaborate their predictions about story events and to use more divergence to do so. Boothby has listed the rewriting of a scene, inventing a new climax, or adding an epilogue to a story as independent activities that encourage such divergence.[4]

- *Language comparison.* Children in upper elementary grades often become interested in foreign languages. It isn't necessary to learn much of a language in order to compare it to English. One appropriate activity for the gifted is to compare and record some of the more common words in several languages, using foreign language dictionaries as a resource. Another is to make a larger comparison between English and one other language, focusing on idioms, slang, or grammar. This is especially appropriate if the students study a foreign language as part of their out-of-room gifted program, if another language is spoken in the homes of the gifted, or if a child in the classroom is from another country.

- *Codes.* Younger gifted learners are often intrigued by "secret" codes. They can easily learn and communicate to each other in such established codes as the Morse system or semaphore. In addition, they are quite capable of inventing their own codes. Of course, the teacher who encourages codes will have to accept the fact that children will be eager to communicate in a language he or she doesn't understand!

TEACHING BILINGUAL CHILDREN

During recent years a new influx of non-English-speaking children has appeared in our schools. Spanish and a variety of languages from Asia have been the most commonly spoken. Usually these children appear at school with very limited, or no, knowledge of English.

Encouraged by new legal requirements, many school districts are responding to this new population with full-time *bilingual* education programs. Based on some rather convincing research evidence, the programs sometimes provide all school subjects in both English and the language of the students. Classes consist completely of students who have the same foreign language, and are taught by bilingual teachers who have proficiency in both English and the students' language. Other bilingual programs combine English and a second language in other ways. An understanding of the students' culture is essential for any bilingual teacher, and training in the specific nature of bilingual teaching is very useful.

In spite of bilingual programs, the number of regular language arts teachers with non-English students appears to have increased in recent years. Even if the school has a program to help these learners with their English acquisition, it is frequently part-time. In addition, regular classroom teachers sometimes have the students while placement arrangements are made in a bilingual program.

What can a regular teacher do to help these children? The highest priorities must be given to helping them overcome any fearful attitudes and to helping them acquire enough English that they can begin to learn from the academic programs. Only then can the educational needs of the individuals be dealt with. Therefore, the following techniques are recommended:

1. On the first day that the children appear in the classroom, make them feel welcome and speak to them in English. Smiles, a friendly voice, attention, and a place to sit among the other children can do a lot to make them feel comfortable. Using English as a part of the communication to them establishes from the beginning that learning English will be important.

2. Begin the instruction of English by teaching them "survival language." This task will be much easier if the teacher can say these statements in the languages of the learners before teaching them in English. The pronunciation of these statements can be obtained from bilingual teachers, members of the community, or sometimes the parents. Gonzales has shown how the teacher who is unfamiliar with the language can write these phrases phonetically on cards for easy reference.[5] This is especially important if more than one non-English language is involved. Although it must be adjusted to individual circumstances, the list of survival language should probably include at least these sentences.

Hello.
Welcome to our school.

Are you OK?

Do you need help?

I need help.

I need to go to the restroom.

I'm hungry.

Do you understand?

Please come here.

What is your name?

3. The way that students learn English as a second language is the same way that anyone learns a language, through using it. At first, this use will be limited largely to listening (except, perhaps, for the survival statements above), but it is through continuous exposure to English that they will eventually come to speak, read, and write it.

4. Once the initial instruction in survival language has ended, the teacher usually can't spend large amounts of time teaching English to these children. However, the other students in the classroom not only have the time but are often better equipped to "teach" English by talking with them. In addition to all of the informal interaction that goes on in a classroom, intentional "peer tutoring" can be arranged. Volunteers can tell the newcomers phrases that are useful on the playground, in getting materials, and in meeting friends. The tutors should be instructed to avoid speaking loudly or slowly, but to use a lot of conversation in normal ways.

5. Make the learners feel safe in their new environment. Don't expect them to do very much speaking in English at first. When they do begin to be verbal, perhaps weeks after they first arrive, avoid corrections and criticisms of their speech. Accept "foreign accents" and mistakes. Experimenting with their new language involves a great deal of risk taking and it will be taken only if the environment is safe.

6. Finally, make every effort to make these children see that the difficulties they are experiencing in learning a language are normal and understandable. Be patient, helpful, and friendly. On the other hand, clearly communicate the expectation that they must learn English. Learn and use the survival language in their native tongue at first, but communicate with them whenever possible in normal, friendly English.

ORGANIZING A SCHEDULE

Once a framework or set of strategies for teaching language arts has been determined, including strategies for dealing with exceptional children, the teacher can begin to develop an organizational plan for the program.

Obviously, if the teacher does nothing for language arts but follow the textbook or curriculum guide page after page, no organizational plan is needed. At the appointed time for class, he or she simply does whatever the book says should be done next. Anyone who attempts to deal with the total child as a communicator, however, must organize teaching and practice activities so that they deal effectively with the learners' communication needs.

The organizational plan that is best will vary from one situation to another and from one teacher to another. The most important consideration must be the learners' needs. These needs will determine not only the objectives and specific activities to be used, but the emphasis of the program at a given point in time.

The three examples of organizational plans discussed next, each with its own situation and emphasis, are based on the strategies described earlier in the chapter.

Oral Language Emphasis

The learners in this example have an inadequate speaking and listening base and might have difficulties with writing. A substantial number of them also lack confidence in their oral abilities. The teacher has decided, therefore, to begin with oral activities for learners with very low confidence (see Chapter Three). The organizational plan at this point is very simple, for the teacher has decided to postpone all other language arts instruction until some oral confidence has been established. Assuming the language arts class period averages about forty minutes, the first week's plan is:

Monday

20 minutes: mime activities

20 minutes: begin puppet construction

Tuesday

15 minutes: mime activities

15 minutes: finish puppets

10 minutes: initiate choral speaking

Wednesday

20 minutes: make plans for puppetry script

20 minutes: read literature to class

Thursday

20 minutes: begin developing puppetry script

20 minutes: choral speaking

Friday

40 minutes; develop puppetry scripts; practice

During the following weeks, puppet shows are given, choral speaking continues, and other oral language activities are introduced. At the same time, a tape recorder is available to those who wish to record their thoughts (see p. 45) during free time. After both the less verbal and the verbally aggressive children have modified their behavior somewhat, writing activities can gradually be introduced. Activities for oral expression continue, however, to be a part of the language arts program.

Writing Confidence Emphasis

The students in this example largely have the oral language background that is necessary to succeed in reading and writing, although attention still needs to be given to oral expression. Their teacher has decided, therefore, to devote about 10 percent of the language arts program to this area.

The bulk of the language arts program is related to writing. However, these students have had so many negative experiences with writing in previous years that their confidence in themselves as writers needs to be built up before much can be done to develop their writing mechanics or written expression. The two areas of mechanics and expression that the teacher has chosen to work on are sentence construction and spelling. The clear emphasis, however, is on writing confidence. The overall plan for the year is as follows:

1. Begin writing by letting students dictate language experience stories.
2. Use a number of confidence-building activities (see p. 130) while gradually leading students to independent writing.

3. Add a second emphasis on creativity.
4. As students are ready, introduce writing mechanics, proofreading, and written expression.

A two-week plan of specific teaching and practice activities for this group of students follows. It assumes that step one above, dictated stories, has begun to be phased out and independent writing has begun to be introduced. The language arts class time, including spelling instruction, is about fifty minutes a day.

Monday

1. Construction of electromagnet as experience related to current science unit
2. Whole-class discussion of procedure and uses of electromagnet
3. Written response to experience—choice of writing independently or dictating experience story

Tuesday

1. Continuation of work on written responses while teacher confers with 4 individuals
2. Volunteer sharing (oral) of written products
3. Spelling pretest for Group 1 and spelling lesson on 5 words for Group 2

Wednesday

1. Completion of volunteer sharing from Tuesday
2. Introduction of idea of oral activity: invention contest (see p. 76)
3. Spelling lesson on 5 words for Group 2

Thursday

1. Lesson on constructing sentences, based on this week's written product
3. Independent work on invention contest while teacher confers with 3 individuals about written products
3. Spelling lesson on 5 words for Group 2

Friday

1. Introduction of poetry to build confidence in writing (see p. 134)
2. Spelling posttest for Group 1 and spelling lesson on 5 words for Group 2

Monday

1. Spelling pretest for Group 1 and spelling lesson on 5 words for Group 2
2. Individual oral presentations for invention contest

Tuesday

1. Provision of information about a local inventor
2. Whole-class discussion on writing an invitation to the inventor to visit classroom
3. Individual responses to experience—letter writing
4. Spelling lesson on 5 words for Group 2

Wednesday

1. Follow-up discussion on letters
2. Review lesson on constructing sentences
3. Introduction of proofreading and practice proofreading for sentence correctness
4. Completion of letter writing while teacher confers with 3 individuals
5. Collection of letters to be mailed

Thursday

1. Confidence-building session using more poetry writing
2. Spelling lesson on 5 words for Group 2

Friday

1. Presentation of idea for making individual poetry and storybooks for parents
2. Discussion of plans for books
3. Spelling posttest for Group 1 and spelling lesson on 5 words for Group 2

Mechanics and Expression Emphasis

The students in this example have a sufficient oral language background and enough writing confidence that they can begin to focus on writing mechanics and written expression. Their teacher has given some attention to writing mechanics through the early parts of the school year, but the emphasis has been upon building writing confidence. The first area of attention is punctuation and proofreading for punctuation errors. The concept of proofreading is not new to the students, but the use of proofreading groups is.

A two-week plan for teaching mechanics and expression based on writing is listed next. The language arts class time, including spelling, is about fifty minutes.

Monday

1. Formation of proofreading groups and instruction in their use
2. Simulated practice with proofreading using passages without punctuation
3. Spelling lesson for Group 1 and spelling pretest for Group 2

Tuesday

1. Lesson on use of punctuation to end sentences
2. Simulated practice on proofreading for punctuation at ends of sentences
3. Spelling lesson for Group 1.

Wednesday

1. Provision of experience related to current social studies—reading of recent editorial related to study
2. Discussion of editor's viewpoint with whole class
3. Written response to experience—letters to editor
4. Spelling lesson for Group 1

Thursday

1. Review by proofreading groups of member's letters to editor
2. Explanation of purpose of polishing and rewriting
3. Individual polishing and rewriting while teacher circulates among writers for brief conferences
4. Spelling lesson for Group 1

INDEX